VERE FOSTER 1819–1900

An Irish Benefactor

Vere Foster

The Life and Times of Mary Ann McCracken, 1770–1866
Little Tom Drennan: Portrait of a Georgian Childhood

Vere Foster
1819-1900

AN IRISH BENEFACTOR

MARY McNEILL

A publication of the Institute of Irish Studies
The Queen's University, Belfast

DAVID & CHARLES : NEWTON ABBOT

ISBN 0 7153 5007 2

HV
28
·F63M32
1971

*Set in 11 point Baskerville 2 point leaded
and printed in Great Britain
by Clarke, Doble & Brendon Ltd., Plymouth
for David & Charles (Publishers) Limited
South Devon House Newton Abbot Devon*

Contents

List of Illustrations

* All from contemporary issues of *The London Illustrated News*

To
Dorothy E. C. V. May

Preface

It has become fashionable to denigrate philanthropy. At a time when all ranks of society claim benefits from the impersonal hands of the Welfare State, and when affluence, typified by the motorcar, the package holiday, and the shorter working week, has become the perquisite of all but the least fortunate, we tend to regard with disdain, almost with reproach, the exertions of those philanthropic individuals whose public-spirited efforts first established, little over a century ago, the right of everyone to decent conditions in which to develop his physical, mental, and spiritual potentialities. If it is true that, at times, philanthropy was made to serve ulterior motives, it is true also that one of the glories of nineteenth-century Britain is the achievement of those outstanding men and women who, sacrificing leisure, ambition, and material gain, established the claims of a vast and underprivileged stratum of society. Moreover, we are apt to forget that it was they who blazed the trail into the then uncharted field of the scientific study of human relations, and that from their labours the sociological advances of the twentieth century have developed. In this sense of the word Vere Foster was, as a contemporary writer described him, 'A Prince of Philanthropists'.

He was, moreover, an Anglo-Irishman who devoted his life to Ireland. No full account has previously been written of his vast schemes to relieve by emigration the distress in Ireland that followed the Great Famine of 1845–47, and the scarcely less disastrous agricultural depression round 1880, nor has his unique contribution to the development of Irish national education been adequately recorded. But there was much more to him than that.

9

Vere Foster's family belonged to the Protestant Ascendancy in Ireland, that section of the Irish population which for centuries had held in its hands supreme authority and considerable wealth, people who were regarded, by and large (for there were notable exceptions) by the 'native' Irish as territorial thieves and ruthless persecutors of the Catholic faith. In 1800, scarcely nineteen years before Vere was born, the Act of Union (and the consequent completion of Catholic Emancipation some years later), turned their comfortable world upside down. The reactions of the old ascendancy to the new Ireland of the nineteenth century were varied and complex. The majority hankered after the old regime, but one of its sons—Vere Foster—accepted unequivocally a changed role in a changed society, an acceptance which he demonstrated by a line of action peculiar to himself.

Without knowledge of his family background much of the romance and colour of Vere's life is lost; the opening chapter, therefore, deals briefly with some of his illustrious ancestors.

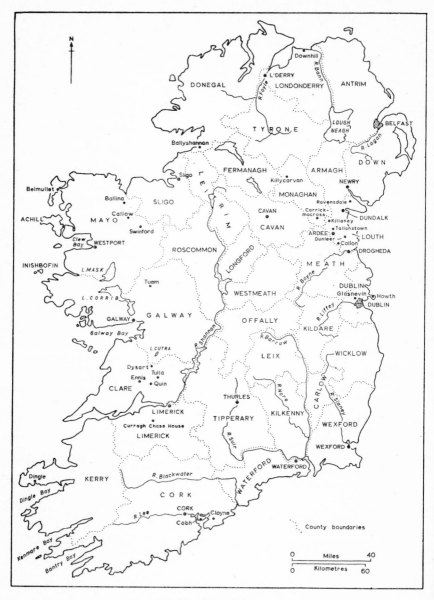

Map of Ireland

I

Introductory

Vere Henry Louis Foster was born in Copenhagen on 26 April 1819. For some days Augustus Foster, British Minister in Denmark, had awaited with impatience the arrival of this his third child, writing to his mother that Albinia was being 'provokingly tedious in giving birth to the new being'. The tediousness was much accentuated by the fact that, having already two sons, both parents longed for a daughter. A few days later the impatient father announced that 'Albinia has at last been safely delivered, but it is of a son instead of the wished-for daughter. However as I assisted this time and witnessed her sufferings the little delivered was made welcome.'[1] The child was named Louis for his paternal great-aunt and godmother, Louisa, wife of Lord Liverpool, the Prime Minister.[1a] The other names belonged to maternal relatives, but it is simply as Vere Foster that he is known to history.

After mentioning this somewhat inauspicious arrival, something must be said of the child's forbears, for they left him a notable heritage, and endowed him with great gifts.

1. The Earl-Bishop
Vere's paternal great-grandfather was Frederick Hervey, the Suffolk clergyman who became Bishop of Derry in 1769 and in

1780 succeeded his brother as 4th Earl of Bristol. This remarkable man, known as the Earl-Bishop—a title invented for him by Horace Walpole—has been remembered primarily as the builder of three great mansions (Downhill and Ballyscullion in his diocese of Derry, and Ickworth on the family estate in Suffolk), as a patron of artists and collector of art on the grand scale, and for his general magnificence. But there was much more to the Bishop of Derry than that.

Frederick Hervey was above everything else a pioneer, an adventurer, in the best sense of that word. In his diocese he strenuously opposed plurality of holdings, and his scheme for abolishing the hated Irish tithe system, formulated in 1774 but never implemented, foreshadowed the Tithe Act of 1838. He established funds to assist aged and infirm clergy and the widows of clergy, and the material welfare of all the inhabitants of his diocese, irrespective of class or creed, was his constant concern. Within a year of his arrival in Derry he laid plans for the first bridge to span the river Foyle at that point, contributing £1,000 to the project. Seams of coal were investigated in the hope of producing cheap fuel. Through the careful management of diocesan lands he became extremely wealthy, spending in the earlier years of his episcopate a great proportion of his wealth within his diocese.

As his estate at Downhill testified, he was an adventurer in land reclamation. Situated on a wild headland in the north of Co Derry, and swept by Atlantic gales, he 'converted'—to use his own words—'sixty acres of moor into a green carpet sprinkled with white clover . . . mountains were converted into arable land and grouse metamorphosed without a miracle into men.'[2] He built cottages and constructed roads on a scale, according to a contemporary commentator, that befitted a Roman emperor rather than a bishop of the Irish Church. In a letter to the then provost of Trinity College, he urged the need for the scientific study of agriculture in the university, and for agricultural education in schools.[3] His practical interest in the natural sciences, especially in basalt formations, earned for him membership of the Royal Society.

It is, however, as the first great pioneer of complete emancipation for Roman Catholics and religious freedom for all denominations that he must ever be honoured. In 1774 he was instrumental in having a bill introduced into the Irish House of Commons, to enable Catholics to take an oath of loyalty to the King without abjuring their spiritual allegiance to the Pope. That this first step towards mitigating the policy of the Penal laws should be taken by a bishop of the Irish Church was, at the time, extremely remarkable. He was an ardent advocate of parliamentary reform, and became a leading figure in the Volunteer movement, where he was strenuously opposed by Lord Charlemont.

Sometime about 1782 the bishop it would seem suffered a lasting and serious mental disturbance. Henceforward a quick and often erratic temperament became progressively more imperious, more extreme and more regardless of accepted conventions and patterns of behaviour. The oft-described flamboyant entrance into Dublin for the Volunteer Convention of 1783 was but one instance of his malady, as were the tragic quarrels within his own family, and the exaggerated friendships with Lady Hamilton and others, follies vigorously exploited by gossipy writers at the time and ever since, though there are no grounds for attributing to them any immoral significance. Vast sums of money were spent on buildings and pictures, and journeys to the continent were frequent. Finally, in 1791, Frederick left his city of Derry never to return, spending his last twelve years constantly travelling in Italy and Germany. He died at Albano near Rome in 1803.

No memorial was raised to this remarkable bishop in Ireland, but the inhabitants of his diocese erected an obelisk at Ickworth. The long inscription setting out his virtues concludes: 'Grateful for benefits which they can never forget the inhabitants of Derry have erected at Ickworth this durable record of their attachment. The Roman Catholic Bishop and the Dissenting Minister resident at Derry were among those who contributed to this monument.' Those who are aware of the depth of the cleavage that separated classes and creeds in Ireland during the eighteenth century can appreciate the uniqueness of this tribute.

2. Lady Elizabeth Foster

In 1776 the bishop's second daughter Elizabeth married John Thomas Foster, only son of the Rev Thomas Foster, DD, rector of Dunleer, in Co Louth, and a cousin of John Foster, the last Speaker of the Irish House of Commons.

The Fosters were extensive landowners in Co Louth. Arthur Young devotes pages of *A Tour in Ireland* to commending the agricultural improvements affected by Chief Baron Foster, the Speaker's father : 'these were of a magnitude I have never heard of before.' In twenty-two years a barren property of 5,000 acres 'deemed irreclaimable' was made to 'smile with cultivation . . . the country is now a sheet of corn.' He planted vast numbers of trees. He bought stock for industrious tenants, 'leaving them to pay as they could . . . He dictated to them what they should do with their lands, promising to pay the loss if anything should happen, while all the advantage would be their own. They obeyed him implicitly, and he never had a demand for a shilling loss.' 'Such are the men,' Young concludes, 'to whom monarchs should decree their honours, and nations erect their statues.'

John Thomas, the nephew of this dynamic personality, had been educated at Drogheda Grammar School, Trinity College, Dublin, and Christ Church, Oxford. He subsequently made the Grand Tour and in the year of his marriage, at the age of twenty-nine, became member of parliament for Dunleer. We do not know how he met Elizabeth Hervey. She was eleven years his junior and for two years he waited patiently for her hand. She was lively, gay, and extremely intelligent. Of all his children the bishop found in Elizabeth the greatest intellectual companionship, he shared with her his political aspirations and it is likely that he viewed very favourably, may indeed have pressed, this match with a member of the liberal and influential Foster family. Elizabeth, for all her high spirits, had perhaps less worldly experience than most of her young contemporaries, for the bishop, strangely parsimonious in some directions, kept his family on a very tight rein, and his daughters do not seem to have participated in the gay, sophisticated social life that the Dublin of their day offered. In the light of what happened it may be that, while strongly attracted by John Thomas's scholarly gifts and gratified no doubt by his patient wooing, to Elizabeth marriage was primarily desirable as the only way in which she could develop her own gifts and personality.

The first months of married life were spent very happily on the continent with the Bishop and Mrs Hervey; the bishop intent on his investigations of the Gallican settlement between the French Roman Catholics and the Papacy, which he hoped might provide a solution for Irish difficulties; John Thomas, no doubt, being schooled for the part he was expected to play in the Irish House of Commons in furthering emancipation, and proving, meanwhile, to everyone's delight his devotion to his young wife. The couple returned to Ireland in time for the birth of the first baby, another Frederick. John Thomas became immersed in his parliamentary duties and loneliness assailed his bride, loneliness not so much for her parents as for the life she had learned to enjoy as she had travelled about in France, Belgium, and Italy. Whatever the cause, and there is no indication that it was anything but impatience with boredom, at the end of three years Elizabeth left her husband, seeking refuge with her mother at Ickworth, where in December 1780 her second son, Augustus John, was born. Two years later the separation was complete, and the two little boys were sent back to their father in Ireland.

For a short time Elizabeth, now in very straightened circumstances, lived in Bath and there her friendship with the Duke and Duchess of Devonshire began. Georgiana, the Duchess, with characteristic kindness, persuaded her husband to employ this unfortunate young woman as governess to his illegitimate daughter, and in 1782 Elizabeth set off with the girl on a long tour through France to Italy. When she returned with her charge after an absence of eighteen months, she and the duke fell deeply in love; she became his mistress, while at the same time the ties of affection that bound her to Georgiana were strengthened. During the next three years she bore the duke two children, but most of that time was spent abroad in order to stifle any suspicion of scandal. The daughter, Caroline St Jules, was born in Ischia, and Clifford, the duke's eldest son, later Admiral Sir Augustus Clifford, first saw the light of day in Rouen.

Meanwhile Georgiana's dependence on Elizabeth increased. Her marriage, though socially successful, had been less than happy, now her fantastic and ever increasing gambling debts widened the breach with her husband. It was indeed owing to Elizabeth's influence with the duke on behalf of Georgiana that he treated his wife with considerable generosity. Strange as it may seem, it was Elizabeth who kept the marriage from ultimate collapse. Inheriting all her father's interest in politics, she became one of the leading figures in the Devonshire House circle. She was the political confidante of the duke, ever urging him out of his habitual lethargy; the Prince Regent sought her advice as did Charles James Fox, Sheridan, and other Whig leaders, advice that was all the more attractive because of the charm with which it was dispensed; and it was Edward Gibbon who remarked that 'no man could withstand her, and that if she chose to beckon the Lord Chancellor from his Woolsack in full sight of the world, he could not resist obedience.'[3a] While all her portraits show a face of great vivacity and intelligence, this rare charm was dependent on something deeper than striking physical beauty. It is noteworthy that strewn as her path must have been with every sort of hazard, she was never unfaithful to her husband while she lived with him, and afterwards she was never unfaithful to the duke.

On the death of John Thomas Foster in 1796 Elizabeth was re-united to her two Foster sons, whom she had not seen since parting with them at Bristol fourteen years earlier. While to both boys the wonderful new-found mother was a source of joy and happiness, to Augustus—a sensitive lad of sixteen—she opened an unknown world, radiant with understanding and affection. From the moment he beheld her he found in her a perfection that he accepted unquestioningly, enjoyed unquestioningly and worshipped unquestioningly till the end of her life. From now onwards their story is intertwined. It is contained for the most part in a long series of enchanting letters that passed between them over a period of twenty-five years, for as things turned out, they were seldom together.

Both boys were warmly welcomed by the Duke and Duchess, and Devonshire House, with its satellite mansions, became their home. Frederick immediately entered Christ Church, Oxford, where he read law. Augustus became a cornet in the Horse Guards, went to Christ Church to study 'the art of War' and then to a military academy at Weimar. It is with Augustus, Vere's father, that we are now concerned.

3. *Augustus Foster*

In 1802 Augustus was joined by his cousin John Leslie Foster —later Baron Foster—and young Lord Aberdeen—the future Foreign Secretary and Prime Minister—on a prolonged tour in France, Italy, Greece, Turkey, and Asia Minor. Armed with the most influential introductions he attended the great functions and military reviews in Paris that welcomed the Peace of Amiens. He was presented to Napoleon and he met many of the prominent political and literary figures of the new regime in France, but it was the stirring of a hitherto dormant interest in classical antiquity in Italy and Greece that altered the course of his life. His letters are full of enjoyment and enthusiasm; the joys of Greece, even the little wild flowers, are almost beyond description. The army career was abandoned; 'diplomaticks' seemed to offer more alluring opportunities for pursuing these peaceful interests, but the first vacancy in the foreign service that his uncle Lord Bristol could secure was, alas, on the small staff of the British envoy at Washington. The appointment was regarded as nothing short of banishment; Augustus declared that he could not quit the 'land of Liberty and Greatness' for more than a year, and Lord Aberdeen wrote flippantly about 'the muddy notions of Americans about Liberty, how unlike our Athens'.[4] No one even yet imagined that the recently lost colonies had any importance whatever.

Augustus remained in Washington for four years. Elizabeth's letters to him record great events, the victory of Trafalgar and the death of Nelson, the death of Pitt, ministerial changes and the death of Fox at the Duke's house at Chiswick. At the same time she followed every detail of his work in America with the closest interest. If, as he wrote, Washington was dull and its society execrable, she begged him to use the time to improve his knowledge of languages, pointing out that 'foreign ambassadors are delighted with Mr Fox, & rejoic'd talking & being talk'd to in french'. Many of Augustus's letters are written in French, his mother correcting the errors in her replies. Dull though it all might be she counselled him 'to work *double tides*, believe me it will tell all your life', and she stresses the value of an enthusiastic interest in whatever he undertakes :

A really true enthusiastic mind will never want an object for its enthusiasm : you may be an enthusiast in friendship, an enthusiast in love, in the forming of one's character to the practice of every virtue and the fulfilling of every duty; and enthusiasm is in fact what, well directed, leads to the attainment of every virtue and enables the possessor of it to walk out of the common track of common characters who rest satisfied with doing what is required of them, but never are equal to that most generous, most rare of all qualities *l'oubli de soi-même* : it leads also to a great indulgence for others, and a great severity to one's self.[5]

There is no better delineation of her own character, no better evidence of her devotion to her son.

Augustus for his part told her everything. He threw himself into his work with all the desired enthusiasm. Mr Merry, the British Minister, disliked intensely the republican atmosphere in Washington; he and his wife were not a very exhilarating couple. There was much that was unpleasantly strange to a young man accustomed to the polished manners of Devonshire House; the rough and apparently boorish behaviour of President Jefferson offended his sense of propriety, but he was, nevertheless, charming and friendly with everyone, and won the hearts of all. He was invited by Jefferson to his country estate at Monticello, and he stayed with the Madisons at Montpellier. He travelled extensively through all the states then constituting the Union, making exhaustive notes of everything he saw. The great forests enthralled him, and many seeds of rare species were sent to the duke for Chiswick and Chatsworth, and to Speaker Foster for Oriel Temple in Co Louth. He acquired all possible information concerning the origin and history of the American Indians, and the collection of paintings by the artist St Memin of members of different tribes which he commissioned is now of outstanding value to students.[6] He was an excellent correspondent; his letters and his notebooks provide a unique commentary on early nineteenth-century American development.

In 1806, while he was still away, the Duchess of Devonshire—his mother's adored Georgiana—died. 'She was', Elizabeth wrote to him, 'the charm of my existence, my constant support in all my sorrows, the doubler and sharer of every joy', and his letters carried back to her a loving sympathy that cheered her stricken heart.

On his return from America in 1808 Augustus was appointed secretary and then chargé d'affaires at Stockholm, a position of importance, for Sweden was England's only remaining European ally in her struggle with Napoleon. Canning, then Foreign Secretary and a critical judge of young men in the diplomatic service, had a high opinion of Augustus, telling his mother 'that he was happy in any opportunity of bringing you forward, certain that you would do yourself credit in it—that you had done so, that he had left a written minute in the Office to mark his approbation of your conduct'.[7] But Napoleon's increasing influence in eastern Europe forced the Swedes to close their ports to British trade, and in 1810 the chargé d'affaires was withdrawn. A year earlier Elizabeth had married the Duke of Devonshire and when Augustus returned to London he found his mother very happy and in a position of great political prestige.

His days were filled with the ceaseless social, political, and intellectual activities that occupied the time and thoughts of the leading Whig families. His half-sister Caroline St Jules had married George Lamb, the younger brother of the future Lord Melbourne, and we may suppose that it was at Brocket Hall, or at the Melbourne house in Whitehall, that Augustus met Lady Melbourne's niece Annabella Milbanke, a wealthy, self-confident young heiress from Yorkshire. He courted her impetuously; she, with tantalising delay, refused to make up her mind. Augustus came over to Ireland to look after his property and to investigate possibilities of representing one of the Louth constituencies at Westminster. While still in Ireland, uncertain about Annabella and about his own future, he received a letter from his mother enclosing a note from the Prince Regent which, she wrote, had been 'handed to me at the Play and you will believe me that I never said one word about you to him or anybody else'. The note read as follows :

> I have pleasure to announce to you my dearest Duchess, that I have this day assented to the nomination of Mr Augustus Foster as Minister to the United States of America. I hope this will meet with your approval as nothing can ever afford me more pleasure than whatever I know can convey satisfaction both to yourself and to the dear Duke.[8]

Elizabeth begged her son to think seriously before throwing away what by now was 'considered an important and advantageous mission' on account of Annabella or the chance of a seat in Parliament, but 'having said what I felt it my duty to do my dearest Child, I can only leave the ultimate decision to you'. His uncle, Lord Bristol, urged acceptance : 'It cannot keep you long in exile', he wrote, 'and it gives you a footing in your profession which opens the brightest prospects to you . . . P. [erceval—the Prime Minister] talked of you with the utmost cordiality.'[9]

Augustus accepted the mission, but Annabella would not accept his proposal. A cordial welcome awaited him in the Washington of 1811, where his friendliness and charm had been remembered, and the new minister determined to perform his duties with the dignity and style befitting his rank and the nation he represented.

The political situation that he encountered in America was ex-

tremely serious. While his friends in England were delighted at
the honour of the appointment, the placing of such a burden of
responsibility on a relatively inexperienced diplomat revealed,
perhaps, the British Cabinet's meagre insight into the ramifica-
tions of the American position. The new ambassador was a young
man, just turned thirty, inclined to the right of centre in his
political views and quite without the Whig predilection for
American ideals. He was faced with a situation that called for
that most mature of qualities, the ability to understand the aims
of those who, while springing from one's own stock, have renounced most of its cherished assumptions. Once again Augustus
applied himself to his task with unremitting diligence and con-
scientious hard work. His meticulous dispatches poured back to
Westminster; the Foreign Office was delighted with its ambassador and praised the clarity of his messages. Were the instructions
sent out to him imbued with the forward-looking statesmanship
that the situation demanded?

Moreover, Augustus was worried about Annabella, and longed
'most anxiously' to get back to England 'to settle that point—
good or bad . . . No Minister ever had such temptations to break
up a negotiation . . . But I can't leave these members [of Con-
gress] to themselves two days together.' In 1811 the news of the
sudden death of the Duke of Devonshire added to his personal
burden, for he knew that, in addition to her grief, his mother's
way of life would now be completely altered. Communications
by sea, so dependent on the vagaries of wind and weather, were
painfully slow, and while, in response to his advice, an order from
Westminster rescinding some of the most obnoxious Orders in
Council against American trade was on its way across the
Atlantic, America declared war on Great Britain, on 18 June
1812.

Augustus was received with every sign of official approbation
when he returned to London in August, but all hope of Annabella had to be abandoned. He came to Ireland and considered
buying a property in Louth. His uncle, Lord Liverpool, now
Prime Minister, anxious to have a spokesman in Parliament com-

petent to deal with American affairs, secured for him the representation of Cockermouth, but Napoleon's dramatic retreat from
Moscow re-shaped the young man's destiny.

In 1814, at a moment of intense excitement, Augustus was
attached to the British Embassy in Paris, and again he shared in
great historic occasions. In the same year he was appointed
Minister to Copenhagen, and immediately represented Britain
on a four-power commission to negotiate the union of Norway
with Sweden. In recognition of his work on the commission he
received the congratulations of the Prince Regent, the thanks of
the Crown Prince of Sweden and the Great Cross of the Order
of Danneborg from the King of Denmark. 'What is this,' he
wrote to his mother, 'but serving God & Mammon, & being rewarded by both & yet I have la conscience nette . . . If such food
could make one fat I ought to be abundantly so.'[10] His long
connection with Copenhagen had now begun.

With Napoleon safely, as they thought, in Elba, British travellers flocked to the continent. Among them was the Duchess of
Devonshire and her eldest son Frederick Foster. Since the duke's
death, London, and indeed England, had become intolerable and
the old craving for the sunshine and warmth of Italy asserted
itself. She left England in 1814, stayed some time in Paris where
she was warmly welcomed by many friends, including Madame
Recamier, and in due course arrived in Rome. Augustus, reaching London on leave soon after she had departed, found everywhere people 'who inquire after you. Everybody, whether they
knew you or not, seems to consider you as a kind of National
Property of which they are proud.'[11] One of the first things he
did was to let his mother's house, No 13 Piccadilly Terrace, to
Lord Byron and his bride Annabella Milbanke, and it was there
that the unhappy year of their married life was spent. His other
important achievement was to become engaged to Albinia
Hobart, a niece of the 3rd Earl of Buckinghamshire, and connected with the Stuart family headed by the Earl of Bute, thus
bringing an essentially Tory flavour into a predominantly Whig
connection. They were married in March 1815, and their honey-

moon was cut short by the landing of Napoleon near Marseilles. By the end of April they were in Copenhagen.

Except for the birth of two sons—Frederick and Cavendish—there was little to disturb the orderly routine of the British Legation in the Danish capital. The steady flow of letters between Augustus and his mother continued. Elizabeth was happily and firmly settled in Rome. From the moment of her arrival she found herself at the centre of the intellectual and political life of the city. Very soon she met Cardinal Consalvi, then at the height of his power, having attended the Congress of Vienna as the papal plenipotentiary. Their acquaintance developed into a sincere and serene friendship that far outstripped political considerations. Consalvi was an accomplished classical scholar; in all probability it was he who first directed Elizabeth's attention to the work of restoring and preserving the ancient parts of the city, an undertaking in which he and the Pope, Pius VII, took a deep interest. Before long Elizabeth was actively engaged in excavation in the Forum, the uncovering of the base of the Column of Phocas and the discovery of its inscription being one of the first results of her labours. Writing to Augustus she says 'the excavation acquires great interest & some celebrity from Consalvi and the Pope having both been to visit it'. 'I long', replied Augustus, 'to see you at work with pencil and spade.'[12] She was one of the pioneers among women archaeologists. She was surrounded by scholars, artists, travellers, and statesmen, while those in need seldom appealed for her help in vain. It was a new life of great happiness and interest.

In 1817 Augustus, his wife, and two baby sons set out on the long journey from Copenhagen to visit her, a visit that brought unbounded delight to both. So great was the joy of companionship that Elizabeth determined to get Augustus moved to a southern mission, and shortly after he left her she set out for England with four objectives: to beg Castlereagh to move Augustus, to see her daughter Caroline Lamb, to further Consalvi's efforts to win British support against Austrian domination in Italy, and to press Canova's request that Britain should make available to Rome plaster casts of the Elgin Marbles. For Augustus she could get nothing more than a promise from the Foreign Secretary—a promise that materialised in a move to Turin three months after her death. For the Prince Regent she had still all the old charm : 'There never was anybody kinder than the Prince has been to me, & he granted me the Elgin casts for Rome with *une grace particulaire*; we got to talk of the dear Cardinal as of a mutual friend, & he said cd there always be a Pope like Pius 7th & a Minister like Consalvi there cd be no hesitation at sending a Minister to reside at that Court.'[13]

In London she was warmly welcomed and lavishly entertained. Charles Kean gave a special performance of *Othello* in her honour. In Paris, on her way back to Italy, she had a tumultuous reception—soirées, dinners, theatres, operas, concerts fill pages of long letters to Augustus. The years could not diminish that incomparable charm. In Rome she was at once immersed in her work and in her rôle as a great hostess. Lawrence arrived to paint the portraits of the Pope and of Consalvi, part of the commission from the Prince Regent for portraits of all the participants in the Congress of Vienna, and it was then that he made the exquisite drawing of the Duchess.* She was sixty-one, an elderly lady by the standards of her time, but there was nothing elderly about her. On another short visit to England in 1822 she met Augustus and his family on leave from Copenhagen, and this time there was the little Vere. In Rome in the spring of 1824 she fell ill, one of her chesty colds which rapidly became more serious, and on the 30 March 1824 she died, loved and tenderly cared for during her illness by her stepson the 6th Duke of Devonshire. She was mourned by rich and poor, her compassion to the needy having known no bounds. Her body was brought to England and was laid beside her husband and Georgiana in the Devonshire vault in St Mary's Church in Derby.

* Now at Chatsworth.

2

Early Years

Vere was five when, in 1824, his father was appointed British Minister to the Court of Sardinia, and Turin was to be his home for sixteen years.

It must have been a sad anticlimax for Augustus to find himself in the longed-for Italy three months after his mother's death, for without her Italy was shorn of half its glory and Turin had little of the Roman glamour. Indeed, Piedmont was involved in the political unrest that was spreading throughout northern Italy; Mazzini, born in Genoa in 1805, had already been engaged in subversive republican movements. The reactionary tendencies of the ruling house of Savoy did nothing to counter such developments; the court and internal politics were dominated by the increasing influence of the Jesuits. The stiffness of official etiquette, the aloofness of the ruling families, the distrust of liberal ideas, presented an unattractive situation to the British Minister, for Augustus Foster was essentially a friendly, sociable person. To his disgust Turin possessed no public assembly room. The theatre was stinted for money and could only afford local talent. Ministers seldom met except in the course of their official duties, the Governor pocketing his entertainment allowance. The King was 'shy and embarrassed and thinks it a bore to be a king'. A

rigid censorship prevented the easy circulation of books. Altogether it was, in Augustus's words, 'poor, dull, uncommunicative
Turin'.[1]

As in America and Denmark it was his delight to maintain the
prestige of the British Foreign Service and, whatever might be the
standards of the Piedmontese, entertaining at the British Legation
was on a generous, even sumptuous scale. 'We gave our great Ball
to-night,' he wrote, 'to which above 800 were invited & not less
than 600 came & we had at one time 17 degrees of heat in the
Saloon. It was a beautiful Ball & they all seemed as happy as
could be. It lasted from 8 in the evening till 6 in the morning.'[2]

Some congenial spirits there undoubtedly were, among them
Plana the astronomer and the frequenters of the 'chymestry lectures', but it was with the Cavour family that the Fosters enjoyed
intimate and stimulating friendship. Many evenings were spent
with the count and his wife, playing whist and discussing
European affairs, and when Camille, the second son, was present,
there was more discussion than whist. The future unifier of Italy
was then a young man of twenty who had left the army and
was devoting his time to improving his father's estates, to making
himself acquainted with new industrial methods, machinery, fac-
tories, railroads and the like, and to studying current political
ideas. His dreams for the House of Savoy were already taking
shape. Vere must often have listened to these engrossing conversations. We do not know if he heard at the time of Garibaldi, the
daring young sailor from Nice who had joined the Sardinian navy
with the sole purpose of spreading revolutionary propaganda,
and had fled the country in 1834 to escape the sentence of death
that his treasonable activities had earned him, but some years later
they were to become closely acquainted in South America.

During the heat of summer the family escaped to their country
house, the Vigna, by the river. There are many references in
Augustus's diary to this delightful resort, its cherished garden and
the earliest spring flowers. Family letters cease after the death of
his mother, and it is from his diaries that all we know of subsequent family history is gleaned. Unfortunately the little red

volumes for the first years in Turin are missing, so information regarding the early childhood of his sons, Frederick, Cavendish, and Vere, is scant. By reason, however, of the irrational fate that hovers over family papers one fleeting glimpse has been preserved; a bundle of childish letters has survived. They were written by the boys to their uncle Frederick during a leave spent by the family at Uddins, a country house in Dorset. The following is the only one from Vere, but its laconic matter-of-factness and insistence on detail and accuracy are curiously indicative of his maturer style—he was nine when he wrote it.

> My dear Uncle,
> If you like to bathe in the sea there is a very nice place near here called Swanage. Papa and Mama are going there tomorrow. We have caught 18 rabbits with the ferret, and papa shot nine and 24 partridges, 7 hares, 1 snipe, 1 landrail, 5 cock pheasants and he saw a spotted rabbit . . . We went to mr bethel's on sunday, it is a very nice situation. Cavy and Freddy ride by turns every evening. Mamma has cut off all her hair and has got a wig.[3]

In 1830, at the age of eleven, Vere followed his brothers to Eton. None of them achieved any academic distinction at school and Vere left in 1834 to continue his education privately in Turin before entering Christ Church, Oxford. Almost the only thing we know about his Eton career is that during it he was smitten with smallpox.

Augustus worried a good deal about the future of his boys. From his various comments it would appear that the scramble for jobs was as ruthless then as now, though patronage rather than examination results was the gateway to success, and in this respect Augustus felt himself handicapped by reason of his distance from London. The great days of nineteenth-century colonial administration had not yet set in and there were too many aspirants for attractive Foreign Office posts. One young attaché in Florence confessed to Augustus that he was afraid to go on leave in case his place would be snatched in his absence for some importunate applicant. Frederick, the eldest son, was destined almost as a matter of course for the diplomatic service,

Cavendish would go into the Church, but what about Vere? Advice regarding the law was sought from George Lamb, who, perhaps wisely, refused to commit himself, and we may suppose that it was with the intention of reading for the bar that Vere went up to Oxford in 1838. No worries about the future appear to have dulled his gay spirits and exuberant enjoyment of life. The few references to him that exist are all of enthusiasm and sociability, whether it be his schoolboy delight in bringing two companions to enjoy a huge meal with his father at the Christopher Inn at Windsor, in planning long and dangerous treks during a family holiday on Mont Cenis, or in enjoying the companionship of the gay young men at Christ Church. During a Christmas vacation spent with relatives in England Augustus sent Vere a letter of introduction to Mr Quintin Dick, explaining to Cavendish that 'I have not included one for you, as one is more likely to be well received than two, & should he still give dinners and invite you, you wd. only be bored with the Men of fashion among whom he lives'.⁴ There was no suggestion that the men of fashion would bore Vere.

Without any previous hint of a civil service destination we read in Augustus's diary for January 1840 that 'Vere had been named a Clerk in the Audit Office—sorry to quit Oxford but pleased to be in the Treasury. Cavendish is offered the living of Hampden.' The next comment reads : 'Vere all gaiety in London.'⁵

In 1831 Augustus Foster had been created a baronet. In 1840, having started all his sons in their professional careers he retired from the diplomatic service, settled in London and some years later purchased, as a summer residence, Branksea Island in Poole Harbour. Before leaving Turin he had begun to prepare for publication the notes he had kept during his two spells of service in the United States. Few Englishmen then living possessed so much first-hand knowledge as he could draw upon of the early days of the now flourishing republic. So with the greatest care and regard for accuracy he extracted from his diaries information about the original states of the Union, recollections of Jefferson and Madison, the two presidents whom he knew intimately, and of the day to day life in political and diplomatic circles. The book failed to attract a publisher, but the manuscript eventually found its way to America where in recent years it has been edited* and is now acclaimed an indispensable source of early nineteenth-century American history.

At this point something must be said of Augustus's eldest son, Frederick, four years older than Vere. Adored by his father, this exceedingly attractive young man graduated from Trinity College, Cambridge in 1837 and immediately entered the diplomatic service. Palmerston, Foreign Secretary at the time, and distantly connected with the Fosters by marriage, arranged for Frederick to work for some time in his office before joining the staff of the legation at Turin as Augustus's secretary. Possessed of great personal charm and social expertise as well as a strong sense of duty, there was, alas, in this young man a strange, crippling lack of self-confidence that encouraged too much introspection and self-criticism. Trained by Augustus to the highest pitch of professional efficiency Frederick found himself, after serving for two years at Dresden, attached to the British Embassy in Vienna in 1844, at the particular request of the Ambassador, Sir Robert Gordon, brother of Lord Aberdeen. At this glittering court he was, contrary to the usual fate of humble attachés, received immediately into the highest ranks of Viennese society. Such seasoned diplomats as Metternich and the ageing Count Esterhazy welcomed him as the grandson of the renowned Duchess of Devonshire, and the owners of great houses showered their invitations upon him. It is worth noting, however, that it was amongst the liberal-minded aristocrats of Hungary that Frederick found the most congenial companionship; Louis Kossuth was already marshalling forces that would shortly drive Metternich from his stronghold in Vienna. Given the temperament necessary to grasp them, one would have said that all the honours of the diplomatic world were well within the reach of Frederick Foster.

Vere had none of his brother's inhibitions. Immensely sociable,

---

* *Jeffersonian America. Notes by Sir Augustus John Foster.* Edited by Richard Beale Davis. Huntington Library Publication. 1954.

he found his friends in every stratum of society, but mere fashionable gaiety had no appeal for him at all. While Frederick delighted the heart of every renowned London hostess, there is no mention of Vere in such orthodox circles. In everything he was adventurous, a pioneer; humdrum ordinariness bored him to death. Unlike his father and Frederick he was a wretched correspondent, the solace of letter-writing and diary-keeping had no lure for him. He could be maddeningly casual, but when the need arose his capacity for hard, relentless work was seemingly inexhaustible. Whatever he undertook was carried through with the utmost intensity, the smallest detail as well as broad outline engaging his attention. He was sturdy of build, with nothing of Frederick's elegant appearance, but he radiated friendship, enthusiasm and assurance.

Between these two brothers, so different in almost every respect and separated for long periods of time, there existed a bond of deep affection, each complemented the other. Neither of them married. Vere, so self-reliant, found in Frederick the one person in whom he wanted to confide, the one person who could understand the impelling motives so soon to drive him to the most important decision of his life; while for Frederick there was nothing but satisfaction in seeing his own unattained aspirations brought to life by Vere's unbounded confidence and drive.

Augustus's second son, the Reverend Cavendish Foster, by now a married man with an increasing family, was the odd man out, having little in common with his brothers.

There is no indication as to why, after just three years, Vere left the Audit Office. His father had evidently taken some steps to effect a move, for an undated letter from Sir Robert Peel informs him

> that it is wholly out of my power to comply with your wishes in respect to the transfer of your son from the Audit Office to the Treasury. Vacancies in the Treasury very rarely occur, perhaps once or twice in the course of the year and I am under such pressing engagements with regard to future nominations that I cannot hope to have the satisfaction of placing your son in the Treasury.[6]

Page 33 : Portrait of Vere Foster

Page 34 : (*above*) Boy and
girl at Cahera searching for
potatoes; (*below*) Sketch in
a house at Fahey's quay,
Ennis—the widow Connor
and her dying child.
(*See* p 56)

Having drawn a blank with the Prime Minister, Augustus presumably tried his friend Lord Aberdeen, the Foreign Secretary, and with more success, for Vere was attached to Sir Henry Ellis's mission to Brazil of which his cousin, Vere Hobart, was secretary. From bare statements in Frederick's diary we learn that Vere sailed from Plymouth on 3 October 1842, that Frederick heard from him 'off Madiera', and a fortnight later directed a letter to him at Rio de Janeiro.[7] So a second Foster son was launched on a diplomatic career.

Family records are silent about Vere's stay in Brazil. By the summer of 1844 he and Frederick were both in England, and in the autumn he set off on a long rambling holiday in Italy, Greece, and Turkey that lasted for a year. Augustus seized the opportunity of a meeting with Lord Aberdeen to ask for another assignment for his son, and then tormented himself because the casual and independent Vere did not write or give any indication of dates or places where he could be found. When, a few months later, the interview did indeed result in another appointment, Augustus was obliged to write hectically to every capital in Europe in wild efforts to locate his son, who eventually arrived in London 'with the haste of a Cabinet Courier from Florence' and just in time not to lose his appointment 'to be unpaid Attaché at Buenos Aires. I had written that very day to release Ld. Aberdeen from his Promise as he wrote me word he could not wait, Mr. Ouseley [the Envoy] having only his Wife and a boy of 15 to assist him.' Frederick, who was in Ireland, came to say goodbye, and there was just time to visit the 'Zoological Museum in Regent's Park' to see the South American animals and 'learn what they do not want that Vere may not send duplicates'. Vere sailed in December 1845. Four months later a letter arrived from the captain of the packet that had carried him as far as Rio de Janeiro, 'full of his Praise, his good Humour & agreeableness', and saying that Vere had already sailed for Montevideo.[8]

Uruguay, whither he was bound, was in a state of chronic civil war. Settled in the first instance by Portuguese from Brazil, the Spaniards in the Argentine could not tolerate these rivals on the opposite shore of the river Plate. Their constant quarrelling occasioned British intervention in the interests of trade, and in 1828 Uruguayan independence was secured, Rivera, the patriot leader, being installed as first President. Internal strife ensued, aided and abetted by Rosas, the Argentinian dictator, who besieged Montevideo from 1845 to 1851. Rivera, in his efforts to maintain independence, received half-hearted help from Great Britain and France, and enthusiastic support from an Italian legion under Garibaldi.

This was the situation when Vere arrived and it aroused all his sympathy for the oppressed. Mr Ouseley, Vere's chief, was an ardent admirer of Garibaldi, and in a short memorandum which he subsequently prepared for Lord Russell he wrote with enthusiasm of the patriot leader's skill as a commander, of his courage and of his outstanding integrity.[9] Garibaldi, the one-time sailor from Nice, now commanded the Montevidean naval flotilla. This small fleet had placed itself under the orders of the French and British admirals, whose governments arranged that all contact with the admirals and all supplies should be handled by the British legation. Vere must, therefore, have known Garibaldi well; many times he must have welcomed the caller who, wrote Mr Ouseley, 'used to come to me generally in the evening, and always enveloped in a Poncho or cloak, which garment he never quitted while the interview lasted. This appeared singular. I subsequently ascertained that his reason for coming after dark was that he had not the means to purchase lights for his own use, and therefore he wrote and prepared his orders, maps, etc as long as daylight lasted and then came to me. He wore the Poncho to conceal the delapidated state of his clothes, for he literally had not the wherewithal to procure a decent suit.'

Unfortunately none of Vere's letters from Montevideo exist. All we have are Augustus's references to them, and this extract, which he copied into his diary, from a letter written by Vere to Cavendish in 1846 :

Rosas is a Man of great Resources & has no opponent in any of these countries equal to him in Intellect. He was originally a

Cattle Tender & is a Man of no Education. He is aware that the Progress of Enlightment & Civilization in these Countries wd. be destruction to his ambitious Projects & his Reign of Terror & Ignorance. He therefore endeavours to exclude Foreigners from his dominions, suppresses literary Institutions & Schools, persecutes Gentlemen and confiscates their Property, thus appearing to favour the Poor, and with the Proceeds buys the Service of the *Press* & of numerous agents in Europe, N. America, Brazil, Chili & Bolivia. Mr Ouseley & Mr Diffaudis arrived here about 14 months ago with Instructions to settle the Dispute between Rosas & the Banda Oriental, amicably if *possible* but by *Force* is necessary. As however the Force was not at hand Rosas despised the Threats & Does not believe that they were made with Intentions to be executed; he believes that differences between us and the French, or between us & the U. States will cause the withdrawal of the Intervention & leave him at Liberty to pursue his Projects of placing his creature Oribe at the head of the Republick. The Rural population, however, are entirely against him & flock in numbers wherever a small force opposed to him exists.[10]

The situation worsened. Augustus considered the method of British intervention most 'discreditable' 'our threats are despised as are those of France . . . and we shall no doubt have to leave the country to its fate. I only wish my poor son were away from it. He complains of great weakness and as the Secretary and the paid attaché are gone away, on him, the unpaid attaché, all the work must fall.' Augustus wrote to Lord Palmerston, recently restored to the Foreign Office, requesting leave of absence for Vere, 'and as they give him no Pay & he works like a Horse at Montevideo, I don't suppose he can refuse it'. Realising, however, the wisdom of having a friend at court he visited Lady Palmerston, who was given some of Vere's letters to read. 'Lord Palmerston was quite unaware of my poor son Vere having undertaken to be attaché at Buenos Ayres in the full expectation of having subsequent pay & promotion; so I was obliged to refer to Ld. Aberdeen's note to me.' After a subsequent interview Augustus recorded :

I was sadly disappointed in regard to Ld P's intentions about Vere. He laughed at a Claim being set up by us for his being a

paid attaché, tho' Vere was pressed into the service at Rio de
Janeiro in 1843 [*sic*] & went to Buenos Ayres last year, the most
busy place certainly at the present time & where he expected
Ld Aberdeen to give him a salary or to move him elsewhere. Both
Aberdeen & Palmerston admitted the work to be important &
heavy & yet the latter will not hear of a Claim & I think in consequence that I may be justified in calling him home or at least
giving him leave to come away . . . Ouseley was highly disapproved of in not settling with Rosas.[11]

In spite of his father's entreaties that he should return from
Montevideo immediately and start reading for the Bar, Vere
refused to move until negotiations, recently opened by Lord Howden's special mission, were completed, thus leaving Augustus in
an agony of worry. More than that Vere had put his thoughts
very forcibly on paper, denouncing Rosas in such strong terms
that his father 'advised him again not to allow himself to be
affected by Party Spirit . . . Diplomats should not be partisans.'
And again : 'Had a letter from Vere on the 9th December, full
of Rosas as usual & containing nothing but Politics of La Plata,
the young man seems bewitched with these matters, & Ouseley
has quite mistaken the wishes of his Govt which was to wash
their hands of the Montevideans.' Vere lived with the Ouseleys,
and 'was indispensable as a man of regular Habits of Business to
him'.

This unrelenting perseverance, this championing of the cause
of liberty and his forthright expression of opinion were typical
of Vere's reactions to most situations. It would seem that his
outspoken 'partisan' comments reached the Foreign Office. Re-
proaching himself bitterly for not pressing Vere's claims to be
included in Lord Howden's mission Augustus writes : 'certainly
it was the thing to do, but H. Ellis observed upon their partisan
feelings—his and Mr Ouseley's—& no doubt had I been Ld
Howden I should have hesitated long before I shd. have agreed to
negotiate thro' a distrusted channel.'[12]

At length, in June 1847, Mr Ouseley and his attaché were
instructed to leave Montevideo. Like everything else about this
unpredictable young man Vere gave little warning of his home-

coming. An announcement in *The Times* that Mr Charles Ouseley and Mr Vere Foster had arrived in England—after a voyage of 75 days—was read with delight by Augustus but no direct message followed, Vere, unknown to his parents, going straight to the Foreign Office with his chief. When, in the small hours of an August morning, he eventually arrived at Branksea Castle, he was welcomed only by a sleepy servant, and when, somewhat later, Augustus crept eagerly into his bedroom 'there he was reposing'—sound asleep, as unruffled as if he had been away for a mere weekend. Further investigation revealed that he had brought with him from Montevideo, 'a menagerie . . . a Coati Mondi for me [recorded Augustus], two Kinds of Vultures, three Curacoa birds or Paraguay Pheasants . . . We placed the birds in the farmyard', and eventually they were transported to the Zoological Gardens in London.[13] History does not relate what happened to the Coati Mondi; he was, Augustus remarked, 'a rather inconvenient present'. Similar gifts had been brought for the Duke of Devonshire.

One wonders what Vere thought of his first Sunday at home, when, prevented from going to church on the mainland, Augustus 'read an excellent sermon from Miss Bowdler on equal duties imposed on all'. Bursting as he was with energy and enthusiasm, and still preoccupied with Uruguay, there were many journeys to the Foreign Office, now made so easy by the new railway that ran from London to Poole, and Vere was ever an enthusiast for the benefits of invention. On a visit to Sir Augustus Clifford at Ryde, the Fosters found Lady Palmerston among the guests. She 'spoke to Vere, making a sharp attack on Mr Ouseley his late Chief whom he [Vere] defended'. The Foreign Secretary's wife knew a good deal about what went on in her husband's department and she was not accustomed to contradiction, especially from a young attaché on whose diplomatic future she could, no doubt, exert considerable influence. Nevertheless she admitted, Augustus noted, 'that he was a nice young man & she approved of his readiness to defend his friend & she invited him & me & Ly. A. to Broadlands between the 20th Sept. & 4th Oct'.[14]

To Augustus this impetuous, forthright son was almost incomprehensible. After long periods of separation 'our little Vere', 'my poor son Vere' had returned a self-assured man, accustomed to gaining his point, uninfluenced by what other people thought of him, and possessed of energy and vitality unknown to his brothers. He was never stationary; within days of his arrival home he had brought young Ouseley to stay at Branksea and together they organised the entire male staff in a complicated manoeuvre to count the deer on the island, the next moment he was off to London.

Vere, it should be noted, had none of his father's passionate enthusiasm for field sports. He was a poor shot, due perhaps to defective vision, for all his life he was troubled with his eyes. Now, on one of their first days out with guns, Augustus noticed 'that he shot away as if they [the deer] were hares, only at a 100 yds. off or 150 as might be'. And a few days later : 'Vere shot the donkey by mistake in the Dusk, not knowing that there was one on the Island & taking it for a Doe grazing—which is not so easily approached.' Patient remarks, in the face of such extraordinary behaviour!

If Vere was not a keen sportsman he was an inveterate and enthusiastic traveller. Every new scene was a fresh interest and delight. Above all it was people and schemes that appealed to him, schemes that would make life easier and more rewarding for those who had few opportunities for advancement. He had many friends in every walk of life, indeed at times his father had been critical of some of the individuals from Uruguay whom he had been asked to befriend on their visits to England. If it was Frederick who inherited so much of the Hervey charm and sensitivity, it was Vere who possessed the mental and physical energy, the unpredictability, the dramatic touch, of the great grandfather who once adorned the See of Derry.

All of which increased the moments of parental bewilderment, as when, on receiving a friendly invitation from the Duke of Devonshire to spend a few days at Chatsworth, Vere electrified everyone by declaring that he didn't think he'd go as Mr Ouseley might require him in London. Horrified at this lack of family courtesy, not to speak of prudence, Augustus instantly wrote to Mr Ouseley to know if Vere—the unpaid attaché—could not be spared for at least a short visit. Of course he could, and the reply letter contained also a sentence 'praising [Vere] as the most unselfish person he ever knew'.[15]

No chances were being taken with the visit to Broadlands. Naturally Augustus judged that for Vere much would depend upon its outcome, little did he know that for himself it would be his last appearance in exalted political society. Everything went well. Vere turned up on time from Chatsworth, there were other delightful guests, and though the Foreign Secretary worked from breakfast till three or four o'clock in the afternoon and then went for a ride before dinner, Vere must have won the great man's confidence, with results that will be evident later in this story.

1847! After leaving Broadlands in October Vere came to Ireland on what was, so far as we know, his first visit—to an Ireland already ravaged by three years of famine and fever. On two occasions Frederick had spent long spells here attending to affairs on his father's property and paying visits to many relations— Massereenes, Dufferins, Farnhams, Portarlingtons, Waterfords, Fitzgeralds, were but some of the names included in the family connection, and he looked forward to becoming, in time, a resident landlord. There is every indication that in his earlier days Augustus Foster intended to have a residence in Ireland; one imagines, though without any supporting evidence, that it was Albinia who did not encourage the idea. From his forbears he inherited a tradition of wise and benevolent landowning, and though, through force of circumstances, he himself was an absentee, he unhesitatingly endeavoured to maintain it. He visited his estates on every leave and when abroad kept in constant communication with his agent. What could be more settled and peaceful than this entry in his diary of January 1845 : 'Sent £35 to aid and assist my Killany Tenants in getting their Cottages into nicer order.' His scrupulous fairness to all, his tolerance of and benefactions to the Roman Catholics, and his abhorrence of proselytising ensured that neither Ribbon-men, Whiteboys nor other manifestations of religious and economic strife molested his estates.

On the great question of Catholic Emancipation, Augustus Foster had never wavered. When on his return from America in 1812 Lord Liverpool wished him to enter Parliament :

> I took care [he writes] to stipulate to my uncle . . . that I should be at liberty to vote in favour of Roman Catholic Emancipation which I thought then as I do now should be gradual but complete. Gradual, because of the respect due to the rooted feelings of a Protestant population that had rendered great services as well to the interests of civilization in Ireland as to the general government at all times, and complete because in the view I took of the question, when the plague against which you have established a quarantine has ceased the quarantine itself should not be kept up to the trying of innocent traders . . . Besides in no other part of the world perhaps does there exist such an anomaly as that of a government without an organ of communication between themselves and the religious feelings of six million of their subjects.[16]

When Augustus visited Ireland in 1828 the issue was once more rocking English politics and the great figure of O'Connell dominated the scene. He had no sympathy at all with the Liberator's methods, and like many another person, was alarmed at his power, but realising the urgency of the situation he wrote urgently to the Duke of Wellington from Dublin supporting the view that immediate relief must be granted.[16a] Three months later the Catholic Emancipation Act was passed at Westminster. Augustus was in Turin during the long struggle to abolish the Irish tithe system, for the passing of the Irish Poor Law in 1838 and for the first stages of the Repeal movement. When he returned to England in 1840 O'Connell's power was being challenged by the much more extreme Young Ireland Movement, and whilst Augustus consistently opposed all militant revolutionaries, he several times spoke of the folly of applying English solutions to Irish problems, and deplored the fact that Ireland must always be governed by English laws. He was heartily in favour of an increased government subsidy to the Roman Catholic College at Maynooth.

Having kept closely in touch with Irish affairs since his return to England, it seems strange that the early stages of the famine do not appear to have alarmed him unduly. It is true that because of its geographical position on the drier eastern coast, Louth suffered less from the actual ravages of the potato blight than counties on the western seaboard. In 1846 he and his brother Frederick had sent money and large quantities of rice for the poor of Dundalk, and in a letter to *The Times* he expressed the view that 'it would cost the country much less, and be more beneficial to send direct relief of this sort than to be employing the people on public works of very doubtful utility, for it is food, not money, that is wanted.[17] And up to a point he was right. As at all times he was a considerate landlord, rents were remitted in cases of hardship, seed was advanced to those who could not pay for it, and where such palliatives were inadequate emigration was the prime solution. 'Colonisation' Augustus called it, planned by government agents who would explore all possibilities in developing countries. 'I think it might be attended with the best effects if such agencies were publically advertised to exist & then Irish landlords were to be heavily fined who eject Poor People & throw them upon the Neighbours.'[18]

It is worth noting that Vere was at home when these words were penned, and that this first visit to Ireland was to carry out his father's plans to assist one of his tenants to emigrate to America.

We have no indication of Vere's reactions to what he saw in Louth and elsewhere. He must have become aware of the unprecedented misery in the south and west. What did he think of the rising storm of agrarian unrest? Of the burnings, murders, and outrages that were daily occurences in Munster and Connaught, and now only less frequent near to the borders of his own county? What did he think of the group of young men, most of them Protestants, for whom O'Connell's pace was too slow—Thomas Davis, Smith O'Brien, John Mitchel, Francis Meagher and the other Young Irelanders? Alas, we do not know. But his independent and liberty-loving mind must surely have read some mean-

ing in the signs and the portentous daily happenings. He went
back to England.

In August of the following year—1848—Sir Augustus Foster
died. During his last months Vere was his constant companion,
his father gratefully recording that 'It is impossible to be more
kind & attentive than Ly. Alb. & Vere'. A long and painful illness was accompanied by tormenting religious doubts—the doubts
of a lifelong believer as to how the orthodox view of the Bible
could possibly stand up to the new developments in scientific
thought just then beginning to confront the world. Frequent passages in his diary, such as the following, show how agonising was
the mental struggle for this perplexed and ruthlessly honest seeker.
Referring to Blanco White's renunciation of Catholicism, he
writes :

> It wd. appear, however, that he was conscientious & in fact
> there is so much that appears nonsensical & incredible in our Dog-
> mas & so much that requires Mental Reservation that no wonder
> Persons of scrupulous minds revolt at the strange declarations
> they are called upon to make or to listen to—and were the whole
> Church not exposed to be broken up in the Effort, how glad we
> should all be to simplify & purify the Service from its incon-
> gruities, its Athanasian Uncharitableness & its unreasonable
> Length & repetitions. But [and here his innate distrust of violence
> intervenes] Reformers are too violent in general & too unscrupu-
> lous to be trusted and so we continue dreading one another's
> thoughts & opinions & dreading to be talked of.[19]

Not even the natural beauty of his beloved Branksea could
banish the doubts and restore his health. In a moment of great
anguish, and perhaps of great courage, Augustus Foster took his
own life.[20]

3

Vere Emerges

On his father's death Frederick, now Sir Frederick Foster, immediately left the diplomatic service and in due course crossed to Ireland. Though famine and fever had been less devastating in Louth than elsewhere, the districts round the eastern ports were at this time crowded with poor creatures who could scrape together the physical strength and the five shillings that would carry them to England, or, better still, the £4 10s that would convey them to the golden gate of America. Frederick's idea of becoming a resident landlord revived, the housing of his tenants and the care of his land engaged his attention, and he became increasingly convinced that the promotion of education—especially agricultural education—provided the only permanent remedy for the backwardness and poverty of the Irish peasant.

For Vere the months following his father's death were, perhaps, the only really unhappy period of his life. Ever since his return from Montevideo there had been problems. His future as a diplomat was uncertain, and for Vere any lack of purpose meant misery. For a few weeks in the winter of 1848–49 he was attached to the British Embassy in Brussels where his cousin Lord Howard de Walden was ambassador, but this led to nothing. Temperamentally Vere was not suited to a diplomatic career. So far as we know his experience of Ireland had been gained on that one short visit in 1847, but in April 1849 Frederick reports: 'Vere seems inclined to settle in Co. Louth and become agent.' In the summer of that year the two brothers were together in Ireland, first in their own county, then on a tour of Cork and Kerry, and finally in Dublin where they visited schools, workhouses, and, most significantly, the new model farm at Glasnevin, ending up with a 'pick-nick' at Howth with Foster cousins. Vere returned to England, and Frederick, after fulfilling his duties as high sheriff at the assizes in Dundalk, was in Dublin for the great occasion of Queen Victoria's first visit to her Irish subjects.

This is all we know, from the briefest statements in Frederick's diary,[1] of a period of important decisions for both men, but especially for Vere. During those weeks of travelling in the south and west, in country still prostrate from hunger and disease, during long discussions with Frederick, Vere made up his mind once and for all. He would 'quit the Queen's diplomatic profession', he would abandon the 'agent' idea, he would become a landowner, but of a new variety. He would, in his own words 'take a farm in the West of Ireland . . . in the hope of making myself useful by falling in with any practicable scheme for giving increased employment to the people, and for providing against a recurrence of similar destitution in the future'.[2] He would, in fact, give himself to the poorest of the Irish people. The idea of farming in the west may have owed something to *A Visit to Connaught* published in the autumn of 1847 by James H. Tuke, the young Quaker who, with his friend W. E. Forster—later Chief Secretary—had visited the stricken areas on behalf of the Quaker Relief Fund. Tuke urged that the wild wastes of country could be drained and developed, giving much needed employment and, he considered, a reasonable return on outlay. Be that as it may, in order to prepare himself for an entirely new life, and no doubt with Frederick's approval, Vere decided to take a year's course of agricultural training at the Glasnevin Model Farm. This was to be the beginning of a lifelong connection with the Commissioners of National Education in Ireland, and something must now be said about what was popularly called the Board of Education.

Ever since the Elizabethan subjugation of Ireland, education had been used by the invader as a weapon of oppression. It is true that in the seventeenth century schools were founded by the State and by the Established [Protestant] Church, but upon principles that of necessity debarred the Catholic Irish from using them. The penal laws of Anne and George I effectively destroyed what Catholic facilities remained by making it an offence, punishable by transportation or death, for a Roman Catholic to act as schoolmaster, or even as tutor in a catholic family, while heavy penalties awaited those who sent their children to schools and universities abroad. Nothing was left to the native Irish but the hedge schools, conducted secretly and forced to move from place to place. When by the end of the eighteenth century various relief acts had removed educational restrictions, the Catholic population was too poor to establish its own schools, and all available state aid remained in the hands of the Protestant ascendancy.

It was inevitable therefore that, following the Act of Union in 1800, one of the first matters to be considered by the newly constituted Irish administration was the provision of education on a national basis, acceptable to the three main religious denominations—the Roman Catholics, the Established Church, and the Dissenters. But it was not until 1831, after prolonged deliberations and one false start that foundered on the rock of religious instruction, that the Chief Secretary Lord Stanley—later Lord Derby—produced a scheme which was eventually accepted. Commissioners of National Education, drawn from the three religious denominations, were appointed, pledged to provide general education for all children together, religious instruction being given outside normal school hours to children in separate groups by clergymen of their own persuasion. A grant in aid was voted annually by Parliament. Though a 'mixed'* Board of

* 'Mixed' in relation to education at this period means a mixture of religious denominations.

Commissioners was certainly a great step forward the Catholic members at the outset numbered only two out of a total of seven, while the Catholic population of the country was approximately five-sixths of the whole. Strict regulations were made 'to prohibit all attempts at enforcing any religious instruction, either on Protestant or Roman Catholic children to which their parents or guardians object'.

Under the scheme all teachers received from the commissioners a small basic salary which it was understood would be supplemented locally by the person or body establishing the school, and by what the teachers themselves could collect in the way of school fees. Two-thirds of the cost of building new schools would be borne by the commissioners, the remaining one-third to be provided by local donors—religious bodies, landowners, and so forth. Such schools, however, had to be vested in the commissioners and their use for other than educational purposes was strictly forbidden. Schools could be held in premises not vested in the board, but in such cases the commissioners gave no initial building grant and accepted no responsibility for upkeep and repairs. A manager must be appointed for every school, vested or non-vested, responsible to the commissioners for its proper conduct, and all schools were to be open to inspection. Parents of children attending schools were expected to pay according to their means, a regulation extremely difficult to enforce. Facilities for training teachers at state expense were provided. Though the National system was not entirely state-aided, nor the education it provided entirely free, under its aegis schools were, for the first time, set up over the whole country, scattered and makeshift though many of them may have been.

The provision of nationwide education for a largely illiterate population was in itself a colossal task, but from the beginning the Board was hampered and harried by extremists from one or other of the three religious groups who were dissatisfied with the non-denominational basis of the system, and who used every form of pressure to further their sectional interests. While it is unnecessary to follow in detail these frustrating struggles they

must be kept in mind, for they recur continuously throughout
our period and influenced profoundly the development of education in Ireland. In spite of them, the exciting work of establishing a national system progressed, thanks to the undaunted
enthusiasm of the Board, the inspectors and—perhaps most of
all—of the teachers. From the beginning great stress was laid
on the importance of adapting the curriculum in rural areas to
agricultural needs, and to establishing wherever possible, 'agricultural national schools' which gave practical instruction in agricultural methods as part of the general programme. In 1837 a
farm was procured at Glasnevin, then a village on the outskirts
of Dublin, where teachers in training would receive the necessary
agricultural instruction. In 1844 the Devon Commission*
strongly supported the provision of agricultural education as the
surest way of raising the standards of those who 'exhibit proof of
the worst possible cultivation and scenes of appalling want'. But
it was the Great Famine that demonstrated beyond all controversy the devastating results of a peasantry entirely dependent on
one source of sustenance, and utterly ignorant, for a variety of
reasons, of the most rudimentary principles of land cultivation.
Writing to the commissioners in 1847 to urge the immediate extension of agricultural education, Lord Monteagle used these
words :

> What before the blight of the potato crop was a matter of
> undeniable usefulness, is now by this casualty made a matter of
> indispensible necessity . . . Had such a system as that now recom-
> mended been carried into effect wisely, but liberally, twenty years
> ago, how many lives, how many millions of money might have
> been saved in the last two years of sorrow. God grant that we,
> our Rulers and Legislature, may feel these convictions and pre-
> pare to act upon them with vigour, and without hesitation or
> delay.[3]

The commissioners did act with vigour. The scope of the model
farm at Glasnevin was extended to include the training of full-
time students of agriculture—young men who, as farmers, land

* Royal Commission of Inquiry into the state of law and practice in
respect of the occupation of land in Ireland. Chairman : Lord Devon.

stewards and so forth, would, it was hoped, do much to reform existing methods. Furthermore, Thomas Kirkpatrick MD, a 'visionary enthusiast' who had given impressive evidence to the Devon Commission in connection with a pioneer scheme for agricultural education operating in Co Antrim, was appointed the first agricultural inspector in 1848. Under his direction the Glasnevin Model Farm* developed rapidly in size and reputation, acquiring international fame, and it was he who initiated Vere Foster into an entirely new way of life.

In September 1849 Vere and Frederick met in Dublin for a couple of days. They dined with Lord Clarendon, the Lord Lieutenant, and before leaving for England Frederick saw his brother enrolled as a non-resident agricultural student at the Model Farm, and established in the nearby lodgings of Mrs Earl.

Vere was thirty years of age. With part of the great load of uncertainty gone we can imagine with what vigour and enthusiasm he threw himself into this new experience. The open-air life, the free and natural contact with his fellowmen—no matter from what rank of society they might come—delighted him, and having seen for himself the devastated areas of the south and west, having listened to Frederick's ideas about education, he was no doubt eager to learn more of the aspirations and mode of living of the Irish peasant. If Dr Kirkpatrick had any qualms about receiving this lively, enthusiastic, extremely friendly ex-diplomat into his group of raw country lads and some rather self-opinionated teachers in training, they were immediately dispelled. Vere was in his element. He rolled up his sleeves and worked in the fields, he sat on hard benches listening to lectures on animal husbandry, the principles of land drainage, the rotation of crops and so forth, and we cannot imagine that Mrs Earl's lodgings offered much in the way of comfort. He and Dr Kirkpatrick were kindred spirits, but it was the lads that won his heart. When at the end of the year the agricultural inspector com-

* Shortly to be renamed Albert College, following a visit by the Prince Consort.

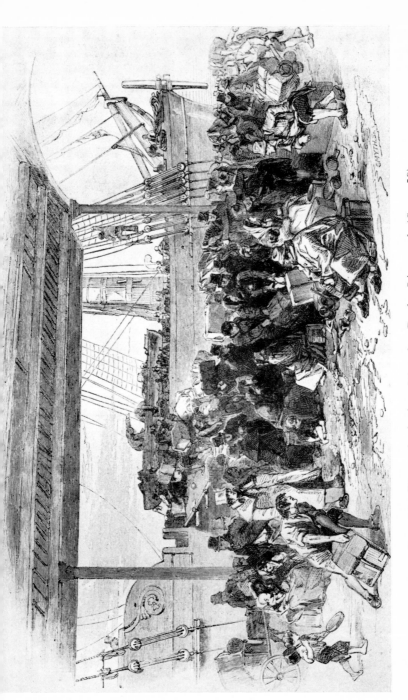

Page 51 : The embarkation, Waterloo Docks, Liverpool. (*See* p 59)

Page 52 : Emigration ship—between decks

posed his annual report for the commissioners, in the course of which he attributed to 'false pride' the reluctance on the part of some pupil-teachers to take part in 'the drudgery of agricultural labour', and maintained that 'the vigour of the body imparts itself to the intellect', he added this comment :

> In proof of this I might cite many instances of individuals of high rank and attainments who considered it an honour and a happiness to share in this employment; but I need not go farther than our own day, our own country, and our own schools, to find an instance in which a gentleman of high acquirements, and independent fortune (the brother of a baronet and high sheriff of one of our eastern counties), in order to acquire a perfect practical knowledge of agriculture, entered as an extern pupil at the Glasnevin establishment, and cheerfully assisted in all the farm operations. I have seen him with his coat off laying tiles in the bottom of a drain, and joining in every other kind of labour on the farm—yet he never thought it any degradation to be so employed; and I think it would be an insult to common sense to ask whether he, or one of the same rank, who would be afraid to soil his fingers, should be entitled to the most respect.[4]

Vere's other great problem was also on the way to being solved.

During the long months of Augustus's illness, Vere more than anyone must have realised the depths of his father's religious doubts and the insupportable suffering they had caused. As he recalled the keen, lively father of his childhood and youth, his whole nature revolted against such wasteful unhappiness. He had seen the valiant struggles to reconcile orthodox belief in the whole Bible with a rational Christian standard of behaviour : was reconciliation, Vere asked himself, really possible? Could any reasonable person accept the hotchpotch of conflicting statements contained in the old and new testaments? He himself had his doubts, so, we know, had Frederick; he would therefore endeavour by intensive study to discover once and for all where the truth lay. In the months immediately after Augustus's death, about which we know so little, the task was begun.

Unfortunately there are few indications of the sources he consulted or from whom he sought advice. We do know however

D

that he read, and was greatly impressed by *Vestiges of the Natural History of Creation*, a book that had appeared anonymously in 1844. In it the author declared that, while not a scientist himself, he had carefully studied the results of the most recent scientific research, and had made 'the first attempt to connect the natural sciences into a history of creation'. That this novel undertaking had reached its eleventh edition before the appearance of *The Origin of Species* in 1859 is an indication of the growing restiveness at the then orthodox opinion. It was in fact a brilliant exposition by a layman of the idea of evolution later to be scientifically propounded by Darwin. A layman's vapourings could, however, be discarded as utterly irrelevant by professional scientists and churchmen alike, and their comfortable bliss remained undisturbed for another decade. Advanced though the author of *Vestiges* was, his new vision did nothing to impair his belief in an ever-present 'Divine Author'. 'Does it not rather appear,' he writes, 'that our idea of the Deity can only be worthy of him in the ratio in which we advance in our knowledge of his works and ways, and that the acquisition of that knowledge is consequently an available means of our growing in a genuine reverence for him?

In what is left of a tattered little notebook belonging to Vere several passages from Hume have been copied: no doubt there were other writers to whom no references remain, and Frederick, we know, was implicated in this spiritual quest. There still exists, however, a ponderous Bible, seven inches by five inches by four inches thick, inscribed with Vere's name and the date, 1848, the gold on its fore-edges still shining, a perfect 'period piece'. The alternate plain pages are strewn with comments, signed chiefly F.F. but occasionally V.F., from which the following are taken at random:

Gen. IX.13. If no rainbow had been seen before this, the properties of light must have been different in the first 1700 years of the world's existence. F.F.
Deut. VII.2. Here's a pretty comment—to show *no* mercy. V.F.
Isaiah LXI. Vengeance!!! F.F.

Hosea VI.6. [extolling mercy] This is a favourite passage of our Lord. F.F.

and so on right to the end of the new testament.[5]

On one of the fly-leaves of this Bible Vere wrote in February 1850, presumably while he was at Glasnevin, this draft of a letter :

My dear

1. If any further argument were wanting to confirm me in my dissent from the religion established in this country, I could derive it from my abhorrence at the thought of believing in the truth of the 31st Chapter of the book of Numbers : our religion inculcating a belief in the truth of the old testament, of course we are bound to believe that the most unexampled atrocities that are to be found in the history of any nation were committed at the command of God, as related in that chapter.

2. 'The miracles' of Christ you say 'are supported by a mass of evidence such as no *jury* could by any possibility resist.' Where is that evidence? If there were such, our ecclesiastical writers would most certainly have treasured up and proclaimed them far and wide. But the fact is that, in the early ages of Christianity, divines alternately shifted their ground, now relying mainly on the evidence of the *prophecies*, and acknowledging that of the miracles to be weak, and again vice versa.

As to the 53rd Ch. of Isaiah, what evidence is there that it alludes to Christ? It seems to me a most far fetched interpretation to quote it as prophesying respecting Christ.

As to the other circumstances respecting the Jews' unbelief, which you say I have not touched upon, I admit that that unbelief was probably on account of their interpreting various prophecies as foretelling a *temporal*, not a spiritual Messiah : but I say they were wrong in expecting *either*.

Now that we have I suppose pretty well exhausted our arguments, convincing to each I believe on both sides, in support of our respective positions, and, as it is but lost time to repeat these arguments a 2nd time, I will state (what I have hitherto suspended, in order to first give time to state my objections, and to hear your answers to them), what are the principles on which, in default of a belief in Christianity, or in any other religion, I think it right to base my conduct in life.

Considering my ignorance of the means of pleasing God, through my inability to believe that he has ever made any revelation of his will to mankind, considering the impossibility, according to universal experience, of pleasing other people, I come to the conclusion that the best religion consists in that most simple art of *pleasing oneself*. That art is to be learned, like every other, only from experience, but the *smallest experience* is sufficient to convince that it is more pleasing, to be at peace than at enmity with one's fellow creatures, and my knowledge of that art tells me that superior pleasure is derivable from doing that which is agreeable to the best interests of society rather than the contrary.

This appears to me to be a practical religion, based on common sense and the best interests of mankind, to combine all the advantages of all other religions, with none of their mystery or faults.

Vere Foster

There is no indication to whom this letter was written. The recipient *may* have been his cousin, Lady Charlotte Hobart Hampden, for a family tradition maintains that some fundamental difference prevented them from marrying. Be that as it may, it was during his time at Glasnevin that Vere's spiritual struggle was fought to a finish. With the certainty of conviction he then recognised and accepted what was to be his way of life. Self-interest was thrown to the winds, doubt became a thing of the past, henceforward he envinced an untrammelled serenity in the face af bitter disappointments, considerable opposition, and continuing ill-health : a *joie de vivre* permeated everything he did.

If any are inclined to criticise the terms in which his victory is expressed, they should remember also the terms in which, only a hundred years ago, the struggle presented itself—both are outmoded today. As has already been mentioned, scholarly criticism, appreciation, and understanding very shortly altered completely the approach to biblical interpretation, as it was to change also the grounds of antagonism and unbelief.

As he worked in the fields at Glasnevin, as he talked to the young men from every corner of Ireland and listened to tragic tales of famine and devastating poverty, as he saw the potential ability, courage and vitality of the Irish peasant, as he sensed smouldering political discontent, he renewed his determination to devote his life, one way or another, to such as these. There was much to be done in every direction, but

> While awaiting the more slow, but I believe sure, accomplishment of that object [the amelioration of poverty], through the operation of the Act of Parliament for the Sale of Encumbered Estates in Ireland, and the Irish National System of Education . . . the anticipated extension of the suffrage to be proposed to Parliament by our Prime Minister in the next session, the substitution of resident improving proprietors for absentees, and other reforms, I believe that the most speedy and effectual *present* means of doing so is by personally aiding and advocating the Emigration of a portion of the population to some other more favoured land.[6]

So already 'education' had taken its place with 'resident improving proprietors' as a long-term remedy, and 'emigration' was to meet the immediate pressing need. We are now to see the speed, the penetrating imagination, the organising ability, the comprehensiveness, the humanity with which Vere translated this idea into action. Before his year of study at Glasnevin was completed he had, at his own expense, sent out forty emigrants to the United States of America, having, as he said himself :

> previously obtained from the police of the district, from their clergy, and from their employers and others in the neighbourhood, satisfactory answers to my inquiries respecting their characters and industrious habits. Having required in many cases a deposit of one pound, as a security of their being in earnest in proposing to emigrate, I then paid their passages in many different vessels, purchased their provisions, cooking utensils, etc., bedding and some clothing, furnished them with some money for their expenses before embarkation, and made arrangements that they should each receive at least their own deposit of one pound sterling on their arrival in an American port.[7]

This was to be the vanguard of a formidable army, and this was to be the pattern of every subsequent exercise.

The appalling horrors of the emigration ships were generally known, and it is strange that Vere does not appear to have consulted those who already had gained some experience of these

nightmare voyages, notably Stephen de Vere of Curragh Chase,
Co Limerick—Lord Monteagle's nephew—who in 1847 made
the journey to Quebec as a steerage passenger, taking with him a
party of emigrants from his own county. This he did, after all
remonstrances with shipping companies about 'extraordinary
sufferings and immense mortality' had proved fruitless, in order
to obtain first-hand knowledge of conditions which he intended
to pass on 'to the public and to Parliament'. His report, read
aloud in the House of Lords, contained such observations as this :
'I have myself when accompanying the emigration agent on his
visit of duty to inspect the [vessel] on her arrival, seen him stagger
back like one struck when first meeting the current of fetid infec-
tion exhaled from between her decks.'* On his arrival in Quebec
de Vere converted a large house into a hostel where his emigrants
could stay until work had been found, and where those stricken
with fever on the voyage 'received from him personally all the
ministrations which they could have had from a hospital nurse'.[8]
As a result of his exposures the Passengers' Act was considerably
amended to require better accommodation.

de Vere returned to Limerick in the autumn of 1848. It is
hard to believe that during that tour of the south-west in the
summer of 1849 Vere and Frederick did not stop at Curragh
Chase, and the fact that during the year at Glasnevin Vere found
time, as will be mentioned later, to visit 'the eight model lodging
houses for the labouring classes erected a year or two ago in
London' by Lord Ashley, suggests that perhaps it was indeed
Stephen de Vere who impressed upon him the need for such
accommodation for emigrants, a need which Vere in his turn was
shortly to impress on philanthropic bodies in America.

There was, however, on crucial point of difference between
them; de Vere's venture was primarily to relieve distress, while
with Vere Foster emigration was in itself, for certain types of
Irish peasant, an inherently good thing. Here his own nature came
into play, his love of enterprise, his intense interest in every new

* For graphic and authentic descriptions of conditions on emigrant ships see
Curiosities in Parliament, by Stanley Hyland.

development, his intolerance of such tradition and convention as condemned young people to lives of poverty, ill-health, and frustration, his fundamental conviction that people were meant to *enjoy* the blessings of this world, to have scope to develop their talents, and opportunity to lead decent, healthy lives. 'Considering,' he frequently declared, 'that it is as natural and desirable for young people to emigrate as for young bees to swarm, I soon became interested in the subject of emigration.' He knew from his own experience the opportunities awaiting enterprising settlers in the undeveloped areas of America, and he knew now the great potentialities of the Irish peasant—these young men and young women must be given their chance to fashion their own lives. It was here that he eventually met trouble.

Meanwhile, whether or not he and Stephen de Vere ever met, Vere Foster's next step was to set out himself on an emigrant ship, not only to experience the hazards of the voyage, but to explore the possibilities of employment in America. On 26 October 1850, accompanied by a Mr Ward, one of the teachers from Glasnevin, he boarded the American sailing ship *Washington*, 'the largest emigrant vessel afloat', bound for New York and carrying approximately one thousand emigrants, 'the largest number of passengers who ever sailed in a single ship'. Two of the passengers, at any rate, must have looked a little incongruous as, encumbered with bundles and utensils, they took their places on the Liverpool dock in that extraordinary collection of humanity.

4

After the Great Famine

The second extant letter written by Vere since the childish missive
mentioned on p 29 was penned on this voyage. It took the form
of a personal letter addressed presumably to Frederick, but
obviously intended for a wider audience. It became an historic
document and is given in full in Appendix I. Packed as it is with
detailed facts related without a trace of sensationalism, any summary is difficult. It must have been apparent from the start that
Vere was no ordinary traveller, and whether or not the Captain
and his officers were aware that his luggage contained a 'weighing
machine weighing so low as two ounzes' so that food allowances
could be accurately checked, they had little cause to welcome a
gentleman who had the audacity to suggest to them within the
first two or three days that life would be a lot pleasanter for everyone, themselves included, if they would treat the passengers with
an ordinary degree of civility. Instances of sadistic cruelty such as
the following frequently occur : 'This morning the first mate took
it into his head to play the hose upon the passengers in occupation of the waterclosets, drenching them from head to foot, the
fourth mate did the same a few mornings ago.' Vere himself was
knocked down by a blow from the first mate. Fearful overcrowding and a total lack of proper hygiene; the withholding of rations

for the first week of the voyage, the extraction of cash 'presents' for services that were due to every passenger, these, and other brutalities are reported in detail with an almost cold objectivity, and constitute a tale of horror that takes its place, along with the barbarities of the earlier slave ships and the later concentration camps, as evidence of the depths to which human nature can sink. Vere's inquiring activities no doubt infuriated the captain of the *Washington* and may have goaded a man of his nature to even greater excesses, but investigations showed that similar brutalities were frequent on emigrant ships, though there were at the same time notable instances of captains who, in most difficult circumstances, maintained perfectly humane conditions. The improved regulations resulting from Stephen de Vere's revelations were evidently disregarded with impunity, as inspection appears to have been non-existent. Vere Foster's health was very seriously impaired over a long period of years by the treatment he received on that voyage.

During the hearings in London of the subsequent Select Committee on the Passengers' Act, 1851, which was the direct result of Vere's report, the British Consul in New York was asked if there was an allegation that Mr Foster had 'harangued the passengers and excited them to complain'. He admitted that while he was not prepared to support such a charge he knew from Mr Foster's own admission 'that he took a very anxious part in the matter; that he took measures which, though founded perhaps on strict justice and right, would not tend to create a good feeling towards him in the ship; in fact he said that the captain said "We know who you are, you are a bloody pirate and we mean to serve you out for it".' When Vere found himself castigated as a spy by a Liverpool newspaper, he replied that he 'would bear with pleasure any odium attached to that appellation if my insight into the management of that vessel shall have proved in any degree conducive to a remedy to a serious public grievance'.[1]

It is true that, theoretically, legal redress for charges of assault and infringement of regulations could be sought on arrival at the port of destination and Vere made immediate inquiries from the

British Consul at New York, but he was dissuaded from instituting proceedings on grounds of expense and delay. What hope, therefore, had an ordinary poor emigrant?

One can imagine the horror with which the fastidious Frederick read this document. Anything more repellent to his nature than the whole performance could hardly be imagined, and yet his feelings are expressed in curiously restrained terms when he wrote to Vere in January 1851 :

> We were, as you may suppose, very much shocked to hear of the treatment you met with on board the Washington, and in the interest of all future Emigrants I thought it necessary to take some steps to make the Ships Companies more careful in their choice of officers.[2]

He wrote immediately to the Emigration Officer at Liverpool, who replied coldly that redress for most of the charges should have been obtained at New York, and to the agent of the Black Star Line, owners of the *Washington*, 'who has not deigned any answer'. Personal calls at Liverpool being equally unsatisfactory, Frederick put the whole affair into the hands of his cousin Vere Hobart, the one-time secretary of Sir Henry Ellis's mission to Brazil [p 35], now Lord Hobart of the Board of Trade, and a sympathetic observer of Irish affairs, who in February 1851 raised the matter in Parliament and a Select Committee under the chairmanship of Sidney Herbert was appointed to examine once again the working of the Passengers' Act. Vere was still in America and could not appear to give evidence, but his now famous *Washington* letter was circulated as a White Paper. Other evidence showed that Vere's experiences were by no means unique. There are descriptions of appalling overcrowding, unspeakable filth, lack of any kind of medical care, that surpass his report. The worse sufferers were always the single women. Utterly ignorant of what the voyage entailed they were the prey of every kind of fraudulent passage-broker, 'runner', and lodging-house keeper, while conditions on board ship were, more often than not, bereft of all decency. The Port Chaplain at Liverpool described how five or six beds [mattresses] were frequently stuffed into a berth made to hold four, and though regulations stipulated that the width of space alloted to each person should not be less than eighteen inches, there was no inspection to see that regulations were observed. Into such berths single people of both sexes might be herded. Sometimes, said the chaplain, beds were divided by a board 'the height of my hand' and had separate blankets, sometimes there was no division but one blanket to cover several beds : 'I have known cases of females who have had to sit up all nights upon their boxes in the steerage, because they could not think of going into bed with strange men.'[3] It was certainly difficult for the captain of any emigrant ship to allocate his berths judiciously; not till the ship actually sailed did he know how many of his passengers were married or single, male or female; the conditions that generally resulted can only be described as barbarous.

After that appalling voyage, and suffering treatment which, in Lord Hobart's words, 'was considerably worse than that ordinarily experienced by brutes', Vere spent his first night ashore as an emigrant, in one of the wretched quayside lodging houses. He visited

a great many others . . . in each of which I found a host of my late fellow-passengers. At all these houses the emigrants are duped, I among them . . . On arriving here [New York] a number (legion) of boarding-house man-catchers pounce upon the passengers, and hurry them off to their respective dens, where they charge them from one-half to a dollar per day, for a portion of a bed and bad food; ply them with drink, and charge them double their agreement, under some pretence or other, and pretend to get them canal or railroad tickets at a discount, while they are all the while adding several dollars to the price, and then ask for a present for having protected them from being cheated . . . There are numerous societies here for the protection of emigrants . . . The complaints, which I understand are general here, about Irish emigrants are, that they are extremely addicted to drunkenness, and put on considerable airs, much to the annoyance of their employers. It is not complained that they are unindustrious; on the contrary, it is wondered at that they are called so in the old country.[4]

If legal redress for his sufferings could not in practice be obtained, Vere, with a tenacity for fair play that was one of his dominant characteristics, appealed to the public in a long letter to the *New York Tribune* which summarised the experiences of the voyage. No doubt this letter formed the starting point of his friendship with the paper's remarkable founder and editor, Horace Greeley.

Next he must look up former friends whom he had helped to emigrate. 'I found out this evening a poor man and his wife from Glasnevin.' They were both doing well—how overjoyed they must have been with that cheery visit. 'I am happy to find that all my emigrants, whom I had any news of at all, are in situations. I got a situation the day before yesterday for a girl whom I had sent out, and who arrived last week; and yesterday a lady friend of mine got a situation for a girl whom I sent out from the North Dublin Union Workhouse . . . I have got places for two servant girls whom I brought from Finglas, with ladies; and also for two I sent from the workhouse. A man I sent from Swords, and who married Catherine Hughes, whom I sent from Glasnevin, earns a dollar a day in the navy yard here, while his wife takes in washing; and I know of three other men whom I sent being in good employment.'[5] There were many more such instances.

Only after all this had been accomplished was any kind of relaxation permitted. Throughout his life Vere was indifferent to physical comfort; to him movement and change, fresh air, and a certain spartan discipline were sources of delight. There was, however, one constant essential—scrupulous cleaniness, and in the oft-repeated references to the filth and stench of quarters on the *Washington* one can sense the acute misery it caused him, and can only hope that his hotel in the as yet uncompleted Broadway provided what he called on another occasion 'a princely bath'. Armed with introductions from his influential relations he found friends immediately. New York delighted him. 'This is a fine city, and I am in the centre of the finest and most stirring street in it—namely Broadway—whose skeleton is already laid out thirteen miles long. I noted ninety-seven omnibuses pass this door in the course of exactly fifteen minutes. It is curious to see the electric telegraph carried through the centre of the most busy part of the town; also the railway in the same street with the omnibuses, etc.; some of the carriages are drawn by horses, and one set by a noiseless steam-engine without smoke . . . I have visited some of the finest houses here, which are furnished in the most magnificent and elegant manner and crowded with ornaments. The owners pride themselves supremely on what they call the style of their houses.'[6]

Allowing himself only a few days to rest and recover from the immediate effects of the illness contracted on the voyage, Vere began, in February 1851, the second part of this enterprise, namely a ten months' trek alone through practically all the states then constituting the Union, in order to make every possible inquiry regarding emigration—the employment, wages, and opportunities awaiting emigrants, where they should go and when they should arrive, and, no less important, how they should behave. With his characteristic grasp of the whole situation he realised that mass shipment of people to America was, from the standpoint of their ultimate welfare, merely the commencement of the operation. To bring it to a successful conclusion advice and assistance on many points, but most especially on employment, was essential.

The only record of this remarkable journey is a series of extracts from letters to his mother and Frederick that Vere published in *The Irish Farmers' Gazette* soon after his return in 1852, the simplest way, no doubt, of imparting to potential emigrants the information he had collected. The letters have all the fascinating detail and wide range of interest that gave so much value to his father's record of an earlier America. In parts of his journey Vere traversed the same ground, and one is quickly aware of the vast territorial expansion and industrial development that had taken place during the intervening forty years, while the brash egalitarianism of the still young republic that so annoyed Augustus did not pass unnoticed by his son. The following incident took place as Vere travelled south from Washington :

Mr King, president of the Senate, and, therefore, Vice-president of the United States, a very gentlemanlike man, who was well acquainted with my father, and has been minister to Paris, was in the train, and I had some conversation with him. He is a senator from Alabama, and is on his way to his cotton plantation. Finding all the seats full in the train, he could not, for some time, get a seat, the passengers remarking to each other how well the principles of equality worked, saying that, though they respected him very much personally, they would see him a long way off first before they would sanction aristocratic preferences by yielding their seats to him . . . As no one moved I assisted him in his search, and ferretted him out an empty seat at last.[7]

In Washington, where his father was still remembered, Vere was graciously received. He was invited to a levee given by President Fillmore, the tenth president, and attended sittings of the House of Representatives. He was

disgusted by the sectional partizan spirit in which everything is debated . . . far exceeding the extent of the same spirit in the House of Commons. Each member is, on the other hand, allowed to speak more uninterruptedly. The greatest and most universal evil *I believe* in this country is the ousting of *many thousands* of persons out of office on every change of President, there being a general idea that each political party has a right alternately to partake of the spoils of office. This reaches twopenny postmasters; so that not efficiency but partizanship is the universal qualification for office : consequently public duties are negligently performed.

He became momentarily engrossed by the dominant topics of the day, free trade and the abolition of slavery. Sections of Henry Clay's speeches favouring high tariffs are quoted for Frederick's benefit with the remark that 'there is no conspicuous advocate for the opposite doctrine'. George Thompson, the English MP who at great personal risk campaigned in the States in favour of abolition, was just then in Boston. Of him Vere writes :

[He] is the scape-goat of a great deal of abuse intended for the abolitionist party here; Henry Clay lending his voice to the denunciation of the Britisher coming to lecture the Americans on their internal affairs. It *may be* indiscreet of Mr Thompson, but no *violent* language has been attributed to him, though, if he had uttered any such, it would infallibly have been published. In fact no words of his at all have been reported that I know of, and I have daily watched for them. As I have observed, the prejudice against persons having the slightest tinge of African blood is *very great*. They are looked upon as quite an inferior race, incapable of intellectual amelioration, and utterly unfit for political or social equality with whites. I have talked to many white Americans of the justice of bringing about an equality of civil and political rights . . . and all invariably scout the idea.[8]

It is here that we get the first glimpse of Vere's admiration for the Queen :

I wish the Queen would come over to visit this country; she is much esteemed here, and would be enthusiastically received, and I am sure that her visit would be productive of vast social benefit, leading as it would, to greatly extended social intercourse.[9]

But interesting as Washington might be to a former diplomat it had nothing to do with emigrants, so Vere sped southward, through the Carolinas and Florida, through Mobile in Georgia— a considerable port of entry for emigrants from Britain—and on to New Orleans, everywhere making inquiries as to employment. In spite of the abundance of slave labour

work for white girls is easier here [S. Carolina] than in the Northern States, and the pay higher. One girl I know is earning, in taking care of children, nine dollars per month; whereas about New York the wages are from four to seven dollars. I would not recommend a great *many* girls to come to this State, and I can get no encouragement from anyone respecting the prospects of *men* emigrating hither, unless as farmers desiring to purchase land in the upper parts of the country, which are very healthy.

In New Orleans he wrote to a local paper describing the manifold pitfalls that faced emigrants on 'their progress from their native cottages to their final settlement in the United States'. As emigration from Ireland was in that year expected to reach record figures he called 'with confidence on the citizens of New Orleans, and more particularly those of Irish extraction . . . to study how they may best perform so noble and delightful a task as that of coming to the aid of their industrious fellow countrymen'. This they could do by providing emigrants with information as to clean, respectable lodgings, and the best way of reaching their destinations, by urging the city authorities to provide suitable temporary accommodation, and by 'being the depositaries of money remitted from the interior to be delivered to friends expected to land at New Orleans'. He pointed out that a German society already provided such friendly assistance to German immigrants, 'yet their circumstances are not usually so needy, nor do they arrive in such large numbers as Irish immigrants'.[10]

From New Orleans Vere took the popular emigrant route, up the Mississippi by boat, in conditions scarcely less dreadful than those that prevailed on ocean-going vessels, as far as St Louis and St Paul. In the days before railroads from the eastern seaboard had penetrated the Allegheny Mountains this great waterway served the vast and emerging middle-west, and the already industrialised regions to the east. From St Louis he went to Iowa and Cincinnati, up to Minnesota and Wisconsin, down to Chicago, over to Ann Arbor, Detroit, Ohio, Pittsburg, Philadelphia, back to New York, up the Hudson valley to Montreal and Quebec to meet the British Emigration Officer, A. C. Buchanan. He spent one night on Grosse Island, where 'in the year 1847 twenty thousand immigrants had died of ship fever . . . In one grave on the island there are 5,424 persons.' There was a flying visit to the Niagara Falls which 'exceeded my expectations however great', then by stages back to New York and Ireland.

The journey lasted ten months. Vere rarely stayed more than a night or two in one place, transport was slow and the methods very varied. In Alabama he travelled 'seventy-two miles of the worst possible road in a heavy, nine inside carriage, taking nineteen hours, with four splendid horses. I had not slept in bed for four nights, and, although sleepy, was afraid, and so were my fellow-passengers, to indulge, lest we should get our faces smashed by the violent jolting and plunging of the carriage.' In Iowa even roads were lacking :

Having landed at Paint Rock . . . I walked [alone] through marshes and woods, along an Indian trail to a creek where there was a ferry; but the ferryman had locked up his house, so I had to make my way as best I could to the top of the valley, to get round the creek, walking through marshes and grasses, and doing so slowly, in order to avoid treading on the snakes, which I started up every fifty or one hundred yards. After journeying eight miles I came to a cottage, where I got dinner of some venison, and then lost my way for an hour or so in a forest, but ultimately got on a road which I followed ten miles further . . . through a region richly timbered with oaks and maples, meeting but one or two houses. Towards evening I saw two racoons in the wood; and succeeded in killing one of them, and took it with me as a present to the master of the house where I should stop the night. I stopped at a farm house six miles short of Marcona, and proceeded there the next morning to breakfast; from thence I got a lift of three miles in a wagon, and then walked eighteen miles over an open, rolling prairie country, and got a lift six miles in a German butcher's buggy to Guttenberg, a village of some 300 inhabitants, mostly Germans, on the Mississippi . . . I took my supper at Guttenberg, and a timber-raft floating by as I finished my last mouthful, I hailed the pilot, got on board, and floated down to Dubuque, forty-two miles, in thirteen hours . . . Four men navigated this little raft, with two or three large oars at each end, with blades twelve feet long. The only shelter was a few planks, leaning on another plank, placed edgeways on the raft.[11]

Eventually he reached Iowa City. Elsewhere he mentions traversing forty-five miles of forest country on foot.

A bare sketch of this itinerary gives no idea of the hazards and privations and, moreover, Vere was frequently ill from the effects of the voyage. He endured great heat and torrential rain and seldom knew where he would find shelter for the night: on one occasion he lost his compass and had no idea where he was. Never robust, and unaccustomed to hardship, one wonders how he bore the inevitable fatigue and exhaustion. But his letters convey only a sense of gaiety and enjoyment, an unbounded interest in the vast variety of people and situations that he encountered. At Minnesota he found himself in the midst of a great concourse of Sioux Indians come to negotiate the sale of territory to the

E

government, and his descriptions vie with his father's in vividness and precision, even to the light-hearted remark that 'Indian ladies', who also wore 'mocassins and trowsers', had 'much the appearance of dishevelled Irishwomen from Connemara'.

But all this was trivial reporting compared with the notes made everywhere regarding the price of land, the price of wheat, rates of wages, canals to be dug, railroads to be laid and lines of 'electric telegraph' to be constructed—work for which the unskilled Irish labourer was pre-eminently suited. Five thousand labourers, masons, stone-cutters, etc, were required immediately for the construction of the Pennsylvania railroad, wages one dollar per day, boarding two dollars per week. Many thousands of workmen were needed for the railroad from Mobile to Chicago. 'Why should not a number of men,' he wrote, 'well known to each other in a district, desirous to emigrate, put into a lottery fund, instead of spending in an alehouse, say sixpence or one shilling at a time, until an amount of £6 or £7 had been made up . . . The prize gainer might bind himself to send home a certain sum from America, say £1 towards the fund for the remainder of the society, and the same process might continue till the whole party had emigrated.' Another long list of railway, canal, and telegraph construction works in Ohio concludes with this paragraph:

> The above information may be relied upon . . . There is no definable limit to the number of labouring men and servant girls who could now find employment on public works or on farms, as mechanics and in domestic service throughout this and the neighbouring state of Indiana; and girls, even grumpy ones, but especially such as will make themselves agreeable, would find permanent homes in a short time, with the greatest facility, and would have an extensive pick of husbands, unlike Limerick, which has 16,000 males and 28,000 female inhabitants.[12]

He was equally emphatic, however, that no one should emigrate who 'is living in comfort in the old country, or is disinclined to work a great deal harder than what he or she has been accustomed to in England or Ireland. The work here is very hard, and the wages very good.' Again : 'No *clerks* should come, nor any one who is *at all* comfortable in Europe.'

About half-way through this journey Vere sent a long letter direct to *The Farmers' Gazette*, headed 'Important to Persons about to Emigrate'. It contained a summary of the information so far collected—the importance to emigrants of leaving the sea-ports as soon as possible, instead of 'lounging away their time' and 'sticking like glue in the large cities'; the relative advantages of different localities; work available; the cost of living; price of land and subsidies towards purchase; crops raised, and so forth. All this was set out with the greatest regard for detail and re-liability. It contains also this paragraph of warning, a warning which Vere repeats again and again in letters and documents regarding emigration :

I sincerely wish that all emigrants and other persons would avoid spirituous liquors, and proclaim their aversion to the prac-tice of drinking them, by following the advice of Father Mathew, taking the total abstinence pledge, which, of course, I have taken myself, or I would not preach to others to do so. I mention emi-grants, especially, because the first few months after their arrival in America prove usually the most trying period of their lives, both on account of its peculiar temptation, and from want of any sympathy with their situation among that class of the population with whom they usually come in contact, and who are immersed in the greedy acquisition of dollars, which makes them thoroughly insensible to the sufferings, and wants, and friendless position of strangers. Besides this, great numbers of the Irish emigrants to this country have, by their drunken, riotous, and quarrelsome be-haviour, and even many of the girls, I am sorry to say, often, by their slovenliness and want of truthtelling, actually brought the Irish name into great discredit among native Americans; so as to render them averse, in many cases, to employ Irish labourers, and domestic servants, and disposed rather to prefer Germans whenever they can get them. This conduct on their part, is very injurious, not only to themselves, but also to emigrants who suc-ceed them. In all my conversations, however, with native Ameri-can farmers, railway contractors, and others, they have always strongly testified to me that, but for that one great failing of in-toxication, and its consequence—a riotous, quarrelsome disposition they would, by far, prefer Irish workmen to those of any other nation, because they are, by far, the most industrious and active of all workmen, very intelligent, and the most to be depended upon, when their employers' backs are turned . . .

I had the pleasure of seeing Father Mathew a few weeks since at Louisville, Kentucky, when he told me that 400,000 persons had signed the pledge to him since his arrival in this country in July 1849 . . . I believe that the great majority have stuck to it, and it is to be hoped that, through their influence and that of their children, this great evil of intoxication, the parent of nearly all the degrading vices of human nature, and of half its sorrows, may, in course of time, be utterly eradicated from the habits of civilised nations.[13]

It was his constant endeavour to increase the self-respect and raise the status of the Irish emigrant.

Meanwhile, there was so much else, besides emigration, that attracted his interest—the letters are bursting with alert remarks and crammed with information. There was the ever-present negro problem. One self-confident fellow-passenger, boasting about the greatness of the American people who would not 'submit' to do any menial work, or be so 'abject' as to allow themselves to be 'designated as servants, which the English and Irish and Germans were found to do', got this retort :

I said that if Americans entertained such notions that it was degrading to perform manual labour for hire . . . that it was extremely inconsistent and degrading in them to expect others to act for them as they would not themselves act for others . . . that in the United States whose population boasted of being the freest nation, half of the States were slave states, where slaves were kept in perpetual bondage . . . In the so-called *free* States coloured persons were not allowed to enter; while those already there were not allowed to leave, even for a day, except to leave the country altogether, never to return . . . That, with these and other evidences of a like nature, not to mention the treatment of the Indians, for an American to decry other nations, and to boast of his own as being the freest nation in the world, was ridiculous.[14]

There was the excellent educational experiment at Oberlin, where men and women were educated together, and women were allowed to take degrees and where an underground escape route to Canada was operated; the Icarian settlement at Nauvoo near St Louis, where refugees from the Paris revolution of 1848 had established themselves in a socialist community under the leadership of Étienne Cabet, in territory vacated by the Mormons who had recently fled to Utah after the murder of their founder Joe Smith (Vere put up for the night in the hotel kept by Smith's widow); there was the Shaker community near Cleveland, reached after an eight-mile walk in exhausting heat—not very appealing, 'their grand principle is a negative'; the famous Girard orphanage near Philadelphia, where no clergyman was permitted to enter; and there was the wonderful reaping machine, worked by two horses and one man and cutting twenty acres a day at a cost of fifty cents per acre. Newspapers were read from cover to cover, those of special interest being forwarded to the 'Mechanics Institute in Dublin to which I belong'; and in the midst of all there is this, in a letter which must surely have been directed to his mother, 'I send you a few flowers gathered at the foot and close about the Falls of St Anthony', some pinks, a very beautiful orange lily, and two other unknown specimens.

When so much can be gleaned from fragments of thirteen letters one realises what an epic tale the whole record must have been, but unfortunately no more of it survives.

At Philadelphia Vere addressed a printed letter to the Directors of the American Emigrants' Friend Society, introducing himself as a son of :

> . . . Sir A. Foster [who] was many years ago British minister in this country, and quitted it, with the United States Declaration of War in his hands, in the year 1812, and was afterwards Minister Plenipotentiary at Copenhagen for twelve years, and at Turin, in Italy for fifteen years; that my eldest brother, Sir F. Foster, is a landed proprietor in County Louth, in Ireland, having quitted the British diplomatic profession when he inherited his estate; and that I have quitted the same profession in order to live in Ireland, which I did for a period of thirteen months, previous to leaving it temporarily, in order to travel in this country.[15]

He then speaks of the likely continuance of emigration for many years, of his reasons for preferring emigration to the United States rather than to the British colonies—the journey was shorter, the country more developed and therefore requiring more workers —, of the emigrants he had already assisted during his short residence in Ireland, of his voyage to America on the *Washington*, and continues :

Having been ill during most of the time that I have been in America, I have not travelled through the country one-tenth part as much as I would wish to have done, and as I otherwise would have done.

I am not connected with any Society, or with Government, but am travelling on my own account, for my own amusement, and at my own expense, having fortunately ample pecuniary means, independent of my own exertions; and I join your ranks in spending my time and money in the service of emigrants, for the simple reason that it is very agreeable to spend time and money usefully.

He then lists the 'most prominent existing wants' in connection with present system :

1. The want of respectable, good temporary accommodation at the principal ports of arrival [and here he describes in detail the model lodging houses promoted in England by Lord Ashley's committee] :

These buildings are well ventilated and amply supplied with water —particulars extremely necessary for emigrants after having been cooped up in the close and filthy hold of a ship during a long voyage. The lodgers are supplied with even separate bed-rooms, beds and bedding, warmth and lights, with the use of a common kitchen, kitchen utensils and firing . . . baths and apparatus for washing, drying and mangling their clothes—the latter being, in most instances, charged extra—the use of a common sitting room and a common library . . . Such buildings might, in the first instance, and under the peculiar emergencies of the time, be put up by the city authorities on the security of the rates, such charges being made as to be remunerative. Baths and wash-houses have thus been erected for the use of the inhabitants of London, by the different parishes, on the security of the parish rates . . . It is expected that the entrance fees, varying from one penny for a cold bath to six pence for a well carpeted bath-room, with look-ing-glass, extra towels and shower bath, will repay both the original outlay and annual expenses.

2. The want of privacy for female passengers on board ship.

3. The want of water closets for female passengers, the conse-quence of which is, that, with the pitching and rolling of the ship, and the upsetting of chambers, it is impossible to prevent the crowded lower decks from becoming extremely filthy—whence arises ship fever, which in its exaggerated form, under the name of cholera, naturally causes so much alarm in this country . . .

4. The want of baths on board ship, which, seemingly a luxury on shore, are absolutely necessary to secure the health of passen-gers on the voyage.

The five following paragraphs deal in similar detail with the need for proper inspection of vessels. Vere constantly maintained that a major necessity was the appointment of 'proper surgeons [then] many essential changes would undoubtedly follow, because no proper surgeon would consent to act unless they were made'. The need for 'respectable intelligence offices' and 'a place of de-posit for money' was also stressed.

It is sad that this long document cannot be quoted in full, for, wordy though it may be, it was written with the deepest convic-tion and sense of urgency, and with a tender understanding that could not be surpassed. No present-day highly skilled welfare officer could have assessed the need in greater detail or more effectively, nor could the plight of the newly arrived, bewildered, cheated emigrant have been more sympathetically expressed :

The brutalizing conduct pursued with impunity towards the emigrants is enough to make them brutes, and it is, therefore, no wonder that they sometimes become very disorderly citizens. Hav-ing been cruelly beggared, they often become reckless and dis-heartened, take refuge in the temporary delirious enjoyment of intoxicating drinks, to drown care; and, after so much misplaced confidence, becoming naturally suspicious of all whom they meet, they reject good advice as well as bad, and so dishearten all those who feel inclined to befriend them, unless the latter are endued with more than ordinary perseverance and leisure time, and determination to benefit them.

Having said so much on behalf of his fellow-countrymen, will the next paragraph contain some admission of their failings?

> The notorious and almost universal conduct of those Irish emigrants who have already arrived in this country, in acts of self-denial and of generosity, in sending to the aid of their suffering fellow countrymen at home the whole of their first earnings, which are not absolutely necessary for the supply of their own wants, should engage our warmest admiration and sympathy. The Irish emigrants to this country may have their faults, and who has not —these faults being attributable to the rotten political and social condition of their native country for several centuries back, and which has but recently been modified—but their generosity, in addition to the laborious industry which they display, . . . is a noble redeeming trait in their character, and no one can on reflection deny, for there is wide-spread testimony to convince him, that the Irish nation are almost universally affectionate, kind-hearted, generous and disinterested, I might perhaps say, beyond any other nation whom we have ever read of in history. The example before our eyes, of the poorest and most uneducated portion of what is termed the civilized population of the world, acting in this noble and disinterested manner, should indeed make the rich and so-called superiorly educated classes of society blush to think how far they are from devoting a proportional part of their ample means to a similar alleviation of the sufferings of their fellow creatures. The amount of the remittances of Irish emigrants from America to Ireland in the year 1850, *of which the British Government has expressed itself cognizant,* was nearly five million of dollars. As much more may have been sent of which the British Government is not cognizant. I believe this money to have been remitted principally by girls in domestic service . . .

Surely the Irish emigrant was never more nobly championed, the Irish peasant more triumphantly defended?

For some reason Vere considered it necessary to conclude his appeal to the Directors of the American Emigrants' Friend Society with two appropriate quotations; the first from Young's *Night Thoughts,* and the second from *Vestiges of the Natural History of Creation* :

> For what is vice? Self-love in a mistake
> And virtue, what? 'Tis self-love in her wits;
> Quite skilful in the market of delight.

Our greatest happiness is not to be realized by each having a regard for himself, but by each seeking primarily to benefit his fellow-creatures.

He could be curiously priggish at times. Perhaps, on this occasion, he considered that the affluent citizens of Philadelphia required some admonition, for he writes to Frederick: 'Poor emigrants here, as at New Orleans and New York, are looked upon as a nuisance.'

There is no mention of the voyage back to Ireland in October and November 1851, but with characteristic exactness he records elsewhere that he had been away for almost a year, had travelled 10,500 miles in America, and that his expenses had amounted to less than £50.

Without a moment's delay Vere hastened to spread the information he had collected. A large broadsheet, headed *EMIGRA-TION*, and dated 'Glasnevin, near Dublin, 1st December, 1851', was widely circulated.[16] One must regret that on occasions, Vere resorted to a tiresomely ponderous and tendentious style of composition, curious in his case, for normally he expressed himself clearly and concisely as befitted his exact and tidy mind. The broadsheet, addressed 'To the Industrious Poor and their Friends in the United Kingdom, and more especially in Ireland' begins with this rather jumbled paragraph:

My Dear Fellow-Countrywomen and Fellow-Countrymen, Necessitous and Affluent.

I say to the former, if you can obtain the necessary means, go away from this distressed country, where you are wasting your precious life in a poor-house, liable to die of neglect and starvation, as is said to have happened to 1,650 persons last year in the Unions of Enistymon and Kilrush, or are getting a bare and precarious subsistence outside of the poorhouse, however hard you work—go to a country where your labour will be well paid, and where you will have ample means to purchase the greatest abundance of the necessaries of life. To the latter I say—circumstances favouring your strenuous exertions, or perhaps merely a lucky accident of birth, have placed you far above want, and its anxious cares and temptations; imagine, however, and feel for the position of your neighbours who have been less fortunate, and give your-self the pleasure of using whatever superfluous means you can spare, *either* in enabling them to obtain a decent livelihood in this country, or in helping them to go to where they can obtain a livili-hood elsewhere;—that elsewhere is America . . .

He then gets down, with no lack of clarity, to the main pur-pose of the broadsheet. He mentions his voyage on the *Washing-ton*, and explains that in aiding emigration he wishes to assist those who stay in Ireland as well as those who leave it, by reduc-ing the supply of labour and thus raising wages, and by

> neutralising, through a kindly spirit of assisting Emigration, those intensely bitter feelings which, naturally and notorously, rankle deep in the hearts of that portion of the Irish American popula-tion which has been driven to the resource of Emigration through being mercilessly, and by wholesale, ejected by wrong-headed landlords, whom I will forbear to name, from their homes in Ire-land*—and which feelings, being a prevailing characteristic feature of the Irish American mind, and a kind of political religion of their hearts, may some day be the means of fomenting some trifling misunderstanding between the governments of the two most free and progressive countries on the globe into a rupture, pregnant with the most disastrous fratricidal effects to both nations.

With great discernment he had sensed the full significance of that intense bitterness. Is this, one wonders, the first public warning of a situation so soon to have disastrous effects?† For those 'bitter feelings' were to find expression in the continuous encouragement and powerful financial backing given by the Irish American to every seditious anti-British movement in Ireland for a hundred years. The Irish Republican Brotherhood, pledged to the com-plete separation of Ireland from England was founded simultane-ously in Dublin and in New York in 1858.

After stating his reasons for favouring emigration to America rather than to Australia, naming the States in which work was plentiful, and again recommending 'no person to emigrate who is

* See pp 133, 134.

† *cf Irish-American Nationalism.* T. W. Moody. Irish Historical Studies. Vol XV.

indisposed to hard labour', Vere launches, with the meticulous care and the sympathetic imagination that characterised all his work, into every detail regarding the voyage : the relative advantage of the different ports of entry to America, the distance from them to centres of employment, modes of transport and their cost, agents from whom tickets should be purchased in Liverpool, the addresses of decent lodgings there, and the provisions due to passengers on the voyage. He continues :

As regards extra provisions, that must depend very much on taste and circumstances. In my recent voyage in the 'Washington' from Liverpool to New York I took the following provisions, which I found sufficient, and which were the same in quantity and quality as I had been in the habit of supplying previously to passengers whom I had assisted to Emigrate to America :

1½ stone Wheaten Flour.	2 lbs. Brown Sugar.
6 lbs. Bacon.	Salt.
2½ lbs. Butter.	Soap.
4 lb. Loaf.	Bread Soda.
¼ lb. Tea.	

These extra provisions cost 10s. 6d. I also took the following articles, for the use of myself and messmate :

	s.	d.		s.	d.
Tin Water Can	0.	10	Two deep Tin Plates		4
Large Tin Hook-			Two pint Mugs		3
saucepan		8	Two Knives, Forks and		
Frying-pan (mine was			Spoons		5
not large enough)		10	Barrel and Padlock, to		
Large Tin Basin, both			hold Provisions	2.	1
for washing, and			Small Calico Bags		—
preparing bread		8	Towels and Rubbers		—
Tin Teapot		4	Straw Mattress	1.	2
Chamber		3	Blanket	2.	0
Tin Kettle		10	Rug	1.	8
Candles		—	Sheets (each)		10½
Lantern		8			

In the case of children, many little extras, which will occur to their mammas, would be, and were found to be, by many of my fellow passengers, a palatable and desirable addition, particularly during the first fortnight, until the stomach becomes inured to the motion of the ship . . . The handles and spouts on all the tin articles should be riveted on as well as soldered; and one should be very particular in trying the different vessels beforehand, especially the water-cans, to see that they do not leak . . . Families would do well to take with them a slop-pail and a broom . . . *Mechanics should take their tools.*

There are warnings that advice and information should be sought only from organisations whose names he gives, including 'those most excellent ladies—the Sisters of Mercy of New York', more emphatic warnings against drunkenness, more strong admonitions to take Father Mathew's pledge with yet another declaration that he, Vere, had taken it himself, and more urgent appeals to quit the sea-ports :

The propensity of Irishmen to remain about large cities, and especially those on the coast, is very much complained of by Americans, and with too much foundation; there they loiter days, weeks and months lazy and indolent, spending in the meanwhile their precious money, and still more precious time, quietly waiting for Providence to turn up something for them . . . They should recollect, that Providence, as a general rule, only helps those who strive to help themselves.[16]

This formidable document, consisting of over 7,000 words, was posted up in villages and country towns. Two months later Frederick wrote from Dublin to Vere, who was with his mother in England :

I have had a copy of your broadsheet stuck up at Dundalk, Collon, Ardee and Drogheda.* I think you might separate that part which is addressed to the Affluent from the rest in the next edition & condense it very much . . . If you are not well yet, you had better defer your expedition to Co. Clare, and have the Emigrants sent up to Dublin by Morrisey.[17]

No doubt there were less sympathetic reactions to this first public pronouncement. In a country dominated by religious cleavage and class distinctions what would the land-owning neighbours think? In spite of notorious cases of extortion and greed there always had been, as generations of Fosters testified,

* All in Co. Louth.

genuinely humane and benevolent landlords; now, in the changed conditions of post-famine Ireland, Frederick was undertaking his responsibilities with a new and forward-looking sense of urgency. But all this thoroughgoing identification of himself with the needs of the humblest, poorest peasants—some of them evicted from their miserable holdings as mere encumberers of the ground—all that was implicit in Vere's broadsheet, and underlined by his declaration of total abstinence, was something utterly and totally different, and there is no indication as to how it was received by his equals. There was nothing here of patronising charity or even of benevolent assistance, and there was in fact a good deal of plain speaking and a demand for considerable effort from those same humble peasants. Nor was there any parade of assumed equality, any dramatically 'democratic' approach. There was, indeed, nothing but unbounded understanding and compassion, and the ability to win confidence, before which all barriers of class and creed simply disappeared.

We hear no more of the farm in the west of Ireland—the idea of becoming 'a resident improving proprietor' had been abandoned. Had Vere sensed that the role of the landlord in Ireland, however enlightened and beneficial, was already outmoded? All these plans had been discussed with Frederick, who wrote in the beginning of 1852 : 'I have been in Collon and think when you settle you had better take up your quarters first in that village . . . At Philipstown there is a cabin which might perhaps be added to and made habitable for you in the course of the summer, but you must build another room to it.'[17]

Vere's identification with the people he was serving was about to take another step forward. He would now live as far as possible under the same conditions.

5

Emigration

When reviewing his emigration activities many years later, Vere declared that he went to America 'at least once every year and sometimes twice' between 1850 to 1857. No record remains of any voyage in 1852 and there are various indications that he was still frequently ill from the effects of the *Washington* experience. In that year, however, he established his 'Irish Female Emigration Fund' to assist 'the emigration to North America of one able-bodied member of each family (in most cases a woman), specially selected on account of her poverty, good character, and industrious habits, with the expectation that she will herself take the remaining members of her family out of poverty'. It was a fundamental principle with Vere to help people to help themselves, in every case some return for assistance was expected, the most desirable being that the person assisted would in turn assist relatives or friends. Amongst the subscribers to this fund were Mrs Caroline Chisholm [famous for her emigration schemes to Australia], Lady Noel Byron, the Duke of Devonshire, the Earl of Shaftesbury, the Earl of Ripon, Earl Granville, and Sidney Herbert, with Horace Greeley, Lucretia Mott, and Henry Barnard from America. The list of donations in which these illustrious names appear includes a column reserved for 'subscriptions of one penny each' and the scrawled signatures of Michael Moloney, Margaret Donaghy,

James Moore, William Finerty and others indicate offerings that must have warmed Vere's heart.[1]

The first party of emigrants to benefit by this fund sailed in 1852, Vere having been assisted in the task of selection by 'my friends Michael and Patrick Morrisey, James and John O'Dea, national school teachers in Co Clare, and by Fr Patrick Quaid, PP'. At the bottom of the certificate handed to each emigrant was this message :

> I expect you will repay the cost of your passage to America by sending for or otherwise assisting your relatives in Ireland. If you have no occasion to do this, I hope you will send some money to me as a subscription to the Emigration Fund, to enable me to help a member of another family, selected like yourself on account of good character.
>
> I entreat you specially to love liberty and fair play for others as well as yourself, without distinction of race, religion or colour.[2]

This is an interesting example of Vere's insistence on shared responsibility, obligations were accepted by the helped as well as by the helper. Nothing that he ever did was prompted by charity in the debased sense of the word; indeed one might almost say that for him philanthropy had no meaning in that he would certainly never have used the word to describe his own work.

Vere was also engaged in compiling a comprehensive guide for emigrants. A detailed questionnaire,[3] requesting information on every conceivable subject, was printed and circulated to friends and emigrants in America. For example :

> What are usually the lowest, highest, and average wages, in dollars and cents, or Halifax currency, of female domestic servants and of Laborers on farms and on public works in your neighbourhood?
>
> What are the usual expenses weekly of day laborers, and of women for board, lodging and washing?
>
> What are the lowest, highest and average wages given (with or without board and lodging) to members of the following trades, and how many hours per day are they expected to work?

and then follows a list of more than fifty occupations ranging from bakers and blacksmiths through coachbuilders, curriers, gardeners, miners, sailmakers, and stone cutters to hotel waiters and weavers. There are queries about tools and clothes, the price of different kinds of land, transport from sea-ports to the interior, the price of a long list of essential commodities such as soap, candles, tea and sugar, a breeding sow, a pair of oxen, flannel for drawers or women's petticoats and strong boots for men. And finally, 'What organisation is there in your town for giving information and advice to all emigrants—shelter, food, or other assistance to those who are destitute?' Vere's address for replies is given as The Post Office, Dublin.

With extraordinary speed a four-page pamphlet entitled *Work and Wages*[4]* and packed with information was issued in September 1852 within eight months of Vere's return from America. A fourth edition, published two years later, contained supplementary paragraphs from Horace Greeley, New York, William Chambers of Edinburgh (co-founder of *Chambers's Journal*), and from Mr A. C. Buchanan, Chief Emigration Agent in Quebec. A letter from Horace Greeley and one from William Chambers, and a few replies from emigrants is all that remains of what must have been a huge and laborious correspondence in connection with these pamphlets, which were sold for one penny each or ten-pence per dozen. Vere appointed agents in Manchester, Norwich, Newcastle, York, Bristol, Ipswich, Birmingham, Edinburgh, Glasgow, and Aberdeen, for he was still prepared to assist emigrants from Britain, and the 'enclosures' on the great estates in the Highlands were, at that moment, rendering thousands of crofters homeless. So far as is known this offer was not taken up.

A printed message 'To the Emigrant Passengers of the Wrecked Ship "Osborne" '[5] written by Vere from Nassau, Bahamas, in March 1853 indicates either that he went to America that year and called at Nassau en route, or went to Nassau in order to regain his health. The message opens with this paragraph:

> As *you* are about to re-embark for New Orleans and as *I* have been there, and have travelled throughout the United States for

* See p 151.

the express purpose of ascertaining by personal observation the prospects of emigrants in that country, and have published a small pamphlet on the subject last year, of which I have circulated gratuitously in Ireland and England 135 thousand copies, I take upon myself to address you now the few following lines of advice and information, remarking first that, having been long in very weak health owing to the exertions which I have from time to time had the pleasure of making on behalf of emigrants, I am unable to exert myself physically on your behalf, but hope that others will.

Occasionally one comes on strange touches of self-advertisement such as this, and they strike, at first, a curiously discordant note. They can be explained perhaps by the fact that Vere was so wrapped up in his work, so whole-heartedly devoted to the cause, so lost in the sheer interest and enjoyment of it, that everything to do with it was significant, whether or not it happened to be his own personal contribution.

After giving the unfortunate shipwrecked emigrants his usual advice he concludes with a little homily—a recurring characteristic :

Finally, follow the advice given by an Irish Emigrant in last Wednesday's Guardian, "Cheer up, Old Fellow! Keep a high head, even though you've empty pockets, remember that darkest the hour is the hour before day. You must not depend on any one to push you forward. Have confidence in yourself, and go ahead", to which I would earnestly add, be honest, just, kind, and charitable, one to another and towards your neighbours, wherever you may be; so shall you spread happiness around you, and obtain it for yourselves.
N.B. A dollar is equal to 4s. 2d. sterling being composed of 100 cents, each of which exactly equals a halfpenny.

Whether or not Vere went to America himself in 1853, parties of emigrants were regularly despatched under his auspices. An old travel permit from the Baltimore and Ohio Rail Road, dated December 1854, has somehow evaded destruction and is the only evidence of a visit that must have extended into 1855, and in a report of the Irish Pioneer Emigration Fund,[6] which seems to have grown out of the Irish Female Emigration Fund, we are told of a long visit which took place in the autumn of 1856

> for the purpose of visiting as many as possible of the emigrants of this and previous years in their new homes, and for the purpose of making arrangements for the reception and direction of others. In my search I travelled over 7000 miles, being courteously provided with free conveyance to and fro by [several Railway Companies], and was successful in finding 130 of our pioneers and 32 others whose passages had been paid for by them . . . I have ascertained that one thousand and fifty-eight pounds sterling have been remitted by 75 out of the 92 emigrants sent in 1852, and 97 additional persons have been sent for by them.

With his passion for lists, and no doubt with a view to publicity, Vere appends the names of those who had remitted sums 'most nobly' and the amounts they had sent, ranging from £15 to £45; the majority of the donors were women and all of them were from the bleak county of Clare.

One highly important result of this visit was the following letter from The Most Rev John Hughes, Roman Catholic Archbishop of New York and himself the son of an emigrant family from Co Tyrone. It introduced Vere to any and all of the Roman Catholic clergy in the United States and Canada thus:

> Mr. Vere Foster, the bearer of this letter, has been introduced to me under auspices highly honorable to himself and to the cause in which he is engaged. That cause is philanthropic and has a reference of the emigration of poor persons from Europe, or, I might better say, from Ireland to this country. As he desires to consult Catholic clergymen and others in the United States and Canada on this subject, I beg leave to recommend him to the kind attention of such Catholic clergymen as he may have occasion to call on.
> New York, Aug. 27th, 1856.   John Hughes.   Abp. of N.York.[7]

Armed with this letter Vere made many encouraging contacts, and returned to Ireland more than ever convinced of the opportunities that awaited enterprising young people in America—six or seven hundred girls, he was assured, could be assimilated annually. But money was necessary, and the report of the Pioneer Emigration Fund[8] indicated that it was at a low ebb. 'As I have but little means of my own, I am necessarily dependent on subscriptions to enable me to carry on the work otherwise than on a very diminutive scale. I am only able to send at my own expense about 50 persons a year. Any person approving of the proposed mode of relieving and preventing poverty, is earnestly entreated to subscribe *something*, much or little.' The 'ample pecuniary means' of the Philadelphia days seem already to be disappearing.

At this stage brief reference must be made to a quite different preoccupation that engaged Vere's attention at this time and is represented by fifteen letters [among the very few that Vere preserved] from Lady Byron. We do not know how this contact was made, and not until many years later did Vere learn of the relationship that had existed between Lady Byron and his father. From scattered remarks in Frederick's diary we know that during the year following Augustus's death he and Vere were frequently at Brighton, where Annabella was then living, and to this period may belong the undated note which she directed to Mrs Scott, wife of the principal of Owen's College, Manchester, introducing 'two Gentlemen who are travelling for purposes well worthy of assistance and which they will state—Sir Frederick Foster and his brother Mr Vere Foster. They would like to know Mrs Gaskell also, but I am not able to give them an introduction.'[9] The next letter is dated Brighton, 14 February 1854. After saying that she wishes 'to contribute anonymously' the enclosed tickets for 480 quarts of soup—and it is hard to know just what these were for, as acute hunger no longer existed in Ireland—Lady Byron continues :

> The entrance of a third person prevented me from expressing all the sympathy I felt in your earnest desire for Truth, and my wish that your Life may be the means of promoting it—for 'the Life *is* the Light' in no mystical sense, but as a matter of fact open to the observation of everyone, — Believe me, with sincere esteem, your   A. J. Noel Byron.[10]

At this time of her life Annabella held very intense and liberal religious opinions and was much concerned about education. Over the next four years her letters continue, chiefly on educational topics. Indeed in 1855 Vere visited Kirby Mallory, her Leicestershire estate, in order to settle some difficulty in a school there for which she was responsible. In the last letter, written in 1859, just a year before her death, she asks Vere for his 'opinion on a question concerning my eldest Grandson, and if you would agreed with me I may ask some assistance from your kindness in promoting the object by kindly communicating it to him, as *your* representations would be likely to have influence'. Her idea was to bring the young, and seemingly unstable, Lord Ockham 'into Parliament for some Constituency to which an Advocate of the Working Classes would be welcome'.[11]

One can only imagine the thoughts that must constantly have been in her mind as, during these lonely, perplexed years, she found herself seeking advice and reassurance from Augustus Foster's son.

But to return to emigration. Encouraged by the widespread support received in America during the 1856 trip Vere, on his return, began an even more vigorous campaign. Conditions in Ireland were improving and some effort was required to counter the growing antagonism to emigration from small shopkeepers in country towns who feared the loss of business, from farmers and landowners who saw their hitherto limitless supply of cheap labour dwindling before their eyes, and from the clergy who saw their congregations being continuously depleted. Why, it was asked, must the best, the most energetic and enterprising young men and women—'the bone and sinew' of the country—be encouraged to leave, when enterprise and energy were precisely the qualities most needed at home?

But Vere was undaunted. He was in excellent spirits; his health seems to have greatly improved, the letter from Archbishop Hughes must calm the fears of any Irish Catholic parent and still the protests of the priests, and above all there were the boundless opportunities to be seized. So more parties were organised, and we have the description of the departure of one of them in the report of a lecture[12] that Vere delivered in Belfast many years later to the Rosemary Street Mutual Improvement Association. It opens with a paragraph from the *Drogheda Argus* :

'On Monday morning Vere Foster, Esq., left Ardee with about seventy female emigrants for Canada. About twenty of them had been inmates of the Ardee Union Workhouse, the remainder were from the town and surrounding country. They were all decently clad with comfortable clothes. The procession (consisting of an omnibus and eight or ten carts), as it moved along the road, with the worthy gentlemen mounted on a common dray amongst his protegees, reminded us forcibly of the patriarch Jacob on his journey to the land of Goshen.'

On my previous trip [Vere continued] I had asked one of my emigrants in America if I could execute any commission for her on my return to the old country. She asked, 'Do you know the big tree of Mullacurry, between Ardee and Dromin?' I replied, 'Quite well'. She then said, 'I spent many a pleasant day under that big tree, and if you would bring me out some of the clay from under its roots I would be greatly obliged to you.' I, therefore, now diverged from the high road, borrowed a spade, filled a flower pot with the desired clay, put garden mould on the top, and stuffed it cram full of shamrock . . .

It must have all been very hilarious and exciting, with Vere the life and soul of the party, directing operations from his vantage point on the 'common dray'. No doubt some of his girls were already tearful and homesick, a little rousing jollity would give confidence and self-assurance all round. Then an unfortunate incident occurred.

On arrival at Drogheda there was the greatest excitement on the quay. Many of the farmers were mad with me for reducing the supply of labourers and servant girls; and alternate entreaties, threats, and force were used to prevent many of my party from embarking, cries being got up that my intention was to make Protestants of them; that they were to be bound for a term of years; to be sold to 'the blacks', to the Mormons, etc., etc.

Among my party was one poor girl who was a 'vert', that is a convert according to some, and a pervert according to others. She had consequently an uncomfortable time of it among her former associates, by whom she was known as the 'souper'. Some kind ladies and gentlemen subscribed to the cost of her emigration, and I promised to get her provided for in Canada. She was to go with the rest of the party as far as Liverpool only, and from thence to America in a different ship. A cry was raised that this girl was to be my instrument for proselytising the rest. Her pockets were searched, and, sure enough, it was found that the over-zealous Ardee missionary had provided her with hundreds of tracts, which were then thrown up in clouds high into the air as proof positive of my crime. I narrowly escaped execution, but succeeded in carrying off nearly all my company.

By a curious coincidence we have additional information about the poor little 'souper', for Vere kept the draft of a letter he wrote from Ardee to the wife of a neighbouring landlord in which he said :

> If Eliza Adams was in the same position as the other girls I would gladly send her along with them at my own expense entirely, but she has no one depending on her for help, and she is said to have many friends among the ladies and gentlemen of the neighbourhood who, I trust, will take as much interest in the welfare of her body as they have exhibited in that of her soul. On receipt of your letter I wrote out a bit of a statement for her and headed a subscription list with £1 from myself followed by another from Mr. McCann. The total amount required will be only £6.10.0 for everything except clothes. The expenses from my own purse for the emigration of the persons from this neighbourhood who will sail the week after next exceed £300. I think it is but little to expect from the ladies and gentlemen above alluded to that they will subscribe amongst them £5.10.0 and clothes for this poor girl who has lost sympathy among many of her former co-religionists by becoming a Protestant and who is said to be a good girl. The Lord Lieutenant sent me a donation of £3 this morning towards the expenses of the other swarm.[13]

Eliza's story furnishes confirmation of the allegations cast at protestants in general, and no doubt deserved in some instances, that during the famine food and assistance were given if the starving recipient would abjure the catholic faith, hence the scornful name 'souper'. As we shall see later the same allegations continued to be made in connection with education. Proselytising in any form infuriated Vere. All his life in one place or another he fought it, and his reply to Eliza Adams' benefactress made this only too clear. He must have regretted the moment when, out of the goodness of his heart, he volunteered to help the poor girl who was a 'vert' as far as Liverpool and though he later turned off the episode with a laugh about execution, he probably knew at the time that there were already those only too ready to use such a story against him.

In May 1857 another large party of 120 girls left Ireland. Vere accompanied them to Liverpool, and having put them safely on the packet ship *City of Mobile* he sailed himself to New York 'by steam' to complete on the spot his plans for their reception. When in due course the *Mobile* berthed he discovered to his dismay that three or four of the girls, in flagrant disregard of his ceaseless warnings, had listened to the beguilements of some members of the crew and had already been surreptitiously landed and hustled off to undesirable quarters. There were also a considerable number of other girls who, for one reason or another, preferred to make their own arrangements when reaching New York—some had relatives nearby and so forth. It should be remembered that Vere in no way bound the emigrants whom he assisted. He paid their passages, he offered them advice, he was prepared to offer them jobs, but having taken his financial help they remained at perfect liberty to go their own ways. Ireland, he believed, had suffered too much from 'charity' that was but a cloak for proselytising and moral enslavement. But the price of the cherished liberty that accompanied his aid was the possibility of just such wayward behaviour. So, having collected the ninety-four 'who entrusted themselves to his guidance' and after spending only one night in the Emigration reception depot where they were provided with food and shelter and were addressed by the Rev J. Kenselaer PP and by Horace Greeley, he proceeded with them on their way westward :

'the greatest thanks being due to the Superintendents of the Hudson River Railroad, New York Central, Canada Great Western, Michigan Central, and Chicago, St. Paul and Fond du Lac

Railroad Companies for their courtesy and liberality in forwarding the company in their fastest trains and in comfortable first-
class carriages at emigrant fare (which is only one halfpenny a
mile), thus enabling them to reach Janesville, Wisconsin, 1,060
miles from New York, in 44½ hours, saving Mr. Foster much expense and the passengers probably some sickness, as they would
otherwise have been seven or eight days on the road.'

At various stopping places parties of girls were met, generally
by the parish priest, who had made provision for them pending
employment. For example at Syracuse the Rev J. McMenony
awaited those bound for Canandaigue, giving them breakfast and
sending them on their way, to be met at their destination by Fr
O'Connor and the Sisters of Charity. Similar arrangements were
made at Detroit and Chicago, while at Janesville, where Vere
arrived with the last batch, the 'hospitable Irish inhabitants of
the city' took the girls to their homes 'for as long as might be
necessary for their comfort to rest to prepare themselves for going
to situations'.[14]

Vere returned to Ireland immediately and without loss of time
printed a handbill giving reassuring information about most of
the girls. He said, quite truthfully, that 'they had *all* landed safely
and in good health . . . Many were forwarded to their friends
in different parts of the country, and many others stopped in
New York contrary to Mr. F's advice.' He gave the destinations
of all the girls who had left New York with him, and the names
of the parish priests in whose care he had left them, and to whom
letters for the girls might be directed. Furthermore, he intimated
that in September he intended to take out another large party
'of girls and a few boys' and would be 'at Mr. Campbell's, Dunleer on Sundays, Thursdays and fair days, and at Mr. Pepper's
at Ardee on Tuesdays to receive applications'.[14]

But the matter was not allowed to rest. In September news of
the delinquents reached Ireland, by which time Vere was again
on the ocean. Frederick wrote to him that he 'must persuade
as many girls as possible to write home good accounts before
your return, to contradict the false impression made by Father

Hughes* & the Drogheda Papers on the parents respecting the girls being taken to a brothel at N. York. Hughes read out the statements in Chapel & you will find it difficult to get any more candidates . . . Thousands must have gone astray of their own accord, but no one hears of them & there is no one to blame, but here they all fix upon you. By the time you return I hope the Parents will have heard such accounts as will quiet them.' But two days later, in consternation, he adds :

> To my great surprise and regret, today there appeared in the *Times* an article taken from *Freeman's Journal* which I send you enclosed. I have written to the Editors of both Newspapers to beg them to contradict so unfounded a statement, which must have been inserted by someone on purpose to stop Emigration. But the mischief is done, and no doubt this article will be circulated in every paper in Ireland.[15]

Both his letters were published, but Frederick remained convinced that 'the Report will be made use of to stop the stream of Emigration' and urges Vere 'to take to some other method of reform, and you might do a world of good in promoting the schools in Louth by giving prizes, etc., or by improving the furniture of the Cottages'.[15]

The *Freeman* article, after mentioning that 'the benevolent exertions of Mr Vere Foster, our countryman' are known to all, proceeded to state with wild inaccuracy, that of the 120 girls taken out in May not more than a dozen had accompanied him westwards and found situations. Nothing, the writer declared, was known of the other hundred :

> . . . how they lived or died—until a kind-hearted gentleman was struck with the appearance of a wretched object in the most fashionable thoroughfare of New York. She was an Irish girl—one who had suffered and was suffering much in mind and in body. Her face was covered with bruises and her body with rags. She told a wild and pitiful story to the commissionars of emigration— that she came to New York in the *City of Mobile* under the care of a gentleman whom she afterwards requited with ingratitude— that she had since lived a life of crime and suffering, and was now

* The Roman Catholic priest at Dunleer.

a wanderer in a strange land without a home, friends or money.
Susan Smith, the Broadway outcast, was one of the girls who went
out under Mr Foster's care, and had been seduced from the ship
by sailors and others to houses of ill-fame, where their ruin was
accomplished . . . Here is a whole cargo of virtue—before it was
subjected to the contamination of sailors—lost for want of
ordinary care. We never heard or read of such a sad story. Out
of 120 who left Ireland in safety, with their characters vouched
for by their clergy, only 12 or so were uninfected, the rest having
been ruined in the short space of one month.[16]

And that is only part of the article!

The Irish-American press embarked on an even more lurid
campaign. For example, under the title of 'Sea Monsters and
Irish Victims', *The Irish Vindicator* declared that

This, of course is the fate of hundreds of our poor country-
women, who, driven by famine, and the oppression of the British
Government at home, are sent to what they consider a Land
of Promise, to find shelter and a home. But alas! they have to
pass the fiery ordeal of the sea passage, in these floating Pande-
moniums [*sic*], called emigrant ships, manned by the vilest of God's
creation! Better—far better—that the mothers had dashed, when
babies, the brains out of these future victims to the lust and
villiany of man. Better that Mr De Vere Foster [*sic*] abandon his
scheme since the cost is so fearful. Better that the poor girls die,
overworked and famished in old Ireland, so that they fill a virtuous,
though pauper's grave. Indeed, in one respect, this emigration,
while it has been the making of America has been the destruction
of Ireland.[17]

In every respect it was a devastatingly cruel blow. Nothing
could have wounded Vere more deeply. All his eager, ceaseless
work, all his high hopes and his great schemes for helping the
young people of Ireland had been wrecked by the wilful folly
of one of his own emigrants, and were now held up to ignominy
and shame on both sides of the Atlantic. Not that it was poor
Susan Smith that really did the wrecking, but rather those who,
for ulterior motives, did not scruple to use lies, calculated in-
accuracies, and blatant misrepresentations.

For Vere the paramount rule governing all his relationships

was an unswerving regard for honesty and fair play. Did he not entreat his emigrants 'to love liberty and fair play for others' as well as for themselves? Very shortly he would write to his brother Cavendish : 'If there is any one thing which I have endeavoured to pride myself in cultivating through life it has been a spirit of fair play.' Now the utter lack of it on the part of his opponents must have caused a savage mixture of pain and anger.

Nothing better displays the essential goodness, sincerity, and courage of his character than his reaction to this great blow. In the first place, in anything that he subsequently wrote about emigration there is not the slightest hint of resentful bitterness or lingering wrath. Secondly, he did not come home, as Frederick had suggested; he stayed in America, set out on a long tour of visits to emigrants already settled, and immediately on his return to New York attached himself to the Women's Protective Emigration Society,[18] recently formed for the purpose of encouraging and aiding unemployed and destitute women in New York to move out to the western states. Elizabeth Phelps was president, and Eliza W. Farnham, formerly matron of Sing Sing prison, its honorary secretary. Horace Greeley sat on the advisory committee. Continuous emigration from Europe, together with financial uncertainty in New York, was resulting in a rapidly increasing number of workless and destitute women who filled the workhouse of the eastern ports while 'the thriving West' was clamouring for their labour. Vere assumed the duties of unpaid travelling agent. He set off in December on another long tour armed with an advertising poster headed HELP FOR WOMEN WITH SMALL CHILDREN, in which he outlined his plans for bringing '100 women with children mostly under two years of age, not to be separated from their mothers, from New York City to the West, provided homes, employment and wages can be secured for them in advance' . . . He asked that all offers of employment, etc, be directed to him at Chicago, and for the information of those not acquainted with him or the society adds the following introduction taken from an article in the *New York Weekly Tribune* :

VERE FOSTER ESQ., honorably distinguished by his philanthropic efforts to diminish the moral and physical evils hitherto attendant on the emigration of poor friendless Women from Europe to America, has just departed on a tour through the West as Unpaid Agent of the Women's Protective Emigration Society. His object is to find places and employment for the destitute Women now congregated in our city, and we heartily commend him to the confidence and co-operation of the wise and good.[19]

He threw himself into this work with his usual ardour. Parties of women were already leaving New York, some 'accompanied by ladies of the society and some by myself. We take cooked meat and fruit and bread with us, and telegraph ahead each morning and evening to wayside stations for hot coffee or tea and milk to be ready in pailfuls.'[20] They must have been very unusual parties!

On one of these trips Vere found himself at Springfield, where 'a distinguished Lawyer had most kindly offered to give a home, certain for a month' to one of the women. This was no less than Abraham Lincoln, and Vere himself stayed with the future President and his wife. On another occasion a young Manchester girl and her baby were in the party. She had been sent for by her husband, already working in the Illinois area, but, having lost his address and directions, was stranded, penniless, in New York. Vere found them a temporary home in the city of Illinois where, by good fortune, the 'servant maid' turned out to be a cousin of the young woman and knew of the whereabouts of her husband.

Frederick wrote early in December that his mother was much disappointed that Vere would not be home by Christmas.[21] Ireland, he said, was weathering the general financial crisis better than most places—conditions in America seemed very 'precarious'. Emigration was now a need of the past, no assistance would be forthcoming, and he himself would not contribute any more. (He had already contributed £1,500.) Again he advised Vere to devote himself 'to improving the schools and cottages';

the call for recruits for the army following the Indian Mutiny 'had drawn some twenty thousand men from Ireland' and would take many more for years to come, for Britain would need to hold India by force.

It was Frederick's last letter to Vere. He died, after a very short illness, in his mother's home at Wimbledon on 27 December 1857. His resolution to live in Ireland had never materialised.

On the first intimation of his brother's illness Vere wrote to Lady Albinia that if he thought he could be of any help he would return 'immediately', but the journey taking so long, Frederick's 'illness would surely be ended for better or worse' before he could reach England, and as he was so busy in New York he would remain for another month. 'I have been greatly fatigued and have exerted myself to the best of my ability every day and night, being most anxious to carry out as quickly and as efficiently as possible the instructions of the New York society . . . I visit a new town every day & in each place I readily find 20 to 40 families, who, notwithstanding their apprehension as to the *character* of the persons whom we may send, express their readiness to open their houses to them . . . Give my love to Fred.'[22]

When the final news reached him a month after Frederick's death, Vere wrote to his mother that he would go home immediately but that he dreaded a winter passage and that he has been in bed with a neglected swelling in his neck. He was glad that his mother had 'the comfort and consolation of Miss Baynes' company at this unhappy time. Were it not for that I would not delay here at all, though I could be of little comfort to you compared to herself.' He then went on to speak of some matters connected with Frederick's property.

Obviously Vere was completely engrossed in his work. Much depended on his ability to launch the new scheme, and his knowledge of conditions in the Chicago neighbourhood must have been invaluable to the society. Cavendish, now the third baronet, living in his rectory in Essex and not overworked with parish duties was, Vere naturally concluded, at hand to help his mother and he wrote him one of his rather prudish letters. Frederick, he commented, had died 'in the pride of health, without care, and in the enjoyment of a handsome fortune . . . Another lesson of the uncertainty of life; another warning to us all to use time & money well while we have it . . . I am pressingly engaged on behalf of a society which is relieving destitution in New York . . . I will make arrangements to return to England very soon to stay there . . . I hope you will now dispose of your living as your property and the poor people on and about it will suffice I think to occupy the whole of your attention.'[23]

Still in America in April 1858 he writes again to Cavendish: he will make one more rapid tour of about fifteen hundred miles in ten days and then sail for Liverpool. He continues:

> I hope very much that you will take up your residence in Dundalk, or some other place in our county, so that the money derived from the property may be spent on it, and that you may add one more to the number of resident landlords . . . What a great pleasure it would be to yourself and the children to be occupied in attending to the condition of the poor on the property, who naturally look to you for employment, encouragement & assistance! A new school house & teacher are wanted at Rathescar, and more new cottages here and there. Do not distribute Bibles or Protestant tracts, or you will injure your power for good, as proselytism is very odious . . . I hope the children will be brought up in association with & to feel an interest in the people on the property.[24]

He then names seven priests in the neighbourhood who are 'especially devoted to the good of the people', and adds four of whom he doesn't 'think so much'—that was all, and Fr Hughes was one of them!

So far as we know Cavendish had never concerned himself with Irish affairs or the Irish property, and he belonged to the evangelical branch of the Church of England. Vere trembled for the line he might take in Louth, but we hear nothing of the reception accorded to this gratuitous advice. Cavendish did shortly make a visit to his estate, and he returned occasionally but never settled in Ireland. He did however, in the course of time, purchase for his eldest son a former Foster property, Glyde

Court, near Ardee, and so after a long absence the descendants of John Thomas and Elizabeth were rooted in their own county.

A severe economic crisis developed in America. Among many other such casualties, R. K. Swift, Vere's banker in Chicago, failed, but, wrote Vere to Cavendish,[25] owing 'to the practical kind of education given to young ladies in *this* country and which I could not but admire' his wife and daughters were able 'to dispense with the services of a servant & do all the cooking, baking, milking, chamberwork, washing & ironing themselves, while in England it would generally be considered beneath the *dignity* of a lady'. They lived in a 'beautiful house on the most fashionable street' in Chicago. He goes on to relate how Miss Swift, 'a very elegant, good-looking, intelligent, spirited young woman of about 19' who had been travelling in Europe for pleasure, returned home to help her mother, while the younger daughter continued at school in the mornings and afternoons and worked in the house in the early mornings and evenings. 'Such persons,' he adds and heavily underlines, 'are independent of revolutions.' One imagines that all this was not unrelated to the training of Cavendish's small daughter Jane! Vere and Cavendish did not bring out the best in each other.

The prospects for emigrants were far from rosy, and though Vere never abandoned the idea of sending out small groups he realised sorrowfully, that anything on a large scale was, for the present, impossible.

He arrived in Liverpool in May 1858, crossed over to Ireland immediately, carrying in his 'parcels' a collection of 'daguerreotype likeness' given him by various of his emigrant protegées, and in his head an amusing idea. He went straight to Ardee, and hired a ground-floor room with a large window in which, at dead of night, he arranged his portrait gallery. Next morning he watched events from inside. 'For some time occasional passersby looked idly at the likenesses, children gathered, till at length a cry was raised, "Maggie", "Biddy," "Arrah! see, here's Peggy Malone, I declare," and "Here's Biddy Cassidy that lived in our lane," and so on, till mothers and all the town came in to inquire

the news of the Ardee girls, and to receive the numerous messages that I had brought home.'[26] The wound of that cruel report still hurt—everything must be done to vindicate his emigrants.

Seizing a last opportunity, he organised a party of thirty emigrant girls. He accompanied them to Liverpool, put them on board ship, and then made his way to London. The first phase of his work for emigration was completed.

During the years 1849–57, Vere defrayed the entire expenses of 1,250 female emigrants from Ireland to America, plus similar expenses for a much smaller number of men and boys.[27] A short list of subscriptions including £1,500 from Frederick amounts to £1,609, but this makes no mention of the sums provided by Vere himself. If we take his own figure of £7 10s 0d as the minimum for each person, the minimum total for the 1,250 would be upwards of £9,000. It is safe to assume that with the additional passages for men and boys Vere must have *spent* out of his own resources at least £10,000 on emigration in seven years, and that quite apart from the assistance he provided in other ways.

6

The Peripatetic Educationalist

Bereft of his absorbing interest, there was now no Frederick to turn to for understanding and consolation. In spite of Vere's genuine charity to all men he appears to have singled out very few on whom to bestow particular affection; so far as anyone ever penetrated the recesses of his heart and mind it was Frederick.

With characteristic indecision, and no doubt in spite of frequent admonitions from Vere, Frederick had made no will. With an equally characteristic energy, Vere, as soon as he returned from America, took up the task of settling his brother's estate, Cavendish remaining singularly inactive in his Essex rectory.

Ironically enough, the only continuous series of Vere's letters that remains is an almost daily correspondence with Cavendish extending over the second half of 1858, dealing in great detail with the apportionment of Frederick's estate. It contains little that interests us today, though here and there, and especially when Cavendish was on his first visit to Louth, brief references occur which show where Vere's real interest lay: 'I hope you will remember James Murray the independent car driver in Ardee. He will be thankful for your patronage. The other cars belong to richer men.' Vere would be obliged if Cavendish would call on

'Mr Quigley, who has a nailer's shop in Wightson's lane, Dundalk' and ask if two letters from Vere had arrived safely. At the time cottage industries were extensively organised as a means of giving assistance to labourers' families, but this in Vere's view did not justify the labourers' wives in overcharging : 'I am very much dissatisfied with Mrs Quinn's price for her shirts. She charges me 30 per cent more than what I pay in London.' Mrs Bunker of the Ardee Post Office was still worse, she 'will be teazing you to take her tattings. She gives me a great deal of trouble through her carelessness & inattention to orders all the time, & at one time caused me loss in this way of £65 . . . I got only 3 weeks ago 24 collars from her at 1/4d. each & have sent her an order for 60 more, so she raises the price to 1/6, so I am to have the risk of selling them & she is to have an *increased* profit, & wants that too to be paid in advance.' Lavish as he was to those in need, Vere, like many another generous person, could not bear to be imposed upon, and here as elsewhere his passion for fair play is evident. Still hankering after emigration, he asks Cavendish to tell any inquirers that 'I am ready to pay the passage of 100 girls or boys who can be recommended to me as perfectly sober & otherwise very well behaved but not able to pay their own passage, but I cannot get places in America for men'.[1] There is no mention of the offer being accepted.

At this time comes the first intimation of the tenants' wish to provide a memorial to Sir Frederick. Money was already being collected. A drinking fountain had been suggested, but Vere hoped that a school would be built. In the end a statue embodying the fountain was erected in the Square at Ardee, and, though the rather crude representation of a Victorian gentleman conveys nothing of Frederick's charm, its very simplicity is a striking testimony to the regard and affection he inspired. Throughout the length and breadth of Ireland not many monuments were erected at this time—1861—to landlords by grateful tenants; that this one should have been set up at a cost of £290 in the lean years following the famine, and at the opening of the bitter land war, is a considerable tribute.

Meanwhile, as Vere worked on his lists and apportioned with meticulous fairness his brother's possessions, pondering on Frederick's achievements and aspirations, his own next move became clear—he would continue what Frederick had begun. So he wrote to Cavendish, who was still in Ireland :

> I intend to lay out the money which I have inherited from Frederick in building as many new schoolhouses as are needed in our county wherever sites can be procured, and the cooperation of the Commissioners of National Education by grants & otherwise can be obtained, the buildings to be the best specimens, with due regard to use, comfort & economy, of what schoolhouses should be, with teachers' apartments attached, the buildings to be vested in the Commissioners, & the education given in them to be conducted strictly according to their rules, & under their superintendence. I hope you may approve of giving me a site for the purpose at Philipstown.[2] *

He reminded Cavendish that 'only last September F. wrote to me in America to ask me to give up emigration and join with him in attending to the national schools. He spent a deal of money first in draining . . . and next in building laborers cottages & in emigration & then he was going to build schoolhouses.'[2]

Cavendish's reaction to the school at Philipstown and Vere's reply are typical of the opposing attitudes of the two brothers. Cavendish's letter is not extant, but apparently he declared that he saw no reason why a Protestant landlord should be expected to donate a site for a school to be attended predominantly by Catholic children, and—more monstrous still—to be under the management of a Catholic priest; a point of view not uncommon among Irish landlords. Vere replied :

> With regard to your observations about the proposed Philipstown school, if there was a Catholic Proprietor in the district where a school was wanted for a population chiefly Catholic I should certainly make application to him for a site, but there is

* This letter, dated 6 August 1858, opens with the delighted exclamation 'What glorious news that the laying of the telegraph is accomplished', a reference to the fact that on 5 August, the first signals were received on the recently laid electric cable between Valentia Island off the coast of Kerry and Newfoundland.

no Catholic Proprietor about Philipstown, & very few in Ireland. *F.* intended to give a site, & had a promise of cooperation from the Commissioners of National Education, who at his request, furnished him with a plan for the schoolhouse. I do not propose it for children of one, but of all creeds, & to secure to all the right of religious teaching according to their own tenets, with the consent of their parents, but no interference with the religious tenets of any of the children except by persons authorised by their parents. I am not asking anything unusual of you as you can learn in Dublin from the Secretaries of the Commissioners . . . at their office in Marlborough St., who will tell you that nearly all the school sites in Ireland are given by Protestant landlords, there being few others, & that half of these schools at least, say 2,500 in number, are under the patronage of catholic priests, the children in them being almost exclusively Catholic, & he being the most natural person in the parish to superintend schools for their education. If you object to giving a site, would you sell me half an acre & then I would give it?[3]

Cavendish relented. Vere expressed his gratitude and said he would not ask for any money towards the building 'as I am prepared to pay all that is necessary for the schoolhouse & teacher's residence there & in at least 20 other places besides in our County, & have written to the Commissioners of National Education to that effect'.

By the end of the year family affairs were settled. Lady Albinia bought a house in Eccleston Square and this and her house in Wimbledon were to be Vere's nearest thing to a permanent address till the death of his mother in 1867. But he was rarely in England. The next three or four years were to be spent tramping the roads of Ireland, as he started his great work for Irish education. He was now thirty-nine.

In September 1858 Vere made a hurried tour of Co Louth, visiting with lightning speed 'nearly eighty National schoolhouses'. Travelling off the beaten track was not comfortable. 'I shall be glad,' he wrote, 'to get back to a dry and solitary bed after so long a sleepless experience of damp & crowded beds (crowded with bugs & fleas enough to serve as snuff for a Brobdignag).'

He was shocked by the bad state of the school buildings and by the complete lack of them in some areas, and he forthwith wrote a second letter to the commissioners, pointing out the various defects in a manner somewhat reminiscent of his inquisitorial activities on the *Washington*, and though on this occasion he diplomatically suggested that 'your inspectors will be better judges', the Board may have felt that this unusual gentleman was undertaking to instruct them in their own business. For Vere awareness of a need was the signal for instant remedial action. A school with a 'damp clay floor . . . no privies . . . no teacher's desk or benches for the scholars . . . and scarcely any school requisites and yet there is an average attendance throughout the year of over fifty scholars', was a situation—and it could be repeated scores of times—that must be rectified forthwith. Delaying administrative regulations he regarded with the utmost impatience and disdain.

And yet for the poor ignorant emigrant, the harrassed underpaid teacher, the child in need of education, his patience was unlimited. Forthright, extremely energetic, even impulsive by nature, the unruffled tolerance—the 'great indulgence'—that characterised all Vere's work with people in need, can only have been achieved by the sternest self-discipline and overflowing charity.

His offer to the Commissioners is recorded in their minutes thus :

13. November 1858. Letter from Mr Vere Foster, Wimbledon, Surrey, offering to contribute 1/3rd of the cost of building as many additional schoolhouses in Co. Louth as may be necessary and also to defray entire cost of erecting teachers' residences : schoolhouses to be vested in the Commissioners.

The Board thanked Mr Foster and informed him that the Head and District Inspectors would make the necessary inquiries.

It should be explained that while the commissioners provided two-thirds of the cost of any schoolhouse built according to their requirements and vested in them, they made no contribution whatever to the cost of teachers' residences, though from the early days of the Board's existence Inspectors stressed the crying need for such accommodation. In country districts a teacher of either sex might have to walk many miles to and from his school in wild, inclement weather, and young teachers on miserable salaries of £20 a year were often

> obliged to lodge in the small public houses, or the confined dwellings of farmers . . . who for a sum of £1 or £1 10s per quarter will 'oblige the manager' by consenting to receive the teacher as a lodger on condition (most generally) that the guest occupy the kitchen during the evening, and at night retire to rest in a bed-room already shared by two or more members of his own family.[4]

By including 'residences' in this his first offer of educational aid, Vere evinced that foresight, that swift and total grasp of a *whole* situation already evident in his schemes for emigration, and declared at the outset that teachers as well as pupils were his concern.

The board's formal minute conveys no idea of the magnitude of the gift—one wishes for some record of the personal reaction of the august commissioners. So far as can be ascertained nothing on this scale had ever come their way before; it was the generosity of a prince. A few exceptional landowners, of whom Lord Monteagle was an outstanding example, had, with the Board's grants, provided one or more schools on their estates—here provision for a whole county was offered by a man who wasn't a landowner at all. There were no stipulations except that the buildings were to be 'the best specimens of what school-houses should be',[5] with 'yard and playground' together with a teacher's residence and garden. Vere had estimated the number of new schools required at not less than twenty and the entire cost of a teacher's residence for each school was included. It was an entirely novel and forward-looking conception: Frederick's idea perhaps in the beginning, but translated by Vere into something of dramatic proportions— Frederick's money, wealth from Louth, being ploughed back in benefit to its people. It is almost unbelievable that such a benefaction should have been thrown back in his face.

Perhaps it was the very magnificence of the gift that caused alarm. If, the Catholic Primate may have thought, the great majority of schools in the county of Louth are to be vested in the commissioners, what chance would the church have of maintaining any specifically Catholic education in the area—for like the ascendancy before them, the Catholic hierarchy now realised the importance of education as a weapon of control.

At any rate, within a week, the commissioners noted another letter from Mr Foster 'enclosing a copy of one from the Rev Mr Tierney in reply to a proposal from Mr Foster to build a new schoolhouse at Tallanstown, in which he, the Rev Mr Tierney, states that he cannot be a party to the vesting of the building in the commissioners as required by Mr Foster, and suggesting that the building should be conveyed to Trustees to be approved of by the Roman Catholic bishop of the diocese'.[6] The commissioners ordered that 'Mr Foster be informed that the Commissioners cannot under any circumstances sanction a deviation from their Rule requiring that schoolhouses towards the erection of which they grant aid shall be vested in them in their corporate capacity'. Vere himself would not have consented to contribute towards building schools not vested in the board 'as that would be the only satisfactory guarantee to *me* that the school should be permanently managed on the liberal system administered by them, & of which I so much approve'. His faith in the vested school was absolute.

In a letter to Cavendish he reported that Fr Tierney had informed him 'that the Catholic Primate had refused to consent that any Catholic priest should be manager of any new school to be vested in the Commissioners of National Education'.[7] This places the responsibility for refusal not on Fr Tierney, but on the Catholic Primate, Archbishop Cullen, with whom no doubt it more properly rested. Presumably all priests in the county were similarly notified for there was no extensive school building in Louth. Vere's great plan was rejected.

Again, one can only surmise the severity of the blow, the bitterness of disappointment and humiliation; not one word of comment, so far as is known, was ever committed to paper. That it should have happened in his own county of Louth, the county to which Frederick and he had determined to give of their best, made the rejection doubly wounding A few weeks earlier Vere had urged Cavendish to throw in his lot unreservedly with his tenants, implored him to avoid proselytising, and, in the face of his brother's opposition, had championed reasonable Catholic demands.* It was little more than a year since a priest in Dundalk had wantonly exploited the folly of one of his poor emigrant girls, here was another instance of that same mistrust of independence and opportunity pitted against Vere's constant and still exuberant confidence in youth. Yet there was no murmur of recrimination, no angry comment, never a harsh judgment on any individual Catholic. Only three months previously Vere had received a letter from Dr MacHale, Roman Catholic Archbishop of Tuam, the most bitter opponent of the non-denominational principles of the commissioners so dear to Vere's heart, thanking him for what is described as 'so seasonable and gratifying a communication. The duty of gratitude [the archbishop declared] will not be confined to me, it will be largely shared by the people of this locality and the clergy of the diocese.'[8] One imagines from the tone of the letter that Vere with unbiassed generosity had sent Dr MacHale some help for one of the non-vested schools.

And yet, strange though it may seem, there was what can be construed as a positive excuse for the attitude of the hierarchy.

It was now thirty years since the Commissioners of National Education had addressed themselves to the task of providing a system of education in Ireland available to children of all creeds, and schools in which Catholic and Protestant children would meet on a basis of complete equality.† The goal had been achieved in principle, though the actual number of schools was not yet adequate, but it was perhaps optimistic to hope, in a country so bedevilled by prostituted religion as was Ireland, that the ideal

* See pp 98, 103
† See p 47

could be pursued unchallenged. In the beginning the scheme was welcomed by the Catholic hierarchy, partly no doubt because the Catholic population, by reason of its poverty, was unable to provide its own schools. At the same time it seems fair to say that in Dr Daniel Murray, Roman Catholic Archbishop of Dublin, and one of the original commissioners, the board had a genuine and able supporter. There had been, nevertheless, from the inception of the system an undercurrent of strong Catholic mistrust led by Dr John MacHale. It was, however, by the Presbyterians that opposition was first expressed. While supporting enthusiastically the concept of national education, the General Synod of Ulster, under the leadership of the Rev Henry Cooke, DD, one of its ministers in Belfast attacked almost immediately the regulations of the board, especially the time allotted for religious instruction, and the content of Bible reading. A bitter battle was waged during the years 1830–1840 in the name of Christianity, and no doubt with a clear conscience, by Dr Cooke. He was a man of magnetic personality, great oratorical gifts. He gained the support of the anti-Catholic element in Ulster, and was largely responsible for propagating anti-Catholic feeling in the hitherto tolerant Presbyterian community. He also won the sympathy of the whole body of evangelical opinion in Britain, engaged as it was in combating the alarming trend towards Catholicism in England, evidenced by the Oxford Movement and later by the conversion of such men as Manning and Newman. This was of immense importance to Cooke and his friends, for they acquired thereby a strong backing at Westminster, and we find, for example, the Bishop of Exeter dogmatising in the House of Lords about education in Ireland. Cooke was successful in securing most of the modifications he desired.

If the opposition presented by the Established Church was less vociferous than that of the Presbyterians, it was no less effective. Because of its comfortable wealth this body was to some extent independent of the board. It had provided, and continued to maintain in many districts, its own schools where its religious tenets were taught. Elsewhere, whilst co-operating with the board, it never wholeheartedly accepted the undenominational basis fundamental to its system, or indeed the need for popular education at all, and through the exertions of Archdeacon Stopford in 1847 regulations were modified, thus undermining some of the safeguards against religious interference.

The situation was further aggravated from outside, for the anti-catholic zealots in Britain could not refrain from entering the fruitful field for action that lay just across the narrow sea. In 1849 the 'Irish Church Mission to Roman Catholics' was founded in England with the express purpose of making converts in Ireland, and it evoked much support from the strongly evangelical section within the Irish Established Church. We can be reasonably sure that the little 'vert' who caused so much alarm on Vere's emigrant procession* had been the subject of such influences. Once again education was used as a partisan weapon. The Irish Church Mission opened schools in the poorest parts of Dublin and in rural areas, notably in the west,† where out of genuine, though misdirected, kindness and pity, the teachers 'feed and caress the children, and distribute among them coal in the winter, and dress them for the school, and teach them daily that the doctrines of the Roman Catholic Church are not the word of God—that what the priest teaches Christ did *not* teach; and the pupils learn anti-Catholic hymns, and join in anti-Catholic prayer'.[9]

As for the Catholic hierarchy—every concession to presbyterians and the Established Church served only to confirm them in their rapidly growing suspicion that once again they had been duped, that the majority of the Commissioners of National Education were—as all 'foreign' rulers of Ireland had always been—proselytising protestants at heart. Death had removed the statesmanlike guidance of Dr Murray, in his place was the far more rigid Archbishop Cullen, while Archbishop MacHale, from his stronghold in Tuam thundered abuse on 'National Education'. Haunted and obsessed by memories of former persecution, the

* See p 89.
† It is not unlikely that Vere's gratifying communication to Dr MacHale [p 108] was to counteract such anti-Catholic action.

Catholics now sought to preserve their faith by adopting a ghetto-like attitude to education. The hierarchy, with notable exceptions, directed that Catholic children should attend only such schools as had Catholic managers, some bishops insisting on Catholic clerical managers; they refused to allow—as in the case of Vere's offer—their managers to accept the terms on which the board granted aid towards the building of new schools; teaching orders, notably the Christian Brothers, were encouraged to open schools; and Catholic teachers were absolutely forbidden to participate in the training facilities provided by the board. As a result Catholic schools, practically all 'non-vested', were, generally speaking, conducted in miserable premises; though nominally open to children of all creeds they tended more and more to have only Catholic pupils, and—most serious of all—Catholic teachers had of necessity to remain in the untrained categories, qualifying only for the lowest of the board's grants and receiving little or nothing from local contributions or parents fees. It was a very high price to pay for church-controlled education.

Such was the background of the fateful rejection of Vere's offer in 1858. He must have known how the tide was running, but in spite of all the portents his never failing optimism, his confidence in the local clergy—Fr Tierney, he had told Cavendish, was 'specially devoted to the good of the people'—and his belief that they had confidence in him, had encouraged him to hope that in Louth, at any rate, reason would prevail.

What was he to do? There was no moaning or self-pity, though there may have been a good deal of suppressed vexation. Instead there was instant action. Within a week or two Vere had decided that if he could not build his fine educational compounds in Louth, he would go to the worst little hovels of schools in the four corners of Ireland, and transform them into something approaching decent schoolhouses. He would mend the roofs, he would replace the earthen floors with wooden ones, he would see that proper privies were provided, he would make the windows open, and he would supply maps and blackboards, pictures of animals and birds, and such other essentials as went by the name of 'requisites'. In the end he did something infinitely more valuable. By his inexhaustible patience and understanding he transformed not only the poor little schools but the entire teaching profession in Ireland.

So he went off to the wild, poverty-stricken districts of the west and south, and the following are inspectors' reports of the sort of conditions that he found :

At Innisboffin there is a shrewd, intelligent, respectable young woman in charge of the school. She has passed her examination, and is very fairly qualified for her position. The house she teaches in, although one of the best on the island, is a mere hovel, and affords breathing space for no more than fourteen, whilst the means of ventilation are wholly unprovided for. Poverty of the direct kind marks the countenances and the raiments and the homes of the 120 people who inhabit the island; the utter wretchedness of their state is manifest even in the badly furnished and neglected schoolroom, and not one farthing can be contributed by them towards the maintenance of the school. With her lot so sadly cast, with misery and loneliness to damp her ardour, with the usual privations of these islands, of having to live solely on potatoes and bread and fish, and deprived of the humblest kind of companionship, this good and brave woman is labouring most assiduously, is attracting to the school-room in the chill of winter, even the adults of the island as pupils, and is a noble example in every light in which her position can be regarded.[10]

Again :

Two per cent of the schools are still, however, wretched hovels —structures under the roof of which it is lamentable to have to gather together as many children as constitute a school, the means of ventilation are so bad, the lighting so imperfect, and the earthen floors so damp and unhealthy.[11]

And again :

In a school in the county Donegal which I inspected last year I found each child carrying a huge slate, four or five times the weight of an ordinary slate, with him every day from home, moving about from place to place in the school during the day, the slate all the while suspended from his neck, and returning home again with it in the evening . . . I visited an infant school in Dublin, not long since, in which I found the same practice prevailing.[12]

It was always Vere's practice to require some measure of self-help as a qualification for his assistance, and in his present plan a nominal sum towards the outlay had to be raised locally, either by the manager or teacher. It is true that a limited free issue of requisites was made by the Board to each school every three years, but otherwise the manager or teacher was obliged to purchase everything required from the board's repository at, as a concession, reduced prices. Such things as slates, paper, pencils, and books, had also to be bought, and were sold again to the children. In the vast majority of cases the managers let this burden fall on the teachers, indeed in very many non-vested schools, the rent of the premises had to be found by the teacher out of his miserable pittance of a salary. That Vere should embark on this kind of help was another indication of the genuiness of his desire to assist teachers as well as pupils. He utterly disapproved of the whole system of non-vested schools; the regulations governing them were less strict, they could be more readily used for proselytising purposes by whatever denomination provided them, and they were generally speaking held in dilapidated premises. Again and again he expresses his confidence in schools vested in the commissioners, but for the present at any rate no other way was open to him. Perfectionist though he was, it was the measure of his altruism that at this stage he accepted a second best.

For information regarding the carrying out of his scheme we are entirely dependent on minutes of the commissioners, reports from inspectors, and letters of gratitude from recipients. No letter written by Vere himself survives, only one of his circulars.

Lavish though his expenditure on any project might be, Vere was always careful to get the best value for his money and never overlooked the business end of a transaction. In February 1859 he asked the commissioners if they would be willing to supply his orders for requisites at a cheaper rate than the reduced prices already available to managers. The reply stated that while the full cost of the articles listed by Mr Foster amounted to £1,072 0s 5d, the price to managers was £735 0s 0d and no further reduction was possible.[13] This gives some idea of the scale of his outlay on requisites alone within the first three months.

Meanwhile Vere sent a circular to teachers of selected needy schools informing them of his offer and asking for particulars of their requirements. Appended to this notification, indeed taking up the greater part of the front page, were, to use his own words, 'comparative tables of statistics [which] may be instructive in view of the present agitation among the hardworked and under-paid national teachers for an increase in their miserable salaries'. These tables set out amounts received from government grants, voluntary sources and local contributions by schools in Ireland and in Great Britain, showing clearly the remarkable disadvantage suffered by Irish schools in the matter of funds from voluntary sources and raised by local contributions. On the other side of the circular was this statement :

> I have on the table before me various statistics relating to upwards of thirteen hundred national schools in the West of Ireland. Sixty-five of these schools are situated on the estates of twenty-eight Noblemen, who contribute towards their maintainance to the amount altogether of £517 : 240 others on the estates of six Marquises, nineteen Earls, eight Viscounts, sixteen Barons, two Bishops, fourteen other Lords, twenty nine Baronets, and six Knights, receive no contribution whatever from their landlords, who are of course mostly absentees. Lest I may be thought to exaggerate I append a list of a good many of these Gentlemen, whose social rank, whose political standing, whose relation to the parents of the scholars and whose *ample* means might lead one to expect that they would be the most liberal promoters of the education of the children of the laborers and tenants on their estates, the sweat of whose brow is the foundation of their wealth.[14]

And there follow, in their appropriate categories, the names of forty-six Irish noblemen and two Irish (Protestant) bishops. One can readily assess the industry required to piece together the 'various statistics', for no readymade list containing this kind of information was supplied by the Board of Education. Here, at the very outset of his campaign, is an indication of his conviction that a national system of education was entitled to demand financial support from three sources, from government aid, from voluntary contributions, and from local taxation. This principle he maintained to the end.

The circular was described as 'very strong language' by the astonished Charles Joly Esq, manager of a school in Co Mayo, who asked the commissioners 'whether it is right or necessary that he should accept the articles proposed to be given'. The even more astonished commissioners replied 'that they do not at all connect themselves with Mr Foster nor are they responsible for any statement made by him, nor have they any power to control him, and it is for Mr Joly to make up his own mind what he should do'.[15]

Judge, therefore, of their feelings when a week later, they received a letter from Vere himself 'requesting the P.O. addresses of all National Schools in Cos. Clare, Leitrim and Tipperary, his object to obtain information from teachers respecting the fitting up of their schools with suitable articles of apparatus, with a view to promoting their efficiency'. The Commissioners' reply indicated unequivocally that the information Mr Foster desired would not be supplied 'as it would give him an opportunity of circulating a document of which they totally disapprove'.[16]

To one so accustomed as was Vere to the normal procedure of official circles, these tactics appear unusual to say the least, except in terms of a definite sympathy with the always smouldering flame of antagonism between peasant and landlord. The section of his circular dealing with the need for increased support for Irish education was certainly relevant, but while the commissioners themselves had been assiduously pressing the British treasury for more generous grants, especially for teachers' salaries, it was Vere's contention that the increased funds should be obtained from a local rate and local donations. But the attack on the nobility! Teachers and inspectors knew only too well that in many instances landlords were either completely unconcerned

about national education or definitely antagonistic to it—giving
neither moral nor financial support—but deliberately to set about
influencing teachers, who were forbidden by the terms of their
recognition by the commissioners to take any part in politics or
express any political opinions, against the aristocracy seemed
nothing short of reckless socialism on Vere's part. Was the re-
pressed anger occasioned by the use of entrenched authority by
the Roman Church, venting itself on the entrenched apathy of
the nobility? It was either an impetuous, ill-conceived gesture, or
a move so far-reaching as to place Vere Foster in the van of the
movement for social reform. Whichever it was the commissioners
were—understandably—horrified, and the incident undoubtedly
prejudiced Vere's relations with the board.

For Vere himself this was to be a period of great happiness.
Again he was continually on the move, from one poor little shell
of a school to another. We do not know where he made his head-
quarters. A few tattered envelopes are addressed to him at the
Post Office, Dublin. A. M. Sullivan, editor of *The Nation*, describes him at this time as 'simply attired in Irish homespun grey,
with knapsack strapped on his back, and a stout blackthorn in
his hand, walking by easy stages through some remote county'.[17]
It is worth pausing for a moment to recall his upbringing; the
decorous luxury of the legation at Turin, the glitter of London
society and Vere 'all gaiety', the manifold interests and connections that even a minor diplomatic post afforded. All these were
now past history and never was there a nostalgic sigh for their
return. Not that Vere forgot his relations. Their names appear
on his subscription lists, and we shall shortly see that even Lord
Palmerston was pressed into his service. In one letter to America
he says he is setting off next week 'for a walk among the promon-
tories and islands of the extreme South West of Counties Cork
and Kerry in Ireland, visiting schools amidst that beautiful
scenery', and we can picture him on the shores of Kenmare Bay,
making his way along the Dingle peninsula and perhaps over to
the Blasket Islands. Here is his own description of a village on
Belmullet in the wilds of Co Mayo: 'I have seen the place. It

was a collection of hovels, built of sods and covered with thatch and large stones. They could not be entered except on all fours, and in stormy weather and in spring tides the owners had to fly for shelter to the neighbouring sandhills to avoid being drowned in their homes.'[18] There must have been many a long wet tramp over bogs and on wretched roads—some stages would be accomplished on a Bianconi car, sometimes there might be 'a lift' on a passing ass-cart, or an outside car, and there must have been many a flea-ridden bed. But there were also the heart-warming welcomes from the Ryans, the O'Deas, the Morriseys and many others of his teacher friends, some of them his fellow students in the days at Glasnevin.

Though the commissioners withheld their help Vere's circulars found their way to every corner of western Ireland : the response was immediate and tremendous. With a burst of rapturous appreciation the often weary reports of enthusiastic but frustrated inspectors are suddenly transformed into paeans of gratitude. The following extracts are taken from reports for 1859 :

As a grand contrast to the indifference of so many to the progress of popular education, it gives me sincere pleasure to mention the noble efforts in this district of a gentleman, whose philanthropic views are not confined to one county, but embrace a large portion of Ireland. I allude to Mr Vere Foster, whose active benevolence was a few years since successfully devoted to the welfare of the poor emigrant, and whose name, identified with the protection of female purity, is as a household word in the cottages of the people. This gentleman has entered upon a new field of usefulness . . . in which he will essentially contribute to advance the moral and intellectual progress of the rising generation. His undertaking is indeed a great one, and more commensurate with the scope of a national effort, or a Parliamentary grant, than with the resources of one person . . . It would appear that with him the knowledge of a national defect is the precursor to the adoption of a remedy . . . With this in view he opened a correspondence with upwards of 4,000 teachers, explaining his plan, and inviting local co-operation . . . In this district 20 schools in the county Clare have been aided with grants varying from £3 to £20. It is to be hoped that this gentleman's unexampled

generosity will have some influence in awaking the interest of some
of his own rank, and in stimulating them to do on a small scale
... the part which he is accomplishing in many.[19]

Another inspector, noting decided improvement in the orderli-
ness of teachers and pupils, continues :

It has been mainly brought about through the voluntary and
unexpected co-operation of a gentleman (Vere Foster, Esq.) who
previously had not, I believe, the slightest connection with the
schools of the District, or the estates on which they are situated.
With princely but discriminating generosity, he has given sums
of money, often very considerable, for effecting the most useful
improvements in the school-houses.[20]

And again :

Mr Vere Foster, a gentleman entirely unconnected with the
district, has, in upwards of thirty schools, presented during the
past year a liberal supply of educational apparatus, and has also
caused the former damp clay floors to be replaced with boards.[21]

Even the commissioners were moved to acknowledge such
generosity :

We take this opportunity [says their report to the Lord Lieutenant dated 1859] of acknowledging the munificent liberality of
Vere Foster Esq., who has contributed from September, 1858, up
to the present date [Dec. 1859] the sum of £2,142 8. 10. in the
purchase of apparatus, which he has distributed among upwards
of 785 National Schools. Mr Foster has also expended large sums
in improving the condition of school-houses in places where
funds were not otherwise available for the purpose.[22]

The same story was repeated the following year : 'the princely
generosity of Mr Vere Foster'; 'Mr Foster's noble example';
'teachers . . . have made personal sacrifices to improve their
school-houses, so as to avail themselves of the liberal donations
which Mr Vere Foster has given for that purpose'; 'Owing to his
[Mr Vere Foster's] prescience and timely aid, the schools in cold
and mountainous districts were, during the winter, crowded
with children, who came for shelter and warmth, if not for educa-

tion. The want of turf pressed so heavily on the poor that even in the winter months the fire was out on many hearths.'[23]

The speed and magnitude of the enterprise was, when we remember conditions of transport and communications, quite staggering. It is true that by this time Vere knew Ireland well. He had toured large areas of the country when selecting his emigrants, and his knowledge of problems on Frederick's estate, with his own acute powers of discernment, resulted in a more than ordinary awareness of conditions of life for the Irish peasant. But he had been in America until May 1858 and was then immersed in family affairs in England. How did he contrive, without the aid of any secretary or such modern aids as the telephone or motor car, to get the vast undertaking 'off the ground' in a matter of weeks? One sees again the ability to grasp a situation instantly and in its entirety, and to act with a 'princely' munificence, not only of expenditure but of conception. Vere swept into the orbit of the national system of education like a fiery comet, and within fifteen months, single-handed, he had improved out of all knowledge almost one thousand school buildings. No one had ever dreamt of doing such a thing before. 'His [Mr Foster's] benevolent and enlightened exertions,' wrote one inspector, 'extend to even the remotest nooks of my extensive circuit.' Between 1859 and 1863 fourteen hundred school-houses had been supplied with wooden floors.[24] The fact that towards the close of 1861 Vere was very ill makes his achievement still more remarkable. So serious was his condition that prayers for his recovery were offered in the Catholic church in Newry and, for all we know, may have been offered in many another church as well. It was said in 1870 that Vere had spent £13,000 on re-roofing, re-flooring and supplying requisites.[25]

Appreciative as were the Inspectors, Vere's action was even more significant for the teachers. The constant references by inspectors to the lack of interest on the part of most managers, and the apathy of those who by their example and position could have done so much to encourage the struggling teachers, are epitomised by one of them in this sentence : 'There is very little super-

intendence of the schools, very little of that personal co-operation
and hearty, warm sympathy with the teacher so essential to success.'[26] Now, suddenly, there appeared this gentleman, known to
many by name, making his way to the most remote habitations,
intimately aware of the difficulties of the teachers and the needs
of the children, offering not only help but 'that hearty, warm
sympathy'. The gratitude of the teachers was boundless and in
some cases very touching. Only a very few of their messages have
survived, though Vere must have received them in hundreds, and
they convey an overflowing thankfulness. This from Belmullet—
where the people lived in hovels that could only be entered 'on
all fours' :

> May it Please your Honour—
> [Here is a paragraph of welcome on Vere's first visit to the
> school]
> Your Honour will, we trust, be pleased to accept our hearty
> thanks for your kind and valuable Gift, the School Apparatus
> which you now see suspended on the walls of our room made so
> very comfortable at your expense.
> Praise coming from so humble a source in this remote part of
> Ireland can be of small consequence to you who are so highly
> applauded by all who know how to appreciate real worth, but it is
> the only way we have in our power at present to acknowledge
> our Gratitude.
> [Here is a long paragraph about the various items of apparatus.]
> In conclusion we truly desire that your Noble efforts in en-
> deavouring to better the condition of all classes, but particularly
> the Working Classes in Ireland may be rewarded with that suc-
> cess which your Honour's Philanthropic exertions so justly de-
> serve.
>   Martin Walsh, Teacher.[27]

The teachers of the county of Longford, in a joint letter of
'gratitude and veneration' for 'active benevolence' over several
years, wished they could procure 'by their united contributions'
some 'tangible offering' to mark their appreciation of 'benefactions almost regal in their unlimitedness', but no doubt the following paragraph, and the fact that he found almost a hundred
original signatures of male and female teachers from all over the

county appended to the letter, were more gratifying to Vere than any gift :

> You sought us in our dwellings and were not discouraged by the contact; you stood by us in our schools and showed your appreciation of our labours by those generous gifts of educational apparatus, hitherto unfortunately beyond our reach . . . startled by the suffering of the poor half clad children, you substituted for the damp, unwholesome clay, the dry boarded floor, and in other important respects, exerted yourself for the promotion of decency,* cleanliness and order in our schools.[28]

In some instances long lists of pupils' names were included in letters of thanks.

Two teachers, at least, found prose inadequate and took to verse. Cornelius Donovan from West Cork composed three pages, of which the following lines are an example :

Honorable Sir, you I most truly thank,
Your donation informs me you are of noble rank.
Pearls, Diamond & Rubies you do value not,
In Africa these treasures are picked out of the rivers by the
    Hottentot.
Your name is exalted in the Emerald Isle,
The noble deeds you performed are spread many a mile.
Deficient in etiquette, overlook my style
In Belles-lettres I'm not versed, for I'm in 'lowest class' of the file.
Your Honourable & Worthy Mamma† May God prolong her days,
And may the *Bards* of Erin of her noble deeds compose some
    roundelays.

*   *   *   *

Now for to conclude, may the Almighty increase your store,
& before very long may it be double more,
& may your flocks & fields with milk & honey flow,
& may he prolong & preserve you from ill where'ere you go.
& may your Honour be happy with the God on high
Singing Psalms & hymns with the Father above the sky.
I hope your Honourable Mamma hereafter will be
In Mansions of bliss among the happy.
I have the Honor to remain your humble servant this day,
Cornelius Donovan—the Author will for ever pray.[29]

* A reference to Vere's insistences on the provision of privies.
† The Lady Albinia Foster had sent a donation.

It was left to Michael Connolly of Killycarvan school,* to compose this less ambitious but more adequate tribute *(opposite)* :[30]

Then, right in the middle of all this appreciation and adulation, with his scheme for roofs and floors and requisites galloping ahead, Vere suddenly decided, in April 1864, to go to America 'for the purpose of endeavouring to save as much as possible of the wreck of my property there'. Like many others he believed that the Civil War would end in the break-up of the Union 'which I think cannot be much longer delayed', and he was anxious to retrieve what money he had previously invested in various American funds. This was no doubt specially urgent in view of the great sums being spent on schools. But, as we shall see, his property was not his only concern. On the trip he kept a brief diary from which the following details are taken.[31]

He embarked from Queenstown. As he had only given the Cunard office one week's notice he was not surprised to find that the second class accommodation allotted to him in RMS *Scotia* was the top berth in a very dark cabin. However, his friend James Rogers, the teacher of Blackrock National School, met him at Cork, and together they went by rail to Queenstown [Cobh] 'where James's sister and a lady friend of mine met us on the pier and came with us on board to see me off', Vere in the height of good spirits showing them all over the ship. If only we knew a little more about the 'lady friend', but she is never mentioned again. This decorous, but no doubt jovial, farewell party seems to have been conducted without so much as a cup of tea between them, for Vere noted that 'when the ship sailed supper was served at 6 p.m.—cold mutton, veal, ham, apple tart, tea, toast—all well enough to eat, I, especially having had nothing since 8 a.m. in Dublin'. Surely there were restaurants in Cork or Queenstown where some simple refreshment could have been had. Was the lack of it really due to Vere's want of cash, or to that streak of strange erratic parsimony?

Notwithstanding the dark cabin the voyage was immensely

---

* Killycarvan school was one of those referred to in the inspector's report quoted on p 118–19.

To Vere Foster Esqr from the children attending Killycarran N. S. Co. Monaghan, Ireland.

We pupils so happy our schoolroom so neat,
Our floor is now boarded, it looks so complete,
Do thank most sincerely, that man of great fame,
That lover of science "Vere Foster" by name,
For his princely donation unsolicited given,
We only can thank, his Reward is in heaven.

And may heaven reward him with blessings Divine,
On earth to be happy in Glory to shine,
Is the wish and the prayer of each child in our isle,
Enjoying such comfort how happy they smile,
And sing – For his princely donation unasked for & given,
We only can thank – his reward is in heaven.

To the emigrant lonely he has been a guide,
To watch oer the poor is his pleasure and pride,
To aid, to improve and to better their lot,
Abroad, on the ocean, or at home in their cot,
His princely donation so freely he's given,
We only can thank – his Reward is in heaven.

Should the great of our isle his example pursue,
How happy the land, Oh! what good they might do,
From the peer to the peasant, without regal rod,
All serving their country and loving their God,
For his princely donation unsolicited given,
We only can thank – his reward is in heaven.

P.S. I recd the 2d half note of your donation yesterday
Yours very sincerely
Mich Connolly
Killycarran. Jany 24th 1861.

To
Vere Foster Esq—

enjoyable, and all sorts of details are recorded—number of passengers, measurements of the ship (she was the largest liner afloat),
distances covered, and so forth. Off the south-west corner of Ireland he writes, 'The weather is supremely beautiful and so is the
scenery'. The voyage took only nine days as against thirty-seven
on the *Washington*! In New York he was at once surrounded
by friends. The day after his arrival he dined with Judge Roose-
velt, uncle of a future president. Horace Greeley and others advised him about his shares. He gazed at the growng city in delighted wonder: 'A great number of very handsome stores built
in Broadway and other streets since I was here 6 years ago. It
seems to me that there are 10 times as many magnificent shop
fronts in New York as in London.' Within a matter of days the
second purpose of his visit was apparent, for we find him in-
vestigating the educational system of the city, and there are
records of schools visited, cost of buildings, numbers of children
in attendance, numbers of classes and teachers, teachers' salaries,
subjects taught, with special reference to handwriting, and how
and when religious instruction was given. In one school he saw
an 'exhibition of Vigorous [underlined three times] callisthenic
exercises by 32 boys'; in another 'books are supplied gratis to
the scholars for use at school and at home. Punishments—marks
and a little rod. Copybooks with printed headlines.'

Then he set off for Chicago, and gives a minute description of
the wonderful sleeping-cars on the rail-roads. 'Chicago never more
prosperous—labourers' wages 2 dollars.' Everything is noted with
that intense interest and pleasure that enterprise and resource
always aroused. Here he stayed with his friends the Swifts who,
it will be remembered, had lost their money. Mrs Swift now took
lodgers, while her husband 'lives in the woods for four or five
days per week, saying he never was so happy in his life. He has
no money except what has been lent to him by some of his former
clerks to be repaid if he succeeds in his speculation of cultivating
cranberries.'

From Chicago there was a long series of visits to emigrants. He
went to Wisconsin to see Thomas Boyle of Glasnevin, arriving

on foot at 10.30 pm to find that the household had retired for the night. However Mr and Mrs Boyle rose from their beds 'lit the stove, prepared supper for me, and made me up a bed on chairs and we conversed till midnight'. The Boyles had seven children, the youngest born 'last Sunday', and the whole family with Mrs Boyle's brother and sister slept in the one and only bedroom in their wooden shack. James Mavorney came all the way to Chicago from his farm in Indiana to meet Vere. He and two brothers had been butchers in Feakle, Co Limerick and were doing well. Vere reckoned that James's capital now amounted to £2,180. He had two little girls, Bridget and Jane. No detail about these people who owed him so much was unimportant. At two stopping-places the parish priests were his hospitable hosts. At Janesville he found that many of his emigrants had scattered and a new list was made of their whereabouts. At St Joseph he stayed with 'Bridget (Cassidy) Dutch, as neat and tidy as ever'. She had married a German husband, they had a baby eight months old, and were very well to do with two bedrooms, 'one of which I occupy'.

Everywhere schools were visited and exhaustive inquiries made about educational facilities. Only occasionally is there any mention of the civil war—somebody's brother had returned with a wounded arm, the principal of a school had gone with many of his boys 'as 100 days men to the war'.

For Vere the fascination of America was as strong as ever, his zest for its boundless opportunities never waned. Undaunted by the disappearance of familiar patterns of society, he revelled in opportunity, in development, in the possibility of a better life for thousands of human beings. The everyday brashness he allowed for, believing it would pass with time; for the men who were shaping the future of the young republic he had admiration and respect, perhaps, indeed, he envied them the very vastness of their task. One feels that had he not committed himself to Ireland very little persuasion would have kept him in the United States. Whether he is describing a great new prison, a highly mechanised bakery, a new method of laying a roadway,

or the extraordinary achievement of moving houses en bloc as
was done in Chicago, there comes the feeling of thrilled admiration.

One incident of this visit must be recorded, for it underlines an
almost remorseless insistence on 'fair play'. In 1858 Vere had
met in Chicago the Rev Dr Dunne, a Roman Catholic priest
engaged in building his parish church and school. 'On account
of the commercial panic he was in a hobble', and he had asked
Vere to lend him 3,000 dollars. Vere, with his usual generosity,
made it 6,000 at the usual rate of interest in Chicago, 10%, adding a further 3,000 dollars two years later. In 1862 Fr Dunne
wished to repay his loan 'but [writes Vere in the diary] availing
himself of the new act of Congress making greenbacks legal
tender, he paid me in greenbacks worth but little more than half
their nominal value. This is very dishonest, though of course he
does not think so, for Chicago, including his congregation, never
was more prosperous than since the war began, trade having been
diverted from St Louis, Memphis & Louisville to Chicago.' A
personal call on Fr Dunne, followed by one on his bishop, brought
no satisfaction, the reverend gentleman declaring 'that he
borrowed current money and repaid current money, that it was a
business transaction all thro', & that there is no injustice on his
part'. Whereupon Vere wrote a long letter to six or seven daily
papers 'complaining of the injustice done him', which was
accepted only by the *Boston Pilot* and the *Irish-American*. In the
latter an even longer letter appeared from Fr Dunne entirely
justifying his transaction. *The Pilot* warmly upheld Vere, declaring that to make the act of Congress 'retrospective and to cover
contracts made years before and with citizens of other countries,
is a hardship and injustice that ought not to be applied', and
called upon the citizens of Chicago to raise the difference which
amounted to 2,835 dollars, 'and thus discharge an honourable
obligation to one who merits only our admiration and gratitude'.
As we have seen, and will go on seeing, Vere would give his last
penny to those who needed it, but to be imposed upon hurt and
angered him exceedingly. He had accepted repayment of another

loan in greenbacks, the man 'having become bankrupt I couldn't expect more from him', but Fr Dunne and his affluent congregation were quite another story. History does not relate how the argument ended. Between various loans to people in America Vere calculated that he had, at this time, lost £3,000.

After spending more than two months visiting his emigrants and looking at schools Vere left New York for home in July 1864, 'Mr E. Cunard having handsomely put a berth in the 1st class cabin gratuitously at my disposal as he did on the occasion of my return to Europe six years ago'. How changed things had become since 1851! Competition between the various steamship companies for emigrant passengers was now so keen that influential customers were worth consideration.

7

Copy-books

Back in Ireland Vere threw himself into his next educational project, the provision of adequate aids for the teaching of 'penmanship'.

For years inspectors had bemoaned the wretched standard of handwriting in the schools and had called on the board for suitable instructions for teachers. The general practice was for the teacher to write a headline on the blackboard which the children, left more or less to their own devices, copied into their 'copybooks'. In the more affluent schools printed head-lines, purchased from the board, were handed round to the pupils for copying, becoming in time hopelessly tattered and dirty.

> Few of the teachers [wrote one inspector] appear to understand how this important branch should be taught. The very arrangement of the desks jammed closely together has not unfrequently led me to anticipate the low estimate which subsequent examination obliged me to form of the penmanship . . . The children were left wholly to themselves, instead of being carefully superintended by the master and hence a wrong method of holding the pen, the maintainance of every posture but the proper one, misshapen, ill-proportioned letters, and soiled copy-books . . . I found young children permitted to make their first attempts in writing with pencils varying in length from half an inch to about three inches.[1]

The following year, exasperated by the apparent lack of interest
on the part of the commissioners, and by the atrocious materials
that they supplied, he wrote again :

> As I have often said, the copy-books supplied to the schools
> might answer the purpose fairly enough with quill, or even good
> broad pointed steel pens; but from the efforts of children merely
> commencing, on soft paper, with points as sharp as needles, more
> favourable results than those I have described could not well be
> expected.[2]

There were countless similar reports. Inspectors knew only too
well the importance of handwriting.

> . . . it enters more largely than any other literary attainment into
> the qualification of a boy for clerkships and kindred situations;
> and furthermore, it is the chief test by which the parents judge of
> their children's progress at school.[3]

And

> The ability to write and read writing is fully appreciated by the
> peasantry and small farmers, as it enables them to carry on a
> correspondence with their relatives and friends in America or else-
> where without the help of a paid or unpaid scribe. Besides he
> who employs another to write his letters puts himself in a very
> humiliating position, as he thereby makes the village teacher, or
> perhaps some doubtful friend, the depository of little family
> secrets which people, no matter how poor, are always anxious
> to hide from the eye of a stranger.[4]

Vere attacked the situation with his usual swift attention to
the most minute detail. He appreciated to the full the inspectors'
remarks about the importance of handwriting to the potential
office boy or clerk, he had made particular note of how it was
taught in America. Furthermore, he recalled how Lord Palmerston, in his Foreign Office days, had insisted that the young men
in the diplomatic service should write distinctly. 'Children,' the
Foreign Secretary had declared, 'should be taught to write a large
hand and to form each letter well', instead of using fine up-strokes
and firm down-strokes that looked, he said, 'like an area railing,

a little lying on one side'.* We do not know how Vere got his first copy lines engraved, but they were beautifully done, nothing but the best ever satisfied him. Within a few months of his return from America he circulated specimen copies to at least forty of the best teachers of writing in the schools and listed their comments in a small notebook, one page to each teacher, with, at the bottom, a line of criticism by Vere of the teacher's own hand, such as 'his own style bad, sometimes illegible'.[5] Samples of the copy lines were also sent to Lord Palmerston, and among the very few letters that Vere preserved was the one in which Lady Palmerston set out the prime minister's comments :

> Lord Palmerston is an Enemy to the upstrokes being two [*sic*] thin and contrasting too much with the downstrokes. He has therefore scratched over with his Pen two of your lines to shew that all the letters should be well rounded and clear—and the Upstrokes sufficiently dark not to deceive the Eye, otherwise the letters seem to be only half formed.
>
> I am very sorry you could not come to Broadlands for a day as I thought it would have been more satisfactory for you to have a word from Lord Palmerston himself, than to have my Explanation. However here it is and when you return from Ireland if you like to call on me, I shall be glad to see you for old acquaintance sake.[6]

Was she thinking only of the incident at Ryde, when she had praised the readiness of the young attaché to defend his chief against the criticism of the Foreign Secretary's wife, or was she casting her mind farther back to the days when she and her brothers and Vere's father had all been young together? By now, *her* handwriting was getting shaky.

A few months later, very shortly before the Prime Minister died, Vere saw him at Brocket. No doubt it was on this visit that he received permission to call the first edition of the copy-books the 'Palmerston Series'. When before had a British prime minister been called upon to assist in the production of copy lines for

---

*Address to the Romsey Labourers' Encouragement Association, quoted in *Freeman's Journal*, 15.11.1865.

Irish schoolchildren? In his passion for perfection Vere could not have done more.

   With incredible speed the first copy-books were circulated in 1865, less than a year after Vere's return from America. They were printed in the machinery department of the Dublin Exhibition, the entire cost of production being borne by Vere. He had wisely decided to ask the blessing of the board 'by submitting (in manuscript) the entire series of Copy Books which he proposes to publish'. These, the minutes of the commissioners record, were immediately referred 'to the Professors [i.e. lecturers in the Training Institute] for their opinion as to the propriety of acceding to

Advertisement: Vere Foster's writing copy-books

his proposal . . . The Professors are to be particular in examining the Sentences and Maxims selected for Headlines and report if there be anything objectionable in them or not'.[7] After the incident of the circular to teachers* the commissioners were taking no chances with Mr Foster, nor running any risks that the minds of children would be inflamed by his subversive notions. The professors agreed that the copy-books 'are deserving of a trial', and the first order of 50,000 copies, at a rate of £6 4s 0d per thousand, was approved. They were sold to teachers at one penny each. 'I needed,' wrote Vere, 'no introduction to them, the demand for the books became immediately so great that in the first thirty-five *days* of their existence the National Board sold more of them than they had sold of their previous publication of headlines on separate cardboard slips during the preceeding 35 *years*.'[8]

The first series consisted of thirteen books, $8\frac{1}{4}$in $\times$ $6\frac{1}{2}$in. At the top of each page was a printed headline to be copied several times on lines below, but the page was shallow so that the child's eye did not have to travel far from his own effort to the pattern. The series began with 'Strokes, Easy Letter and Short Words', working up to Nos. 8 and 9 which contained sentences in the shape of those 'proverbs' which have stuck in the minds of hundreds of thousands of users of Vere Foster's copy-books; such sayings as 'The good is the enemy of the best'; 'He that cannot bear a jest should not make one'; 'Friendship multiplies joys and divides grief'; 'Property has its Duties as well as its Rights'. Still more advanced numbers had rules for book-keeping, simple accounts, and business terms, all so necessary for 'the clerkships and kindred situations', all part of Vere's vision of educating children for life. The writing paper was specially made, of excellent quality, smooth and firm—none of the 'soft woolly' abomination issued by the board. The stiff paper covers were decorated with a border of shamrocks, roses, and thistles in the best Victorian taste, incorporating the two medallions depicting children *playing*, and a crowned harp was surrounded by the motto 'A Nation's Greatness Depends upon the Education of its People.'

* See p 114.

Page 133 : The ejectment. (*See* p 78)

Page 134 : The day after ejectment. (*See* p 78)

Pages 2, 3, and 4 of the cover were packed with information—a brief history of the art of calligraphy, practical instructions about having 'a loose piece of paper under the hand while working, to keep the work clean', advice as to nibs, etc., all compiled by Vere. Not one inch of space wasted, not one detail overlooked. The amount of preparation was prodigious.

Very soon the title of the publications was changed to 'Vere Foster's National School Copy Books', and later and finally to 'Vere Foster's Copy Books'.

The result was a triumph for Vere. Once again his name is in every inspector's report. In 1865, the year of publication, one of them writes :

> In all good schools the whole of the second class now write on paper [as opposed to slates], from Vere Foster's No. 1 and 2; the higher classes using the more advance numbers of that excellent series. There is scarcely a school in the district [Westport] in which these copy-books have not come into use during the year, and the teachers one and all appreciate them highly. The acquisition of a good and fluent hand by the pupils of National Schools, so long a desideratum, now appears easy of attainment; but will be still more so if Mr. Foster's project of a supply of superior pens (some of the 'nibs' now sent out are exceedingly bad) and *ready-made ink* shall be approved by the Commissioners.[9]

Vere had already taken up the matter of poor ink with the board, whose ink powders resulted in a 'pale watery fluid quite unfit for school purposes'. His first effort was unsuccessful, but he returned to the subject in 1868, offering to supply 'Arnold's Superior Ink in casks or jars of any size at less than what the Board is paying for their inferior ink.[10] The commissioners relented so far as to put the item out to tender. In the matter of pencils he was more successful, his offer of Paraviso's Pencil at 4s 3d a gross being accepted. These bore the name 'Vere Foster', being specially manufactured. He also had inkwells manufactured to his design.

To do the board justice the question of monopoly had always to be kept in mind. In the very early days two well known

London publishing firms had strenuously opposed, as a use of public money to the detriment of private enterprise, the board's production of cheap school books for use in their own schools. They carried the matter to the House of Commons and won their point.[11] Vere himself relates that as soon as the copy books were launched 'the Dublin Press teemed with the cry of monopoly, and representations were very naturally and properly made to the National Board that they ought to throw the competition open to the trade. They, therefore, advertised for tenders, and, after examination of forty tenders, submitted by the principal school-publishing firms of London, Manchester, Liverpool, Birmingham, Edinburgh, Glasgow, Dublin and other places, decided on sanctioning the use of three different series of books, including mine.'[12] But there was never any real competition; Vere's books 'supplanted all others'.

Praise of the copy-books continued year after year in scores of reports, though it must be admitted that some teachers considered the bold, round hand unsuitable for girls—polite young ladies still hankered after the 'area railing' style of handwriting abhorred by Lord Palmerston. 'Female pupils, especially those whose parents are in comfortable circumstances, object to the roundness of style which characterizes the advanced or "finishing" headlines . . . headlines of angular hand . . . would render those copy-books more popular in Girls' schools than they are at present'.[13] Vere did not pander to such outmoded snobbishness, and 'angular' headlines were never produced.

It was not only within the confines of the Irish National schools that the copy-books were acclaimed, for their success was instantaneous in Britain and widespread throughout the English-speaking world. Orders poured in from America. Again, nothing like it had happened before. There were other copy-books on the market, but it was Vere's stroke of genius to provide something that attracted the child's interest, thereby uniting instruction with pleasure, that was a real help to the teachers, and that swept its way to a supremacy unchallenged in its field for more than fifty years.

Orders speedily outran the capacity of the original printer. After extensive investigations in London, Dublin, and Belfast, and having made the acquaintance of John Ward, one of the partners of Marcus Ward & Co. of Belfast, Vere arranged that this firm should undertake all his work; a fateful step as we shall see.[14] The firm, owned by three brothers, with offices in Dublin and London, was one of the foremost printing concerns in the British Isles, and the Wards threw themselves enthusiastically into Vere's project. Their technical skill and commercial ability delighted him, and they shared a similar intellectual outlook. Between Vere and John Ward a very sincere friendship developed, one of the few real friendships that he ever formed, and when in 1867 Lady Albinia's death meant the loss of a base in London, Vere made the seemingly extraordinary decision to settle permanently in Belfast. Not that he so far renounced his principles as to burden himself with a house and staff—such needs were met by inexpensive lodgings. In making this choice he must have been influenced by his business connection with Marcus Ward & Co., and by his friendship with John Ward and his brothers, for there seems no other reason why he should have fixed on the rapidly growing industrial centre of the north, where, so far as we know, he had no previous connections at all. Why did he not choose Dublin, the seat of all government administration, the home of the Board of Education, the central point from which his travels in Ireland would be undertaken, and the meeting place of all those who should have been his friends? Perhaps it was the realisation of how separated he had become from the social life in which he had been brought up that helped to direct his choice, and that made the friendship with John Ward all the more welcome.

Having come to the decision, Vere threw himself wholeheartedly into the life of the town. The *Belfast News-Letter* of November 1867 reporting an exhibition of painting organised by Messrs Ward describes a case of small antiquities : an ivory carving of Adam removing a thorn from Eve's foot, a medallion by Tassie, a miniature of Napoleon by Augustin, another miniature of Napoleon set in a ring, and acknowledges the 'kindness of Mr

Vere Foster in lending these to enhance the attractions of Messrs
Ward's gallery'. One imagines that these were family treasures
collected by his father and his grandmother in Italy. There was
a growing interest in art in Belfast, and it is likely that Vere
served on a committee set up in 1870 to establish a school of art,
with special classes for artisan students. He certainly contributed
£20 towards the initial expenses, and guaranteed the salary of
the teacher for some years.[14a]

From another newspaper report we learn of his connection
with Charles Sherry, a prominent Belfast architect, and, in a
town where religious affiliations have always had great significance, a Roman Catholic. The story does not open, regrettably,
until Mr Sherry's death, when immediately after the funeral 'a
meeting of his friends and admirers' took place to consider some
lasting tribute to his memory. Vere presided and opened the
subscription list with a donation of £20. His suggestion as to the
form the memorial should take was set out in a letter to the press
as follows :

> As [Mr Sherry] had made it an object of special study to prepare
> plans of labourers' dwellings of suitable and economical construc-
> tion, and had actually made arrangements to devote his time con-
> tinuously to the elaboration and maturing of these plans to com-
> mence with the morning after that on which he died, I suggest
> that an appropriate form for the proposed tribute would be—
> first, to erect the monumental cross, the cost not to exceed a
> limited sum; and secondly, to apply the surplus of such amount
> as might be raised by subscription to the erection of a row of
> labourers' dwellings, according to his own plans, to call them by
> his name, and the proceeds of the same to be appropriated as
> the subscribers may determine.
>
> Should this suggestion, combining an object of urgent public
> utility with a private memorial meet with approval, I shall have
> much satisfaction in subscribing £100 for that purpose, in addi-
> tion to the amount I promised, as I believe that 'they mourn the
> dead who do as they desire.'
>   Vere Foster.[15]

It is all perfectly in character—the overstepping of religious
barriers, the sympathy with any plan to help the working man,

and the instant lavish generosity. Vere's suggestion was adopted, but it has not been possible to discover if the project was completed.

But it was the Royal Hospital* that engaged Vere's active sympathy during practically the whole period of his thirty years' residence in Belfast. When he arrived the hospital, despite the strenuous efforts of the committee, was in dangerously low water financially, due to the serious decline in the voluntary contributions on which it was entirely dependent. Vere joined the committee in 1874 and two years later offered to become an honorary collector and to work up a large district. (It will be seen later what important matters were at the same time engaging his attention, but the call of the hospital could not be ignored.)

The task to which he addressed himself is set out in a letter to the hon. secretary, as follows :

Having this day completed my canvass for subscribers in the districts which were assigned to me by the Board of Management, and having closed my accounts with the Treasurer, I herewith return the collect-books, containing my journals of receipts, and an alphabetical list of subscribers arranged according to streets.

Taking as I do a deep interest in the Belfast Royal Hospital . . . I have used my best efforts to obtain for it increased support, and regret greatly that I have not been more successful . . . In the course of my canvass I made nearly 9,000 personal calls, besides posting large numbers of circulars, and I have collected £559. 8. 2 from 1,043 persons. This sum includes £210. 8. 2 obtained from 693 new subscribers, and with £12. 4. 0 paid to other collectors or to the treasurer, and after deducting 96 discontinued subscriptions amounting to £65. 1. 6 represents a nett increase of £147. 2. 8 over the amount, £524. 10. 6 collected in the same district last year.

Although so small an increase seems scarcely worthy of the labour involved and time devoted to its collection and it might have been cheaper for me to have paid the whole increase myself, and to have devoted the time to attention to my own business, yet I think it justifiable in the expectation that those persons who have kindly commenced to subscribe this year will increase their contributions next year, and others will be encouraged by their example, and that, the fact of large numbers of the work-

* Now the Royal Victoria Hospital.

ing classes of Belfast contributing according to their means to the support of this excellent charity will stimulate other persons possessed of ample means, who have hitherto subscribed sparingly or not at all to give a generous support in the future.

I have much pleasure in subscribing a sum equal to the nett increase of my collection, and enclose herewith a cheque for £144. 18. 8.*

Nine thousand personal calls! He must have gone systematically from house to house over a large area. The sentence in his letter censuring the niggardliness of the well-to-do and appreciating the generosity of the poor reiterates sentiments he had often expressed before.

The following year he set out again, taking with him a small printed leaflet to push under doors where his knock was unanswered. This set out clearly the needs of the hospital and stated that 'Mr Vere Foster will add 10 per cent to all sums under £1 which he may receive from new subscribers . . . Mr F. will feel greatly obliged to persons willing to subscribe, and whom he may not find at home, if they will send their subscriptions either to him at No. 43 University Road, or to the Treasurer.'[16]

He was to continue to make his annual collection, in the midst of all his other commitments, practically up to the close of his life, though at the end the circumstances were very altered.

There remain two small cash-books—Nos. 3 and 31—obviously part of a sequence.[17] Each of these relates to the 'beat' of a collector, and has pasted in the inside of the cover a section cut from a map of the town with the streets allotted to the collector clearly outlined in red. There is also a list of the streets and the returns from each one, all in Vere's clear handwriting and executed with the meticulous neatness that was the hallmark of everything he did. Again one is amazed at the enormous amount of detailed work carried on simultaneously, and single-handed, in a variety of causes. In 1897, when the hospital committee was considering rebuilding on a larger site, Vere collected reports 'from all the general hospitals in the principal towns of the United King-

* I am much indebted to Dr R. S. Allison, FRCP, Royal Victoria Hospital, Belfast, for bringing this letter to my notice, and for permission to use it.

dom'; furthermore, he sent to the *Belfast News-Letter* a detailed comparison of funds expended on the various branches of hospital services in Belfast and Dublin, much to the discredit of the former. In the *Northern Whig*, October 1889, there is reference to a letter written by Vere when a public school for boys (Campbell College) was about to be built near Belfast, declaring that the large bequest would have been much better employed in providing adequate hospital accommodation for the poor. But this is to anticipate.

Getting back to the 1860s, and before returning to the copy-books, something must be said about Vere's excursions into the political world. Politics were in his blood, and at times he could not resist sallies into the territory in which he had been born and bred.

One such occasion was the Louth election of April 1865 when Vere vigorously supported the liberal candidate—and sitting member—Mr Tristram Kennedy, whose declared radical policies had already merited Vere's confidence. In an open letter to Mr Kennedy, which he published as a handbill, Vere announced his wholehearted support of the candidate's principles—'Religious Equality : Justice to tenants, without injustice to landlords : The furtherance of Popular Education on terms of equality to all denominations.' He continues :

I share with Mr Gladstone the opinion that the present position of the Irish State Church Establishment is unsatisfactory and false.

I agree with opinions expressed a few years ago by Viscount Palmerston [and others], that Protestant ascendancy in Ireland cannot on principle be defended.

I believe that justice to tenant-farmers requires that, in cases where they have no lease they should have a legalized right to compensation for their unexhausted improvements in case of eviction . . .

My sentiments as regards the National System of Education are well known to you . . . The maintainance of that system in its purity as originally established by Lord Stanley would leave but little further to be desired as regards the action of Government.

The principles of the Conservative party as regards the above subjects, I believe are :

The maintainance of the Protestant ascendancy.

The preservation of the landlord's right of confiscating his tenant's improvements.

The duty of the State to educate the people of Ireland on Protestant proselytising principles only.

I cannot doubt which of these opposite sets of principles will receive the sanction of the free and independent Electors of the County of Louth at the approaching election.[18]

It was a declaration of very radical views.

Mr Kennedy was returned for Louth, but within three months there was a general election and the seat was again contested. Vere presided at an open-air meeting at Mullacrew fair, again in support of the Liberal candidate, Kennedy. It was a hot summer day in June, and everyone 'suffered much from the heat which was intense'. A band from Dundalk enlivened the scene before the meeting began. Vere was 'loudly cheered' and one senses from the report in the *Irish Times* that he entered into the spirit of the meeting with great zest and his infectious gay spirits. He urged the right of the tenant to compensation for improvements in cases of eviction—a burning question of the day :

> he touched on the question of religious equality, and condemned the Church Establishment of Ireland. He did not want any ascendancy at all, but equality, and if they had that there would be a great deal more union of persons of all denominations for the common good. He thought a Catholic as good as a Protestant, and a Protestant as good as a Catholic. One was as as good as another. The matter of their religion was between them.[19]

He appealed for an orderly election, he would rather it was lost than that it should be carried by any violence. He reminded them of O'Connell's words : ' "He who commits a crime gives strength to the enemy". Don't let it be said that even tenants would not allow tenants to vote as they pleased. That might apply to the landlords, but it must not refer to the tenants.'

Little wonder that at a subsequent meeting at Dundalk Mr Foster was received 'with thunderous cheers'. He could easily have been a political leader—what an enlightened Chief Secretary he would have made! We shall see later that the question of land tenure occupied his attention over a long period.

On the subject of Irish nationalism Vere expressed himself clearly in a letter to the *Freeman's Journal* dated 19 April 1865, contradicting a report that he had been on the platform at a meeting of the Irish National League; he had in fact been in the audience :

> I consider [he wrote] the organisation and objects of the League, no doubt well intended but mischievous and delusive . . . I know it is the darling desire of immense numbers of Irishmen and women in America to help to make Ireland independent of England; that, but for the civil war in America, it is probable that a war between England and America could not have been much longer delayed, and that, should a war unfortunately break out between England and America, the people of Ireland might welcome an invading army; but I believe that such an invasion . . . would inflict unutterable misery. I cannot bring myself to approve the shedding of human blood for any purpose, however righteous. To avoid so great a calamity as a civil war through an abortive attempt at revolution here, I desire not disunion, between Great Britain and Ireland, but rather a more perfect union.

From all this it is clear how deep was his concern for the welfare of his country, how intimate his knowledge of her situation, and how progressive his thought. There were not many people in the middle of the nineteenth century to whom war was so abhorrent.

Earlier in the same year the *Cork Reporter* had published a letter addressed by Vere to the Prince of Wales 'respectfully suggesting to your Royal Highness that it would be an act of political wisdom, and worthy of your Royal Highness, to purchase an estate in Ireland, and to reside upon it a portion of each year. The Queen has residences in England and in Scotland, and your Royal Highness has recently purchased estates in both these countries; but no member of the Royal family has residences in Ireland.' He admits that the people of Ireland are disloyal 'for reasons on which it is unnecessary to enter'; but suggests that

Advertisement: Vere Foster's drawing books

the prince could 'take a considerable step in a very simple manner towards rendering them contented and loyal'. The London *Daily Telegraph*, 10 January 1865, commenting on the letter, poured scorn on that 'benevolent but eccentric gentleman' the well-known Mr Vere Foster, but if his idea had been accepted it might well have altered the course of Irish history.

But always it was through education that he saw the greatest hope for Irish progress—education conducted on a non-sectarian basis. As the Established Church and the Roman Catholic Church continued to clamour for the modification of the national system on a denominational basis, Vere returned again to this theme in 1865, upholding what he ever regarded as a fundamental principle—the maintenance of the non-denominational system 'in its purity as established by Lord Derby in 1831'. This he stressed to the utmost of his ability in a letter addressed to the Lord Lieutenant, the members of both Houses of Parliament, and to the press which he circulated widely—Vere was never averse to publicising his views—begging them to preserve intact the original principle of 'combined secular and separate religious instruction'.[20] He also wrote to his friend the Rt Hon Alexander Macdonnell, Resident Commissioner of National Education, stressing the same point and deploring concessions already made 'to solicitations from opposite quarters . . . especially the multiplication of schools under managers of different creeds in places where the population was not more than sufficient to form one united school for each sex'.[21]

Meanwhile the annual sale of writing copy-books was counted in millions. A series of drawing copy-books was now started. Though primarily to encourage the teaching of drawing, a subject that Vere considered most useful for boys entering mechanical or clerical work, the books were used as a means of widening education. Inspectors had frequently lamented the ignorance of the average child about anything outside his immediate range of observation, and, to encourage teachers to dispel such ignorance, Frederick, as far back as 1855, had given £20 per annum to be used as awards to teachers in national schools in Louth 'best acquainted with the Knowledge of Common Things'.[22] Now the drawing books were to help in that direction; the book on horses, for example, contained drawings of a Clydesdale, a dray horse, a mule, an American trotter, an Arab, a hunter, and so forth, with distinctive harness, etc., in the background. In a letter to the *Irish Teachers' Journal*, dated July 1868, Vere intimated with his usual candour, that he had :

engaged the services of an able artist to take likenesses of a large number of the Cattle, Horses, Sheep & Pigs for which the first premiums were awarded at the Annual Shop of the North-East Agricultural Association, held this week in Belfast. The likenesses will be published in my forthcoming Half-Penny and Penny National School Drawing Copy Books. I am sorry to have to add that I was refused permission for the artist to enter the Show Grounds at any other than the regular crowded public visiting hours, unless on the condition of my becoming a member of the Association, which illiberal condition I, of course, complied with.

Whatever may be the present reaction to such a method of teaching drawing, Vere's 'Drawing Copy Books' were immediately approved by the Department of Science and Art in London.

Encouraged by all this success and anxious, no doubt, to explore the new techniques of colour printing, John Ward urged Vere to embark on 'Water Colour Copy Books'. Vere was sceptical about the wisdom of this but allowed himself to be overruled, and there followed a series on the painting of trees, landscapes, marine views, flowers, the human figure, etc., illustrated by coloured plates produced by the very latest process of lithographic printing, with accompanying detailed instruction for making copies. The production was exceedingly costly. Vere, with his passion for perfection, engaged 'eminent artists' to execute the original watercolours, and their fees were commensurate with their status.* All the necessary experiments in colour printing were made by Marcus Ward & Co at Vere's expense, indeed Vere mentions that to meet the cost of elaborate new machinery the firm borrowed any available capital he possessed, and the reflooring of schools had to be temporarily discontinued. The united efforts of Vere and John Ward resulted in productions as nearly perfect as was then possible, the colour printing exciting amazed admiration, but the costs were exorbitant and these coloured books were never a financial success.

The sale of the writing copy-books continued to increase fan-

---

* The plates depicting flowers, birds, animals, and ships were from drawings by St John, Tweekler, Harrison Weir, Whittaker, and Callow respectively.

tastically. Distribution in Great Britain and elsewhere was carried out by the publishers—Whittaker of London and Marcus Ward of Belfast—but the orders from the National Board, amounting to perhaps two-thirds of the whole and to tens of thousands of copies, were handled entirely by Vere. A room in Marcus Ward's premises was put at his disposal, and there he carried on this stupendous work, without clerk, assistant, or aid of any kind. The sums of money alone that passed through his hands were very great.

Nor was this all. The copy-books were bringing in great profits, and with the utmost integrity every penny was ploughed back for the benefit of the pupils, in the shape of 'Vere Foster's National Competition in Writing, Lettering, Drawing, and Painting'; 'instituted by me in 1870, and open to Pupils of either Public or Private Schools throughout the British Empire'.

There is neither time nor space to dwell here on this additional undertaking, suffice it to say that entries were received from India, Burma, Malta, Constantinople, Australia, New Zealand, Jamaica, Grenada, Newfoundland and the Cape of Good Hope, as well as from Ireland and Great Britain. In 1872 there were over two thousand competitors from Ireland alone. Competitors were divided into classes, prizes ranged from £5 to 2s 6d, with books for children under eleven, and such as could not reach this standard were given cards of commendation. By 1898, 9,140 prizes had been awarded amounting to £3,356 11s 6d in all.[23]

Vere loved children—it was a family characteristic—and he knew how much they enjoyed a competition, especially if there was something for everyone to win! Out of all this mass of organisation one trifling but significant incident has survived. Three girls from the little school at Ravensdale in Louth gained between them two prizes of £5 and one of £1. How nice it would be, thought Vere, if Lord Clermont, on whose estate the school was situated, would present the awards. Lord Clermont was delighted to do so. Vere apparently was not present at the function and, when the girls wrote to thank him he replied that he was much gratified to be able to recognise 'distinguished merit. I thought [he continued] it would be most agreeable to you to receive the prizes from the hands of Lord Clermont, and feel most thankful to his Lordship for the honour he conferred on us by undertaking the distribution.'[24] The honour conferred on *us* : always that knack of associating himself closely with those he was helping, always that delight in giving pleasure. Judging the entries, and all the organisation and clerical work entailed, was carried out single-handed by Vere.

If Sir Augustus Foster at one time bemoaned that his 'poor son Vere' was working 'like a horse' at Montevideo, what would he have said to the work that was being carried on now?

Bank clerks were the next target. There exists the draft of a circular letter in Vere's clear writing [with a note in John Ward's to the effect that the type had already been set up] headed with the address of the head office of the Ulster Bank in Belfast, to be sent by the directors to all bank managers, deploring 'a deteriorating tendency in the character of writing and figuring in the service. Instead of neat, careful, distinct, businesslike, and easily legible handwriting the prevailing style is too often careless and slovenly. The Directors think the time has come when it is necessary to impress upon every Officer the importance of writing and figuring carefully at all times, but especially in Bank books and all official documents, letters and returns, so as to guard against mistakes, economise time, and facilitate the proper despatch of business.'[25]

The directors of the Northern Banking Company were even more explicit. Forwarding supplies of the copy-books to their branches they requested that these be returned, 'written up', within three months.[26]

8

Organising Teachers

Absorbing though all this might be it was secondary to the major preoccupation of these years, Vere's unparalleled exertions on behalf of the teaching profession. The production of copy-books had been undertaken to meet a present urgent need; the same was true of repairing the schools. It is, however, through his work for teachers that we can appreciate Vere's long-term aspirations for education, the most cherished dream of his life.

Addressing a meeting of the Limerick Teachers' Associations in 1874 Vere spoke of an interview he had had in America with Mr Edward Everett, a former Secretary of State. On discovering that this gentleman sent his children to 'the common public school' Vere inquired why a private school was not preferred. 'Because,' came the reply, 'the best teaching in this country is in the public schools.' Mr Foster hoped, says the report of the meeting, 'that the day would come when the nobles of their own country would be able to say the same of their children—that they could send them to the ordinary schools, where they would get the best education to be had in the country'.[1]

Education was to him the supreme benefit. Without doubt adequate educational opportunities for all was his ultimate aim, though he may not have expected to see it realised in his lifetime.

He was one of the first to emphasise that the national system for primary education must be followed by a national intermediate system,[2] and to urge that university education be available to all who would benefit from it. In the meantime, he himself assisted several poor students to make their way through Queen's College, Belfast. It requires some effort to appreciate how advanced this educational policy was only one hundred years ago.

With these visions before him, what was the actual situation in Ireland? A non-compulsory system of primary education, initiated and fostered by the state, in which Vere had unqualified confidence; a lay population, unconcerned or antagonistic in its higher ranks, pitifully apathetic in the lower; clerical interests intent on manipulating the system for their own ends; a band of teachers who, from his first contact with them at Glasnevin, he loved. No other word describes his feeling for them—men and women with no social background, with little enough education themselves and seldom with any professional training, whose services to the community were generally regarded as being adequately rewarded by the token salaries of a few pounds assured them by the Board of Education, but never supposed in themselves to constitute a living wage.*

Inspectors' reports of the early 1860s give some idea of the teachers' plight. One of them writes :

> Removed above labourers and artisans in their tastes, sympathies and general culture, though somewhat superior to the former, they are yet inferior to the latter in their means and modes of living . . . The average annual income for their schools is £28.3.2., of this £5.10.5. is derived from local sources, leaving the average income from the Board, £21.5.0.[3]

And another :

> The majority of teachers are very poor, and find it hard to keep up a respectable exterior—such as becomes their profession . . . The wonder is not that teachers are not more respectably dressed,

---

* Salaries assured by the Board were rarely more than £30 and often as little as £18 per annum; they were intended merely as a basic wage to be supplemented by voluntary contributions which seldom materialised.

WORK AND WAGES;

OR, THE

𝔓𝔢𝔫𝔫𝔶 𝔈𝔪𝔦𝔤𝔯𝔞𝔫𝔱'𝔰 𝔊𝔲𝔦𝔡𝔢

TO THE

United States and Canada,

FOR

FEMALE SERVANTS, LABORERS, MECHANICS, FARMERS, &c.

AS I WAS.   **AS I AM.**

Containing a short description of those countries, and most suitable places for Settlement; Rates of Wages, Board and Lodging, House Rent, Price of Land, Money matters, &c.; together with full information about the preparations necessary for the voyage, instructions on Landing, and expenses of Travelling in America. With Appendix, containing rates of Farm Laborers' Wages and Board in 88 districts.

BY VERE FOSTER.

LONDON:—W. & F. G. CASH, 5, BISHOPSGATE WITHOUT.

Manchester, Heywoods; Norwich, J. Darken; Newcastle, Barkas; Liverpool, Shepherd; Glasgow, Gallie & Sons; Edinburgh, Menzies; Dublin, M'Glashan, Mason; York, J. Brown; Bristol, W. H. Cook; Birmingham, White & Pike; Ipswich, Ridley & Grimwade, Druggists; Aberdeen, A. Brown & Co.,

AND ALL BOOKSELLERS.

PRICE ONE PENNY EACH; OR TENPENCE PER DOZEN.

Page 151 : Illustrated advertisement : *Work and wages, or the Penny Emigrant's guide.* (*See* p 84)

Page 152 : (*above*) Glyde Court, Ardee, Co. Louth; (*below*) No 115 Great Victoria Street, Belfast—a house in which Vere Foster lived

but that they are able to appear at their work with anything
like becoming decency at all.[4]

Even in Dublin, we are told :

> Their means of living, I fear, are very narrow; as to their
> dwellings, such as I have seen of them are comfortless, and too
> small to preserve the separation of sexes, so essential to the
> morality, or even decency of the household.[5]

From the outset these teachers were Vere's 'friends', and though
wooden floors and proper requisites were immediate needs which
could be satisfied immediately by his own magnificent generosity,
his very first circular* indicated that the long term effort for
teachers had already begun. He knew they were not all good at
their job, some of them he admitted were very bad, 'not being
worth a farthing a year', others were able and accomplished,
most of them were doing their best in intolerable circumstances,
all of them were 'miserably paid', and at any rate how could one
expect 'misfits or old worn-out teachers' to retire when there were
no pensions, and all that faced many of them was the workhouse?[6]

Successful though the Board of Education had been in establishing primary schools, it was clear by the 1860s that modifications in the expanding system were necessary, and such points as
teachers' salaries, teachers' residences, pensions, irregular attendance of pupils, and managerial power called for immediate consideration.

At this time teachers were appointed without any accepted
form of agreement. In cases of inadequate teaching the inspector's report was accepted by the board, and the salary grant
withdrawn, which in turn led to dismissal by the manager. In
matters unrelated to teaching the managers had full control, and
at times teachers were summarily dismissed without any means
of redress, for alleged misdemeanours that had nothing to do
with their professional work. This prerogative was jealously
guarded by—in particular—the Catholic managers and the hier-

* See p 114.

archy, who insisted on retaining the right of summary dismissal in order to deal with cases where the teaching of the church was contravened; that it may not have been very frequently used was perhaps due to the natural reluctance of the teachers to expose themselves to such treatment. For all teachers this situation produced a general feeling of insecurity.

Over the years various attempts made by teachers to organise themselves with a view to seeking redress for their grievances had failed to get any permanent foothold, but by 1868 new developments had taken place. Education was very much the topic of the moment. An education act for England had been carried at Westminster; a Royal Commission, under the chairmanship of Lord Powis, had been appointed to look into the position of national primary education in Ireland, with special reference to the points mentioned above; the Roman Catholic Church, carrying its desire for denominationalism to university level had endeavoured—unsuccessfully—to establish a catholic University in Dublin under the guidance of John Henry Newman, in opposition to the government-sponsored, so-called godless, colleges of Belfast, Cork, and Galway, which constituted the Queen's University in Ireland.

In 1867 the National Association for the Promotion of Social Science held its annual congress in Belfast. For the first time for many years Lord Brougham, a prime mover in the founding of the association, was prevented by failing health from presiding, his place being taken on this occasion by Lord Dufferin. Education was one of the subjects of a very impressive programme, and Vere, already well known for his progressive views, was a guest speaker in the section on primary education. Emphasising the success of the National Board of Education in Ireland, the superiority of its system over 'the Privy Council system in England', and upholding its non-sectarian principle, he said:

> As regards the religious difficulty, I have travelled a great deal through the country—I dare say I am acquainted with more teachers and managers of schools than perhaps anybody else in the room—and I maintain that the religious difficulty does not

exist excepting in the minds of theorists; that it is unknown to the teachers and to the parents of the children. That is my experience on this matter, and I have visited fifteen hundred schools, and have been in correspondence with the managers and teachers of a great number of them; and I have just now returned from a journey through several counties, in which I have visited several hundred schools within the last few weeks. I will content myself with having made these references to the comparative popularity of the two systems in England and Ireland, to the fact that in Ireland the mixed system has been successful, and to the fact that the religious difficulty is a myth.[7]

That was the way he saw it.

In the section devoted to the status of teachers Vere urged the need for higher salaries, for teachers' residences, for monthly instead of quarterly payments—'they ought not to be kept so long waiting for their money'—and for a local educational rate. He strongly condemned

the great multiplicity of schools. In one district, for example, where there is really only a sufficient population for one school, the Catholic priests set up a school and the Presbyterians and the Episcopalians set up another, and the result is that it is impossible to keep up the status of the teachers, and the efficiency of the teaching. The Commissioners ought to be very careful in not taking on schools unless in districts where they are absolutely required . . . Then I think it would be very desirable if we could have a Teachers' journal or Magazine; there are, I believe, teachers' magazines in the United States and in Canada, which are found very useful for diffusing information among teachers on subjects connected with the improvement of education, for discussion on the different methods of instruction, and for advertisements by teachers wanting schools, and schools wanting teachers. Such a magazine might be very useful in this country, both as a means of improving the status of teachers, and of increasing the efficiency of teaching.[8]

Sometime between September 1867 and the beginning of 1868 Vere must have met Robert Chamney, a journalist publisher in Dublin who may have already been considering launching just such a journal as Vere visualised. On the first of January 1868 the first number of *The Irish Teachers' Journal* appeared and, in response to an invitation from the editor, A. E. Chamney, Vere contributed a letter in which he welcomed the new publication and set out his own views with clarity and emphasis. This statement forms the basis of all his work for teachers. After mentioning the social science conference in Belfast, and noting that one of the special subjects for discussion was 'The best means of improving the position of teachers, and for securing to the public sufficient guarantees for the efficiency of their teaching', he continues :

> I consider the most important means to be by an increase of voluntary local contributions in aid of teachers' salaries, or, failing such voluntary contributions, then compulsory local taxation, specially for educational purposes—not a tax on income only but on capital, so as properly to fall most heavily on the rich, and yet only in proportion to their means—not in the place of, but in addition to Parliamentary grants. The average pay of Irish National Teachers is only about one-third of that of English National Teachers, and should be brought up to the same level, in order to retain the services of such well qualified teachers as we have, and to secure others. Most of the Irish gentry take no interest whatever in, and pay voluntarily nothing, and in taxation but a miserable small share of the expenses of, popular education. Take, for instance, the county of Longford. The average annual amount of annual contributions from the gentry and clergy to 85 out of 93 national schools in that county (see last official report) is three-pence *per school*, not per scholar observe, but per school. The average per scholar is about one-twelfth of a farthing for each. A very moderate tax should produce on an average at least £30 per school. It is to be regretted that the Commissioners of Education refused to receive a deputation empowered to present a memorial on this subject, signed by between two and three thousands of their teachers. Under such circumstances an appeal to Parliament seems to me to be the proper course.
>
> There should be an increase of local superintendence. This would be a natural consequence of voluntary or compulsory local contributions.
>
> Suitable school-houses should be provided rent free to the teachers, in place of the numerous rented thatched cabins, which abound chiefly in Connaught and Ulster. Building grants may now be obtained on very easy terms from the Commissioners of

National Education, in those dioceses where their acceptance is not prohibited by episcopal authority.

Teachers' residences should be provided . . .

Teachers' salaries should be paid *monthly* instead of quarterly.

A system of pensions should be organized for superannuated teachers, as for officers in other branches of the civil service. Unless retiring allowances be secured it is cruel to oblige old teachers, worn out in the service, to resign, yet, if they are retained, the efficiency of their schools may be seriously impeded.

There should be improved arrangements for the supply of school requisites . . . I believe this could best be done through the agency of a wholesale bookseller or stationer in the metropolis, with agencies in every town. I have recently endeavoured to bring under the notice of the Board some improvements as regards exercise books, also liquid ink, slate pencils, clocks, etc., but have met with no encouragement.

A teachers' journal is greatly wanted.

It is highly important that a network of Union High Schools should be established within walking distance of *senior* children, for instruction in higher branches of education. These would serve as intermediate links between the elementary schools and the various colleges, whether in connection with the Government or otherwise, and would serve as goals for the more ambitious teachers of elementary schools . . .*

Teachers' Associations should be multiplied.

Vere's insistence that support from central and local statutory funds, involving as a natural corollary representation on school boards, constituted the only satisfactory financial basis for a national system of education has already been noted.† His suggestion of a tax on capital was extremely radical in days when a tax on income was still regarded as an innovation.‡

We have no idea to what extent Vere and Chamney co-operated. There seems to have been complete agreement between them as to their aims for Irish education; no doubt Vere provided Chamney with much of the information that appeared in the *Journal* regarding developments in Britain and the continent.

* Legislation to promote Intermediate Education in Ireland introduced 1878.
† See p 115.
‡ Income-tax was extended to Ireland by Gladstone in 1853.

Vere, with his international outlook and wide contacts, continually stressed that Irish education must at least equal the best standards found elsewhere, and he was a frequent contributor to the correspondence columns, but there are no grounds for supposing that this was one of the schemes that Vere, in his generosity, rushed to subsidise. In after years, when it was insinuated that he was thus able to use the *Journal* to air his own views, the charge was resolutely denied by Vere and Chamney. When, however, in 1872 this excellent publication landed its publisher in bankruptcy, it was Vere who instantly inaugurated an indemnity fund, to which he no doubt contributed generously and of which he was hon. treasurer.

Further evidence of his established position as an authority on education in Ireland came in July 1868 when he received an invitation to give oral evidence before the Royal Commission on Primary Education (Ireland), already mentioned. This Vere rather surprisingly declined, requesting that a list of 'the special points on which information is desired' be sent to him, which information he would endeavour to obtain from reliable sources. 'Having been subject for some years,' he continues, 'to inflammation of the eyes I have scarcely read anything or visited schools. [it was a different story when he was addressing the Social Science Congress not twelve months earlier], but have devoted my attention exclusively to certain publications, namely, the preparation of good and cheap writing and drawing copybooks, I therefore, do not consider myself competent to be a *direct* witness, but would prefer being a medium for inquiry, and could leave my business here & travel through the country without any expense to the Commission, if by so doing I can further their important object.'[9] The secretary replied that what the commission wanted was Mr Foster's own views; but he was adamant and in the end got his way, for specific points were sent to him, and these, with four additional queries of his own, Vere embodied in a formidable questionnaire which he addressed 'to the secretaries of the numerous Teachers' Associations which have been recently organized in nearly every county'.

One wonders, at first sight, why he adopted this attitude. Stephen de Vere, the only individual who came near to rivalling Vere Foster on educational affairs (as he did on emigration), accepted a similar invitation and gave exhaustive and valuable evidence. Why did not Vere? Did he really consider that he was unfitted to be a helpful witness? The answer is indicative of his approach to the whole situation; he was determined that the teachers themselves, through their associations, should have an opportunity to state their case in written evidence. When, in the course of a few weeks, he learned that the commission was prepared to receive a deputation from the Teachers' Associations he contemplated calling off his own line of action, more especially as some of the harrassed secretaries, confronted by two unusual tasks, had not yet replied to Vere's questionnaire; he was apt to get a little impatient if people didn't come up to his own exacting standards of punctuality. Nevertheless, he still wanted this written evidence from the teachers as a whole, so : 'Should, however, even a majority of the associations from which I have received no replies, think proper, even yet, to empower me to express their views, I will proceed, and if too late for the reception of my report by the Commission, I will publish a blue book for presentation to each individual member of Parliament, at my own expense, omitting, of course, all reference to names of localities of my correspondents, unless receiving express permission to refer to them. This will put me to great expense, which should have been rendered unnecessary [had they replied in time].'[10]

Sixty-nine of the hundred or so teachers' associations, together with 37 individual teachers connected with notably 'mixed' schools, responded to the questionnaire and by September Vere had assembled their statements in a report of 74 pages entitled *Evidence of the Irish National Teachers' Associations in Reply to Queries addressed by the Commissioners to Vere Foster, Esq., and submitted by him for their consideration.*[11] This title and Vere's introductory remarks make it clear that he was transmitting evidence from the teachers themselves.

Again one is impressed by the speed with which he worked—

less than three months to collect and print evidence from every corner of Ireland! The pamphlet is well produced and of great interest; it is in fact a report in miniature of education in Ireland in the middle of the nineteenth century. Over five hundred copies were circulated to the Government, the Irish press, Irish MPs and a selection of some three hundred English members, and it put the Irish Teachers' Associations on the map as nothing else could have done.

Meanwhile a small conference of teachers had met in August 1868 to prepare for a much larger meeting to be held at the end of the year at which Vere presided. This December conference was an enormous success and an historic occasion, for at it the Irish National Teachers' Association took shape, the first professional organisation of teachers in Ireland on a national basis.* Over one hundred delegates attended, representing some seven thousand teachers. Reports were given by the various associations who had interviewed their MPs on the matter of salaries, etc. A feeling of purpose animated everyone. The editor of the *Irish Teachers' Journal* commented :

> We have reserved for the last another topic of congratulation namely the good which resulted to the whole proceedings by having such a gentleman to preside over them as he who filled the chair upon the occasion. Those who witnessed the patience which he showed and the more than judicial impartiality with which he comported himself, never suffering for a moment the slightest indication of his own private opinion of the subject under discussion to appear, and who also considered the amount of fatigue, both physical and mental, which he had to endure, must agree with us that if anything could raise Vere Foster higher in the estimation and affection of the National Teachers of Ireland, it would be the Congress of Christmas 1868.[12]

Another report gives a description of Vere's appearance :

> The august assembly was presided over by the illustrious Vere Foster, the munificent patron of popular education, and the idol of the teachers. The distinguished gentleman seems verging on sixty years of age,† of a tall, graceful figure, fair complexion,

* The precursor of the Irish National Teachers' Organisation.
† Actually he was 49.

with a mild, benevolent expression, the index of his innate goodness.[13]

The congress concluded with a banquet 'which the teachers from all parts of Ireland had ordered on Wednesday evening at the European Hotel, Bolton Street, in honour of Mr Vere Foster'. How a 'banquet' came within the scope of recipients of less than £30 a year it is difficult to say, but we may be sure that Vere responded to this generous hospitality by being a most jovial guest.

It may all sound flamboyant and perhaps a little extreme, yet when the delegate from Carrickmacross got back to his home in Co Monaghan and had time to reflect calmly on the whole exhilarating experience he was constrained to write thus to the *Journal* :

> On the part of the Carrickmacross Association I take this opportunity of returning our most grateful thanks to Mr Vere Foster for his unceasing exertions and self-denial in favor of the Irish National Teachers. Titus was called the delight of mankind, and I often thought the same appellation would not be inappropriately applied to Mr Foster by the teachers of Ireland.[14]

Exacting though his standards might be that was how they felt about him. Envy had not yet raised its horrid head.

In the spring of 1869 Vere led a deputation of five teachers to wait on the Lord Lieutenant. They were received by Earl Spencer in the drawing room of the Vice-Regal Lodge in Phoenix Park. After introducing the deputation Vere handed the Lord Lieutenant a memorial with more than three thousand signatures attached. He had briefed the chosen five with care, and according to the report in the *Irish Teachers' Journal* they spoke on the usual points with clarity and assurance. In supporting their pleas Vere upheld the Government's contention that national education should be financed to a considerable degree by local contributions, but stated that, in his opinion, the only way of obtaining such contributions was by a compulsory local rate.[15] This was to be his constant argument.

The year 1869 saw also the condemnation by the Irish Hierarchy of the whole national system of education, in spite of the fact that the appointment of a larger proportion of catholic commissioners on the board had removed a genuine catholic grievance, *viz* the domination of the board by protestants. This condemnation, described as Dr MacHale's greatest triumph, was ratified by the pope at the Vatican Council at the end of the same year.

At the close of 1869 Vere again presided at what was now regarded as the annual congress of the Teachers' Associations. While denominational schools and managerial power were subjects too dangerous for public discussion by teachers naturally afraid to air opinions that differed from clerical policy, Vere, in a statement of his own views, firmly grasped the nettle of managerial control. He outlined procedure in other countries and declared, 'I cannot too strongly express my opinion that no single person should have uncontrolled power to dismiss a public servant. There should be a right of appeal either to a local committee or to a central authority, or both.'[16]

The following year was crowded with activity. Schools were still being re-floored; the handwriting competitions were being inaugurated; the series of writing and drawing copy-books was being increased, and there was continued discussion regarding the type of handwriting best suited for use in girls' schools. 'I am still,' wrote Vere, 'on my travels round Ireland collecting judgments as to the style of writing most desired for use in girls' schools. As there is great diversity of opinion I expect to be so occupied for some months longer.' He himself was perfectly satisfied that in order to take their place in a changing world, girls as well as boys should be taught to write a clear, round hand, so it was with considerable satisfaction that he sent to the *Irish Teachers' Journal* the following extracts from a letter written by the head of 'one of the largest commercial firms in this country':

Scarcely a girl that we get can write her name creditably. The consequence is that we cannot advance their position the way we can that of lads who can write a good *round hand* . . . Girls are half-taught a bad scratchy style that is *useless* to business folk . . . so I consider that your present effort to improve female penmanship will do more to give employment to women than half the society work (for amelioration of women's position) that is now going on : and women's wrongs that we hear so much about are more the wrongs of their bad education than anything else.

All our book-keeping and clerking might be done by girls, no reason, save this horrid sharp system that cramps their hands, to prevent their writing and counting as well as males. Really, I consider it of supreme importance, and I hope you will go on with it heartily.[17]

Not content with 'collecting judgments' on the subject in Ireland, Vere dashed over to England in the autumn and in two months visited 'nearly 700 schools' in towns and cities so far apart as Bristol and Newcastle-on-Tyne. 'I have found,' he reported, 'angular penmanship decidedly condemned, and round legible handwriting . . . in use in every one of these schools, excepting two, so I presume no long time will elapse before the scratchy "area railing style" will be completely banished from all schools, public and private, in Ireland also.'[18]

One wonders how it was possible, with mid-Victorian transport, to visit nearly 700 widely separated schools 'within two months'.

Nor, in the midst of all this to-ing and fro-ing, were the needs of teachers forgotten. One little note has been preserved. It is written on most elaborate Victorian stationery and signed by three female teachers-in-training in Dublin on behalf of the whole class. It conveys thanks for 'your great kindness in supplying us with the sewing-machines, which we are sure will prove a great boon, not only to ourselves, but also to the female children in the remote localities to which many of us are now returning. If you ever visit our schools we trust you will find us successful in carrying out your intentions, and that the little pupils, who may come under your notice, will show in their appearance that the machines were not bestowed in vain.'[19] The use of sewing-machines had very recently been introduced into the training department, and it required great efforts over the next few years to induce managers to acquire them as part of the essential school equipment. Inventions were always a delight to Vere, and anything that curtailed drudgery was hailed with joy; it is typical that he should immediately arrange for these latest mechanical aids to be sent to 'the most remote localities'. Nothing was too good for the poorest little schools.

Another letter may be mentioned here. It came from Sister Mary Louis of the Ursuline Convent in Thurles. Once Emily Davenport of New York, she was now a drawing teacher in the convent school, and when a parcel of newly arrived drawing copy-books were given into her charge she was amazed to see thereon the name Vere Foster. 'I had last,' she wrote to him, 'the pleasure of meeting you [at my home] in New York, a wild school girl then, sobered however more than you could believe, but your description to me of a certain voyage à l'emigrant [was] a graphic sketch sufficient to dispel self . . . Years of continental as well as conventual life have not effaced the memory of many beautiful theories, many bright doctrines for the weal of others, which were given from the heart of "Vere Foster", and which may not have been, it is hoped, cast upon rocky ground, but brought back to Irish soil, there to be thought over, an incentive "to labour unto the end".'

Emigration still made demands on his time and thought. A little notebook headed 'Family Emigration from the East of London' contains lists of subscribers in Vere's handwriting for the years 1869–73 and sums amounting to around £750 annually, with a corresponding annual expenditure, to which emigrants made some contributions, of approximately £12,000. Vere was treasurer of this fund, but there is no indication of how many families were assisted.

9

Organising Teachers (continued)

But the greatest event of 1870 was the eagerly awaited publication of the report of the Royal Commission on Primary Education (Ireland)—the Powis Commission—and when it came it filled the teachers with apprehension. Trifling improvements in salaries were recommended, and the statement regarding managerial control was unsatisfactory. Vere at once headed a deputation to the Chief Secretary, Chichester Fortescue, to express the teachers' concern, but the result was so inconclusive that he advocated an immediate interview with the Prime Minister, Mr Gladstone, which was however postponed till after the December Teachers' Congress at which Vere again presided.[1]

Discussion on these burning questions was inevitable and a resolution calling for modification of existing managerial control was adopted at the Congress and had far-reaching effects. A teacher of a small country school in Co Monaghan courageously voted in its favour. News travelled quickly, and very shortly the manager of the school, the parish priest, received a letter from his bishop, informing him that had this not been the teacher's first fault it would have been necessary for the manager to remove him forthwith and to see that he did not teach in any other school in the parish. As it was he must be severely reprimanded. 'Tell him,' wrote the bishop, 'I would much prefer his school were closed up altogether and that his pupils were dependent for their education upon such humble instruction as, unaided by Government grants, the piety of your parishioners with the help of the clergy would secure for them, rather than accept his doctrine that teachers should be independent of their managers' control, a doctrine which I find shadowed forth in that monstrous recommendation of the Royal Commission on Primary Education . . . The Manager must be authorised to dismiss a teacher *instanter* for any fault or misdeed on the score of faith or morals. Upon no other terms can we have relations with State-aided schools.'

This long letter was published in the press.[2] Vere replied immediately in the *Irish Teachers' Journal*. 'I solemnly protest,' he wrote, 'against what I cannot help designating as an unjustifiable interference with the liberty of the subject,' which drew from the bishop a still longer epistle. Mr Foster's letter, his lordship wrote, calls for a few remarks, 'the more so as I learn from the journals of yesterday that he is just now operating in London as the representative of this province and the mouthpiece of the national Teachers of Ireland . . . For all my sincere admiration for his character and undoubted services I cannot consent, aware as I am of his views on school management and mixed education, that Mr Foster's testimony should be accepted as the system of education that will respond to the convictions and wants of our Catholic people; and I warn Mr Gladstone and his colleagues to beware how far they take counsel from Mr Foster on this important matter.'[3]

'Operating in London' referred to the deputation consisting of Vere and three teachers appointed by the congress to wait upon Mr Gladstone in February 1871. He 'received them most affably and shook each of them by the hand. He also caused them to be seated and made them perfectly at ease.' So much so that, in closing the interview, the prime minister said 'nothing could be more intelligible or more fair than the manner in which the deputation had put their case, and he was very glad to have obtained such valuable information from their own mouths. They would of course take care to make their views known to Lord Harting-ton.'*[4]

This Vere did on behalf of the others before leaving London, 'supporting to the best of his ability the views that had been so ably and faithfully laid before the Prime Minister' on salaries, pensions, residences, and managerial power. To illustrate the need for residences close to the schools he 'instanced the fact that one of the deputationists, Mr Burke, had for some years walked a distance of ten miles daily to and from his school which he now reaches by means of the latest novelty in locomotion, the veloci-pede. I advocated compulsory powers to obtain sites for public schools from unwilling landlords such as the authorities of Trinity College,† etc.'

The teachers' indebtedness to Vere was expressed with touch-ing insight by the editor of the *Irish Teachers' Journal* when commenting on the good impression made on the prime minister by the deputation :

> Of the teachers' unwearied and indefatigable friend, Mr Vere Foster, we need say nothing. He has so thoroughly identified him-self with the cause of his humbler countrymen that they look upon his co-operation as a matter of course. This, perhaps, is the best tribute we can pay to his active and untiring benevolence, though it may sometimes cause us to underrate, or rather not to perceive in a proper light, the real value of the services he has rendered to Irish Education.[5]

And his services were not confined to official undertakings. Believing that a 'knowledge of progressive educational thought in Britain is so essential to Irish teachers' he inquired of his cousin Lord Ripon, Chairman of the English Council of Education, if the council would accept for posts in England teachers with certificates from the Training Institute of the Irish National Board. It has not been possible to trace the answer.

* The Chief Secretary.

† Trinity College had recently refused the Commissioners of National Education a site in Co. Louth.

In the autumn of 1871 Vere made one of his lightning expeditions to America. All we know about it is that he visited more than one hundred schools in the States and in Canada. He was back in Dublin in time to preside as usual at the 1871 congress in December.

In August 1872 the eagerly awaited government proposals to implement the findings of the Royal Commission were announced. It was a time-gaining programme, the chief points being the provision of an interim grant for three years of £100,000 to be used in part for increasing basic salaries, the remainder to be disbursed as 'payments for results'. This system of paying teachers on the results obtained by their pupils, already established in Britain, had been frequently mooted as applicable to Ireland, and had provoked much opposition from Irish teachers, who declared that local conditions made the scheme entirely unacceptable. Many rural schools were so small as to make qualification for 'results' virtually impossible, thus penalising the worst-paid teachers. Vere himself was apprehensive, insisting that the system would constitute a grave injustice to some teachers and would encourage concentration on the bright children, to the detriment of those who most needed help.*[6]

In an effort to meet the demands for modification of managerial control, 'result fees' would be paid only to such teachers as had completed a form of agreement with their manager which would include the stipulation 'that the teacher should not be dismissed without three months' notice or three months' salary, unless the National Board of Education affirmed, upon enquiry, that there was good cause for such dismissal'.[8] This, in effect, made the Board of Education the final judge on matters of faith and morals. The majority of Protestant managers were prepared to accept the government's form of agreement, Protestant teachers, therefore, would have no difficulty in getting

---

* That he later modified his views somewhat is evident from his suggestion in 1878 that result fees should be taken into consideration when determining the salaries of the headmaster and second master of the Belfast School of Art, provided a minimum salary of £300 and £150 respectively was guaranteed by the Department of Science and Art.[7]

their 'results' fees. From the Roman Catholic managers there was almost general refusal, though it must be said that three of the bishops were prepared, at the outset, to sanction acceptance. Undoubtedly this would be the vital issue at the forthcoming congress, with the lamentable probability that it would split the associations on religious grounds—Roman Catholic teachers being in a difficult position *vis-à-vis* their managers—the very situation, in fact, that from his earliest association with teachers, or indeed with Ireland, Vere had sought to prevent. It is easy to imagine the sense of tension as the eighty or so delegates from every 'nook' of Ireland converged on Dublin in December 1872.

In the autumn of that year Vere had written to the secretary of the Central Committee of Teachers' Associations expressing the view that the time had now come when a teacher should preside at the annual congress, and that, accordingly, he wished to retire. The letter was received with consternation in Dublin, the secretary writing 'without delay', begging Mr Foster to 'continue to occupy the position he has filled in past years at their annual congress with such great advantage to the National Teachers of Ireland . . . from past experience they are convinced that Mr Foster's presence, advice and invaluable assistance are indispensable for the successful prosecution of their claims'. He consented to remain, replying that 'Whatever services it may be in my power to render . . . shall be cheerfully given as my sympathies are entirely with the National Teachers in their justifiable agitation'.[9]

There is no clear indication as to what prompted Vere to make this move. Did he fear that his own strongly held views on local taxation and managerial control might embarrass discussion at the forthcoming congress, eventful as it certainly would be? Did he want to be free to speak his mind? Did he sense a feeling, amongst some teachers, of resentment? We do not know.

The Congress assembled at 5 pm on 26 December in the Assembly Rooms kindly placed at its disposal by the Lord Mayor, the first time that such civic recognition had been bestowed. In spite of this evidence of public confidence, and owing no doubt

L

to the tension already described, the gathering got off to a bad start, three hours being consumed by disagreements over procedure and arguments as to who were or were not delegates, until the chairman, when making certain rulings, 'intimated that if they had squabbles to settle, they should have settled them somewhere else, without taking up the time of the Congress, and bringing discredit upon the proceedings by such unseemly exhibitions'. At 8 pm a delegate suggested that, as time had been 'so uselessly squandered . . . upon topics of no interest, but upon which each man thought he had something to say and insisted on saying it', the chairman should postpone his address till next morning, but on Vere informing them that the Lord Lieutenant might wish to see him during the following day it was decided to keep to the programme, and Vere was permitted to retire 'for a few minutes respite'. Meanwhile, under the guidance of a temporary chairman, the secretary proceeded to read his annual report, in which he permitted himself some pious hopes on business not yet transacted. Instantly a fresh storm arose, delegates protesting that the offending passage contained 'too nice a point for the secretary to deal with in his report', that 'a report [should not be] turned into a sermon or an oration', that it was impossible to 'catch the words about which all this discussion was going on, gentlemen discussed the matter with such sound and fury that it was difficult for anyone to know what was being discussed'. The confusion continued, 'many delegates complaining that they had been kept there now for a number of hours without fire or comfort'.[10]

When Mr Foster returned he was loudly applauded, but such tiresome behaviour in view of the seriousness of the situation must have caused him dismay. With skill and forbearance he succeeded in lifting the disorderly discussion to its proper plane. He emphasised that 'no crisis like the present had ever arrived in their fortunes since first they were called a congress', and he begged them to act with 'good sense and unanimity'. After outlining the government's proposals regarding increased salaries and managerial control, and accepting that there was much division of opinion on the latter, he stated his own view that the true solution of the difficulty would be . . . to place the system of primary education upon a more secure basis, similarly as in England and Scotland. Whenever that took place there must be local taxation . . . and local representation on a board of Managers or a School Board (cries of 'No School Board').

Power of dismissal would then lie with the school board and not with individual managers.

He felt very much the responsibility he had undertaken in having anything to say upon this question. He had endeavoured to avoid it;* but was pledged to meet it, and he felt bound to make the remarks he had made. Perhaps he had given offence to some, perhaps to many (cries of 'Not to any just man') upon this managerial question. He had many intimate and respected friends amongst the Catholic clergy in this country. He knew he differed from them in opinion upon this—he must differ from them, and differing must give offence when he spoke. He was sorry if he should excite any unfriendly feeling, but he felt bound to speak out. He had said enough about this question, he had now done with it.[11]

He had drafted for the consideration of delegates a memorial on the form of agreement to be presented to the chief secretary, but discussion on this was postponed, and after further remarks on less controversial issues Vere 'resumed his seat amidst prolonged applause and cheering, which lasted for some minutes'. The session closed at one o'clock in the morning.

When the delegates re-assembled at 9 am duly refreshed, they were annoyed to find that the reporter was absent. When he eventually turned up he had to 'defend himself' against 'one or two of the gentlemen [who] upbraided him with being late', explaining that he had had to sit up well into the morning to write out the speech of the previous evening before taking it to the printer. 'By this arrangement he had but taken a few hours' rest before he had now again to go to work. Men who came fresh from the country and rushed into a room as soon as they had light to see each other should have some consideration for a reporter, who had to keep his attention on the stretch for many hours together,

* Perhaps a reference to his attempted resignation (p 169).

to catch the arguments of some 60 or 80 who took up the question
by turns . . . He did not mean to say that they were not the best
talkers he ever came across in his life, but he had only the physical
powers of endurance of any other human being, and would feel
relieved if members would meet within reasonable hours of
the day, and keep to the regular business, instead of flying off
into long discussion upon nothing.'

This trifling contretemps is included to illustrate, as does the
arguing on the previous evening, the very human limitations with
which Vere had to contend. The congress eventually settled down
to two days of pleasant business, welcoming delegates from England, listening to long, congratulatory speeches and enjoying an
official dinner.

On the fourth morning Mr Foster took the chair at ten o'clock.
The first business was the election of president and vice-president
for the ensuing year. The report in the *Irish Teachers' Journal*
baldly states that 'Mr Vere Foster having expressed frequently
his wish that his place as Chairman should be filled by some
member of the Congress, the meeing now proceeded to elect a
new President and a Vice-President'.[12] Vere withdrew from the
meeting, and immediately one delegate ungraciously declared that
he 'thought they had plenty of men at that Congress, or of their
own number, quite as competent to fill the position of Chairman
as Mr Foster . . . and he moved that a teacher be now elected
to act as President'. The motion was seconded and it was evident
that it would have considerable support, though, as reported in
the *Journal*, most of the speakers were anxious that Mr Foster
should continue as their head. 'Mr Ryan said that if Mr Foster
did not preside, he would not attend the Congress. Mr Foley
[evidently the one realist in the place] said they would never get
a man to give them so much of their time as Mr Foster did'.
Another delegate hinted that 'efforts were being made by a clique
to deprive them of Mr Foster'. It was finally decided to ask Mr
Foster to remain as Honorary President to preside at Congress,
and to appoint a Vice-President from among the members to
preside 'on all occasions on which Mr Foster could not attend'.

On Vere's return he was greeted with prolonged applause but there is no record of how the foregoing decision was communicated to him, or of his reply. The congress proceeded with the business of proposing, seconding, and speaking at great length to many resolutions.

Not until the very end was Vere's draft memorial on the form of agreement discussed. It expressed gratitude for the government's efforts to 'remove some of the more prominent of [the teachers'] universally acknowledged grievances'. It pointed out that by constituting the National Board of Education as the arbitrator in cases of disputed dismissal, the form of agreement between managers and teachers would be unacceptable in many cases, thus depriving the teachers concerned of the 'additional grant so generously voted by Parliament', and it called upon the government to treat the various grievances separately and independently of each other. The draft was modified to include the suggestion that 'the legal Tribunal of the Land' should be substituted for the National Board of Education as the final arbitrator. When after more discussion the memorial was put to the congress an amendment, stating that it 'was unwise and injudicious' to send any memorial at all, was proposed and seconded.[13]

Such vacillating tactics annoyed Vere who considered that the government, having met the teachers' constant grievance regarding managerial control by a specific solution—ill-advised though it was in one particular detail—expected, and was entitled to get, the views of teachers assembled in congress. Possibly he was working on some hint gained during his interview with the Lord Lieutenant, which he was unable to disclose. After a great deal of discussion the voting took place. 'The Chairman read the resolution and the amendment slowly, and told them to remember that they were going to vote first of all upon the amendment, which was virtually whether or not they would accept the memorial. As he called the roll let each member go past and drop in his paper, folded with the word "yes" or "no" written within.' There he stood, tired after four days of endless talk, supervising a vote that might very well go against him.

The result was the rejection of his memorial by thirty-three votes to sixteen, a two-to-one majority, and it was received with 'tremendous cheering'. It was the first time, so far as we know, that his advice had been spurned, and Vere took it as a definite rejection of his policy and leadership. 'The meeting soon after broke up in a rather disorderly fashion some members being apparently much chagrined, the majority exulting as in a signal victory.'[14]

That there exists not a single personal letter or note of any kind written by Vere at this time makes an assessment of his feelings almost impossible. One longs for some intimate expression of the thoughts that assailed him as he made the cold, dreary journey back to Belfast by train, some letter, such as fifteen years earlier he would have sent to Frederick. Instead we have only press reports—not always unbiased—of his public utterances, and the reactions of his hearers. In spite of his great self-confidence, did the loneliness of his position sweep over him? For so long he had been isolated from those who by upbringing and family ties should have been his friends; now he was isolated from his chosen friends by the very foresight and ability which enabled him to be their incomparable leader, and by an inviolable integrity which forebade the slightest exploitation of that leadership. One hopes that he found in John Ward a companion in whom he could confide and with whom he could confer.

Alarmed by the gravity of the situation, Mr Chamney took immediate action and, irregular though it was, he circulated Vere's modified draft memorial to all the Teachers' Associations, with a covering note of great urgency. The draft was carried by the associations, accepted by the chief secretary, and a form of agreement thus amended met with the approval of the Catholic bishops.[15]

From the somewhat disjointed report of the congress in the *Irish Teachers' Journal* it is difficult to discover why Vere's modified memorial failed in the first instance. One fears, alas, that the whole issue at the congress was vitiated by the undercurrent of dissension and intrigue, already apparent in the effort to remove

Vere from the presidency, that was bent on undermining his leadership.

Be that as it may, agreements between managers and teachers were speedily completed, and 'result fees' were shortly received with delight in many a household. But the dissension at the congress engendered a sense of consternation and dismay among the great body of teachers scattered all over Ireland who looked to Vere, and to Vere alone, for guidance. One of them, writing in the deepest concern to the *Irish Teachers' Journal*, recalls not only Mr Foster's 'princely expenditure in promoting National Education' but also his work for emigration—how 'Moses-like he opened a passage for thousands to the land of promise'—and, with overflowing admiration, recalls this incident, which is nowhere else preserved :

> In another capacity I shall place him before your readers. It is well known that in London there are Irish families depending on the labours of young women who sell fruit through the city. The police often annoy these poor creatures, and drive them from street to street to prevent them from following their humble but honest industry. They even beat them and then summon them before the magistrates for obstructing the thoroughfares or for some other imaginary crime. On a cold morning in the month of February, some fifteen or sixteen years since, a gentleman observed a scene such as I have been describing; he watched the cruel treatment a poor Irish girl received from a policeman; he followed them to the courthouse, and heard the charges preferred against her. He requested to be examined against the peace preserver, and in defence of our poor countrywoman. Need I say who this gentleman was? No . . . If ever again I visit the metropolis [Dublin], I expect to see his statue not so far from those of Burke, Moore and O'Brien. As soon as a secretary and treasurer are appointed I shall send my subscription.[16]

In November of that year, 1873, the Dublin Teachers' Association organised a large public meeting to press their claims. More than a thousand people filled the Exhibition Room of the Rotunda and, on the motion of Mr Vere Foster, still president, the Lord Mayor occupied the chair. In supporting the resolution calling for increased salaries Vere once more, and very forcibly, expressed his conviction that the necessary funds could be raised only by a local rate.* It was hopeless, indeed wrong, he declared, to expect any more money from the British Government, which already contributed much more per head for the education of Irish children than for English children.[17]

This may have caused further dissatisfaction, for in that month he again tendered his resignation. In a letter to the *Irish Teachers' Journal* informing the teachers of his decision, Vere stated 'that his resignation was necessary as his advocacy of local taxation and the necessary concomitant—school boards—might prove an embarrassment to the teachers' organisations'. Once more there was general dismay. Letters poured into the office of the *Journal* and the editor 'felt it to be his duty to forestall the action of the teachers by intimating to Mr Foster the number and the nature of the communications we have received, and are daily receiving from all parts of Ireland; and urging him to be prepared to resume his post at the head of the teachers' movement in obedience to the universal appeal which will be made by the associations'.[18] But this time Vere was adamant.

Hardly was the ink dry on his letter of resignation than the Belfast Teachers' Association held a large and enthusiastic public meeting, emulating, no doubt, their brethren in Dublin. The Mayor presided; the Moderator of the General Assembly of the Presbyterian Church, representatives of other churches, and many prominent citizens, having been specially invited, were present on the platform, but no invitation or communication of any kind had been sent to Mr Foster. He pocketed his pride and joined the unprivileged audience, but next day, in legitimate wrath he sent the following letter to the *Northern Whig* and to the *Irish Teachers' Journal* :

> Sir,
>   As I take a lively interest in the just agitation of the National Teachers for the redress of their many grievances, and am conscious of having given practical proofs of my sympathy for up-

---

* Vere's constant advocacy of local taxation was supported by the Inspectors of the Board of Education. R.N.Educ. 1870 pp 288, 297.

wards of twenty years previous to the existence of Teachers'
Associations, I request your permission to explain to friends of
the cause that the only reason for my not having taken part in the
proceedings of the public meeting presided over by the Mayor last
night was because such was the deliberate wish of the Belfast
Teachers' Association, who not only did not invite me to speak,
or to take a place on the platform, but did not even extend to me
the ordinary courtesy, so profusely scattered amongst the rest of
the community, of inviting me to be present.

On inquiry of the president and the secretary for the reason
of my exclusion, I was informed that it was because, in consequence of my well-known opinions, it was feared that, in my
utter hopelessness of any further grant for the Imperial Treasury,
I would advocate that mode of supporting public schools which is
common in all other countries—namely, local taxation—as in my
opinion the only likely or practicable source of increase.

I observe that at least one of the speakers at the meeting expressed a similar opinion, which is ably supported by argument
in your leading article of this day.

I had supposed that the teachers would welcome an increase
of income from whatever source, and would wish their friends
to be free to advocate methods of increase each from his own
point of view. I think it should ever be borne in mind, when making comparisons between the incomes of Irish and English
teachers, that the sole reason for the enormous disproportion between them lies in the fact that two-thirds of the support of
schools in England are derived from local contributions, but only
one-seventh part in Ireland. I cannot be content to go on beat-
ing the wind and whining to Government for what I know to
be perfectly hopeless, and I wish to see my countrymen more self-
reliant.

Vere Foster.[19]

The *Belfast Morning News* [a Catholic paper] expressed dismay 'that one who has done so much for the cause of education
in Ireland, and who in an especial sense has made himself the
champion of the National school teachers, should have been overlooked in the manner which he describes . . . Mr Foster is kind
enough to furnish them with an excuse, but it is scarcely one
under which the officials can shield themselves . . . His views are
his own; and assuming that the teachers' associations are un-

favorable to the scheme of having a local tax struck for the purpose of having them properly paid is no reason why Mr Foster should have been denied the opportunity of showing he was at issue with them on the point . . . Indeed authorities like Mr Foster properly form opinion; and though the teachers' associations may think his plan unpopular, yet this does not provide for its being unsound in principle, or that it would be unacceptable to the public, who wish to be enlightened on the education question.'[20]

From all this it must regretfully be concluded that the Belfast teachers were antagonistic to Vere and were prepared to press their opposition by any methods—it had indeed been hinted that they were responsible for the rowdyism at the conclusion of the December congress. As far back as 1868 the Belfast Teachers' Association, of which Mr Boal and Mr Cullen were, even then chairman and secretary respectively, suggested forming an Ulster National Teachers' Association. Granted 'the Belfast men', as they came to be called, may have had a spirit of independence that resented the overlordship of Dublin; that they should have acted with such calculated insolence to one who had sacrificed practically everything in the interests of education is incredible if one fails to acknowledge how strangely jealousy and ambition can drive smaller men. We can only imagine the suffering that such wounds inflicted.

When the congress met in Dublin in December 1873, Mr Boal was elected president for the ensuing year. Intrigue was thus crowned with success.

In such circumstances it was easy to be benign; Mr Foster was invited, as principal guest, to the congress dinner. With quiet dignity he replied to the toast in his honour using a phrase that might have been spoken by his father—he hoped he had been able to 'set an example'.[21] Deep in his nature, the foundation in fact of all that he did, was that inherited, powerful sense of personal responsibility, expressed in his case with originality and fantastic generosity. The seemingly light-hearted assertion made years ago in Philadelphia, that it was amusing to do good, covered a fundamental belief in the responsibility of the individual towards his neighbour.

Nevertheless the wound had cut very deep. With a sort of bravado Vere continued to voice his conviction that it was wrong to seek an increased parliamentary grant for Irish education, going so far as to declare, in a letter to *The Nation*, that 'if I had the honour of being a M.P., I would decidedly vote against any such increase'.[22] Government, he maintained had been more than generous to Irish education, 'they already pay to Irish schools nearly twice as much per pupil as they do to English or Scotch schools'. The extra money must, in his view, come from other sources, and, as the possibility of obtaining it voluntarily had for one reason and another decreased the only solution lay in local taxation.

Letters of affection and confidence reached him from every quarter of Ireland, and associations throughout the country begged him to address their meetings. At a great gathering in Limerick of teachers from the whole county, supported by the Roman Catholic bishop, other clergy and many prominent people, he spoke his mind on local taxation for the last time 'exercising that freedom of speech which has been denied to me in Belfast and which I did not feel at liberty to exercise at the Congress in Dublin'.[23] But, pursued by opposition, there was no alternative but to withdraw completely. 'I now desire,' he wrote to the *Journal*, 'in the interests of general harmony and goodwill, and in supplement to my retirement from all official connection with the Teachers' Organisation, to express my intention of refraining from taking any part whatever at public meetings, such as those above referred to [Limerick], as I cannot conscientiously do so without touching on the subject on which I differ from my Belfast friends.'[24]

It was ardently desired that he would offer himself for the presidency the following year. With one gesture towards return he could have split the movement from top to bottom—instead his concern was for 'harmony and goodwill'.

Perhaps his work for the teachers of Ireland was completed. In

1849, when he had made his first connection with Irish education, he found them depressed and disorganised. Over the intervening twenty-five years he had, by his sympathy, his personal
contact, his readiness to experience their poverty, the genuineness
of his encouragement, his knowledge of the world, his social position, and his great gift of leadership, no less than by his 'princely
generosity', integrated them into a national movement, able to
take their place among their professional brethren elsewhere. His
hope now was, as he told them at that last congress dinner, that
'they would continue in their course of self-improvement, and in
peaceful agitation for a redress of their grievances, a non-
political and non-sectarian body, composed of teachers of every
denomination'.[25] But one of his heartbroken adherents ex-
claimed : 'if this [Vere's complete retirement from the teachers'
struggle] be the first development of the decapitated Organiza-
tion, it augurs very badly for the future of our present agitation.'[26]

IO

Personal

It is now necessary to go back to the copy-books. While there were still complaints about the board's wretched, thin pointed nibs, poor quality ink, and unsteady, crowded desks, inspectors in 1873 were able to write: 'all the good writing is Fosterian'; 'the teaching of writing has now become a reality'; 'copy writing shows manifest signs of progress, and the books are better preserved'. The last comment refers to the 'Copy-Book Protector' which Vere, in his abhorrence of untidy, slovenly work, had invented. Even in the girls' schools 'a compromise between the round, which they dislike, and the small, cramped, angular style, which girls think "genteel", has been effected, and a large, bold semi-angular hand is now written'.[1] Entrants for the Penmanship Competitions increased every year and 'the annual sale of copy-books was around four million. Everything', said the Master of the Rolls in the case of Foster and Ward v. Marcus Ward & Co, 'went on in the greatest harmony until 1876 when, without action on the part of Mr Foster at all, but I rather think positively brought about by the enormous success of the firm and the vast sums of money they had realised, they began amongst themselves to differ'.[2]

The long tale of this unnecessary litigation can be briefly told.

The quarrel arose between the three Ward brothers over their relative status in the firm. It had nothing whatver to do with Vere, but as the work on his orders constituted by far the largest single contract handled by the firm, it naturally affected him very closely apart from his friendship with all three brothers. 'Very large sums of money [the judge remarked] passed between him and the firm of Marcus Ward & Co in relation to these little publications. In fact such an extraordinary amount is scarcely possible to conceive when one looks at the nature of the copy-books themselves; and it is only when one considers the enormous demand that was on them that you see the immense sums realised out of the transaction.'[3] Vere put the value of his orders from first to last at over £150,000, and the firm's annual profits on the manufacture of the copy-books amounted to £4,600, with almost another £2,000 on sales.[4] It is evident from statements made during the trial that Vere did everything he could to help the brothers to arrive at an amicable settlement, and when legal proceedings had been instituted, to facilitate both sides in the interests of peace and goodwill. 'Mr John Ward is most anxious,' writes his solicitor, 'to adopt any suggestion made by Mr. Foster, who has always proved himself to be a sincere friend to all members of the firm.'[5] When in 1876 John Ward, as a result of the quarrel, retired from the partnership, intending to set up another printing business, Vere informed the two brothers who continued the original firm, that 'while he must in honour and in gratitude continue to do business with Mr. John Ward', he would, in order to assist them to carry out their financial obligations, give them for two years orders for 'a supply of writing and drawing copy-books to the value of about £36,000'.[6]

So much for a short-term arrangement, but surveying the undertaking from the longer viewpoint it seemed to Vere that it was now time to pull out from this fantastically successful venture, which he never intended should serve any purpose other than that of raising the standard of penmanship among young people for whom good handwriting was an essential qualification when seeking employment. Besides, he had other schemes in his mind. So in 1877 Vere wrote to John Ward saying that 'in consequence of what has happened and of the embarrassment which I anticipate, as I have achieved my original purpose of making my publications—with your hearty and wise co-operation—a complete success, I am now inclined to retire from the enterprise'. He would continue the system of prizes as heretofore, but 'is disposed to part with copyright, plates, blocks and all interest in my publications'. This was followed immediately by a second letter in which 'having thought the matter over and without consulting anyone' he offered to John Ward 'the entire concern for the sum of £3,000, to represent blocks, plates and plant of every sort and goodwill, the stock and goods on order', an extremely generous offer which John Ward eventually accepted.*[7]

At the termination of the above-mentioned two-year agreement with Marcus Ward & Co, Vere vacated the room at the Ulster Works which had for almost ten years been his one and only office, requesting the return of all his property—stock of books, copperplates, electrotypes and the lithographic stones used for the production of his colour drawing books. These last the brothers refused to hand over, maintaining that they belonged to the firm, though the costly process of preparing the stones to reproduce the artists' pictures in colour had been borne by Vere. Repeated requests elicited only the public declaration by Marcus Ward & Co that they would not part with the stones 'even for payment, unless they can be compelled to do so by process of law'.[8] These stones were part of the property that Vere had already sold to John Ward, for that reason, and also in common justice, they must be retrieved. So in 1878 Vere and John Ward sued Marcus Ward & Co for the return of the lithographic stones. The case was heard by the Master of the Rolls, who in 1882 gave

---

* As things turned out, John Ward did not start again in business; Messrs. Blackie & Son became the printers and distributors of the copy-books. When this arrangement was being made Vere insisted that the printing should continue to be done in Dublin, in order to maintain the employment that he had been able to provide. Blackie accordingly opened a branch in Dublin which, in 1910, became the Educational Company of Ireland.

a verdict in favour of the plaintiffs and awarded them costs. The case caused a considerable stir in the printing world and as Marcus Ward & Co decided to appeal, Vere produced a pamphlet entitled *Origin and History of Vere Foster's Writing and Drawing Copy-Books*, in which he included the judgement of the Master of the Rolls. This he circulated 'among all members of the lithographic trade in the United Kingdom'. It is important now as the only authoritative record of the copy-book enterprise. Though the Appeal judge upheld the first verdict, with very slight modifications, there was a further appeal in 1886, this time before the Lord Chancellor; the respondants were again successful. It then became evident that Marcus Ward & Co had defaced the stones, and Vere was awarded £700 damages as well as costs. The firm had spent vast sums of money to no avail.

For ten years this sorry controversy dragged on, and though Vere by no means allowed it to monopolise his time and thought, the particular circumstances must have made it a very unhappy experience.

In 1877, immediately after the sale of his 'enterprise' to John Ward, Vere embarked on a fresh building scheme.

Though the general standard of school building had greatly improved, many black spots still remained, as the following extract, written to Vere in 1880 by a teacher in Co Mayo, shows:

> I have this day an attendance of 253 pupils in a school 36 x 18 ft., and I can honestly say that they are very much in need of food and clothing . . . I need not point out to you how injurious it is to the health of both teachers and pupils to have so many human beings together in so small a space.[9]

With the help of the National Board, Vere made a list of 619 schools conducted in unsuitable premises and offered 'to subscribe £30 towards the small local balance required to entitle each [of them] to building grants from the National Board'.* In his circular to managers announcing this offer,[10] and naming the six hundred odd schools he was willing to assist, he explains at

---

* The local contribution required by the Board towards erecting a school for 60 children was £75, for 75 children £83, and so on.

some length that while his publications had been 'a complete and unqualified success as far as the quantity sold is concerned' he had, nevertheless, owing to 'a disagreement between members of the firm who had for many years printed my books, and who had been up to that time my most intimate friends', decided to dispose of the whole concern for 'a sum considerably less' than he had put into it, and he now proposed 'to expend the proceeds, together with a further sum, in subscriptions towards the cost of building proper school-houses in poor rural districts throughout Ireland'. While the sum at his disposal would not be sufficient to cover quite all the 619 buildings, applications would be considered as they were received, and all applications should be made before June 1881. It seems probable that he was prepared to spend something in the neighbourhood of sixteen or seventeen thousand pounds on this project! Vere stipulated that the schools thus aided should be vested in the Commissioners of National Education, but he added this pregnant footnote: 'In those few Dioceses in which the Bishop does not permit acceptance of the National Board's building grants, I am willing to waive the condition as to Vesting.'

If anyone is disposed to 'write off' Vere Foster as a kindly, well-intentioned, benevolent person, whose life—unassailed by the world's temptations—was an uneventful sequence of good works, let him pause to consider the unspectacular courage required to forego willingly, and for the benefit of others, a fundamental and widely publicised principle—a courage enhanced in this case by the solitariness in which the mental struggle was conducted by a man naturally sociable, headstrong, and violently impatient of sectarianism or of anything that raised barriers between human beings. Vere's dream for the advancement of nation wide education—the dearest ambition of his life—rested on the acceptance of two essential concepts—financial assistance from local rates as well as national taxes, and the working together of all classes and creeds on a non-denominational basis, typified by the vesting of schools in the Commissioners of National Education. Everyone in the educational world knew that these were the principles he

M

stood for and had fought for with unremitting tenacity. We have seen how he had had to accept the refusal by teachers of the first principle*—a refusal that meant also the repudiation of all that Vere could give them in the way of leadership and counsel at the very moment when he had raised them to a point of unprecedented self-confidence and prestige, and which forced him to relinquish his most important public commitment. Now three years later, with a dignity and a poignancy that no sensitive person can fail to appreciate, he voluntarily renounced, in certain circumstances, the second principle. There is no hint or suggestion as to how the decision was reached. As he sat in his Belfast lodging, making his lists and visualising in his mind's eye districts all over Ireland with wretched little schools into which children were still being herded, he realised that if the need was to be met, if as many children as possible were to be helped, either he or the bishops would have to give way. Never, never had he asked anyone to do anything that he would not face up to himself, so without one recriminating remark, the words were penned : 'In those few dioceses . . . I am willing to waive the condition as to Vesting.' It was perhaps the most magnanimous action of his life; and there was now no one at all to commend it, no one, perhaps, even to understand how much it meant. But renunciation is not synonymous with defeat.

Unfortunately it has not been possible to trace the results of this scheme with any accuracy, but the gratitude of the parish priest from Swinford, Co Mayo gives some indication of how it was received. He writes :

> Many thanks for your cheque £40 to hand this morning, towards the building of the new Schools at Callow. I was very fortunate to begin building them at the time I did, as the Bishop wont allow priests for the future to undertake the building of vested schools.

Then listing the six schools he has been instrumental in erecting in the parish within the last eight years, he continues :

* See p 174.

Of course I could not think of undertaking the building of so many schools without your substantial cooperation & aid. Your subscriptions were so liberal that you always enticed me to go on with the good work, and enabled me to overcome difficulties. I must therefore feel for ever grateful to you.

The letter concludes with this significant PS :

Only this morning I got the order form from the Board of Works that I can go on with the building of T. Residence at Killesser, to be built on the School Plot.[11]

Vere was fifty-nine when he launched this scheme.

Time and again, as one follows his remarkable story one longs for the personal letters, the intimate touches that enrich our knowledge of the Earl-Bishop, of Lady Elizabeth Foster, and of Sir Augustus Foster. In Vere's case there is so little, so desperately little, that one lays tenacious hold on any fragment that remains. Is it, for example, too fanciful to read into the reference [in the above-mentioned circular to managers*] to the disagreement between those, 'who up to that time had been my most intimate friends' a pathetic indication of how much the friendship with the Ward brothers had really meant to Vere, a perhaps unrecognised longing for sympathy that could not be denied expression even in a formal circular? The role of the pioneer and leader can be very lonely. For all his independence where there moments of bitter isolation? In a short note, accepting an invitation to dinner from a prominent Belfast citizen who sympathised with many of Vere's interests, he writes : 'I keep early hours and do not go to dinner *parties*, but shall be much pleased to make the acquaintance of your son and his wife.'[12] One recalls his father's remark of thirty years earlier, 'Vere all gaiety in London', and the praise earned on the voyage to Buenos Aires for 'his good humour and agreeableness'. Why, one wonders, had life become quite so lonely?

There is however this delightfully happy picture. With that deep personal interest in all that affected anyone who crossed his

* See p 185.

path Vere, on hearing of the death of the father of a young Cork girl who had gained a prize in his drawing competition, immediately wondered what could be done to assist the orphaned family. The girl obviously had talent, John Ward was persuaded to offer her work in his illuminating department, and up she came from Cork. In due course she married the head engraver, John Vinycomb, and to their home on the shores of Belfast Lough Vere was ever welcome. Members of the family[13] still living recall his eagerly anticipated Sunday visits, when the old 'humour and agreeableness' delighted both children and parents. When a baby daughter was named Vera in his honour, Vere gave her one of his few remaining treasures, a little silver measure that had belonged to his grandmother Elizabeth, Duchess of Devonshire. One is thankful for that glimpse of real, natural happiness.

Writing of him after his death someone who had known Vere well described him thus :

> He was courtesy and geniality themselves. Endowed with no inconsiderable fund of humour, gifted with great natural intelligence, an excellent raconteur of the good things garnered in a very wide experience of the world of men, he was indeed a charming companion. His contact with the world left him quite unspoiled, his genuine kindliness pervaded his whole character.[14]

What a vivid glimpse of lovable personality—one only wishes there were more.

II

Emigration Again

In 1879 Ireland was facing another crisis. After several bad har- ~~the appaling tale of evictions was repeated, it is said that between~~ vests the potato crop failed in that year as it had not failed since the Great Famine. Once again starvation threatened. Once again the appalling tale of evictions was repeated, it is said that between 1874 and 1880 more than ten thousand families were turned out of their homes.[1] Such legislation as had been enacted since 1848 to grapple with the problem of land tenure had made little impact on the lamentable situation. The Encumbered Estates Act of 1849 had facilitated selling, but the new landlords were in most cases less sympathetic to the tenants than were their predecessors, and the two acts of 1860 which followed the Ulster Tenant Right Campaign failed to promote any general benefits. In 1870 a land act which owed much to Chichester Fortescue, the Chief Secretary, was introduced by Gladstone. It embodied the 'Ulster custom'* and a considerable degree of compensation for improvements, but unfortunately the severe agricultural depression of the 1870s rendered it largely ineffective.

Reactions to the crisis were various. Agrarian outrages increased in violence and in numbers and yet another Coercion Act

---

* A traditional arrangement between landlord and tenant, which gave to the tenant some measure of security and compensation.

reached the Statute Book. In 1877 Parnell became leader of the Irish Party at Westminster. In 1879 Michael Davitt, peasant-born advocate of land nationalisation, founded the Land League. In 1881 Gladstone introduced the first really effective land act, with its three 'F's'—fixity of tenure, fair rents, and freedom to sell. In 1882 Lord Frederick Cavendish, on whom so many high hopes were fixed, was murdered in Phoenix Park the day after he had arrived in Ireland to take up his duties as Chief Secretary; an act perpetrated by the Invincibles, the most violent of the subversive organisations. In 1886 William O'Brien inaugurated his 'Plan of Campaign' to withhold rents from extortionate landlords, and in that same year Lord Randolph Churchill made his famous anti-Home Rule speech in Belfast. In 1880 Vere Foster turned once again to emigration.

The first thing he did was to write, in January 1880, an open letter to Parnell, then in America collecting funds for the relief of distress in Ireland. In this long epistle Vere warmly supported the view that 'the prosperity and happiness of the people of Ireland would be greatly advanced by [a] large increase in the number of freehold properties in land'. He believed, however, that this should be achieved 'by the abolition of the laws of primogeniture and entail, and by the simplification of legal proceedings for the transfer of ownership of land', and was totally opposed to 'the course proposed by some theoretical enthusiasts —namely the compulsory purchase by Government of the estates of all landlords, and their subdivision among the present tenants, who would thereafter themselves become landlords'. If the present rent was burdensome, he argued, the necessarily increased rent covering the cost of purchase would be 'intolerable'. Still less did he approve of Parnell's constant advice to tenants not to pay exorbitant rents, keeping meanwhile 'a firm grip of their holdings'. This 'calculated invalidating of contracts' could only result in 'pandemonium', and

> it is quite inconsistent with your position in society as a legislator, for lawmakers should not be inciters to lawbreaking. While however, I dissent from compulsory dispossession . . . and from social

disorder, I desire to invite your attention to assisted emigration as the most practical and certain mode of, not only temporarily but permanently, relieving the present poverty and ever-recurring distress in the West of Ireland . . . It is unstatesmanlike and cruel to the poor to contravene the laws of nature by decrying emigration as some people do.

After referring very briefly to his own work in this connection 'between twenty and thirty years ago', the letter continues :

I am now too old to resume the necessary labour, but I believe that, if you would apply your acknowledged talents and influence to solicitation of public subscriptions, and to organising a scheme of assisted emigration to the Western States of America and to Canada, you might be eminently successful in conferring lasting benefits on great numbers of poor people whose normal state is ever verging on starvation . . . In proof of my sincerity, I hereby express my willingness to subscribe towards the proposed Emigration Fund at the rate of £2 for each young man or woman between eighteen and thirty-five years of age, in the proportion of one of the former to two of the latter, because, as men earn higher wages than women, they are usually better able to provide for themselves. This offer to hold good until the end of the present year, and not to exceed £15,000 in all, and to be paid by me in instalments as may be hereafter arranged on information reaching me from yourself or your agent of the embarkation of each such emigrant from the province of Connaught or from the counties of Donegal, Clare, Kerry or Cork, with particulars of name, age, and parish.

As always every detail was worked out. The letter was printed in *The Northern Whig* and afterwards distributed widely.

As for Parnell; the Irish leader, Vere said, 'simply ridiculed my suggestion of assisting emigration on a magnificent scale from the smaller Ireland of Europe to the greater Ireland of America, and struck out for himself the path of political agitation which he has since pursued'. From the few comments that remain one gathers that Vere Foster, at any rate, did not succumb to the spell of 'The Uncrowned King'. Political agitation might go on, Michael Davitt might add thousands to his Land League, the Irish Party at Westminster might continue its course of obstruction and keep the House sitting continuously for hours on end, but meanwhile the Irish peasant starved, and *that* was what mattered to Vere. 'Old' though he might think he was [he was only sixty-one], he had now no alternative but to resume the 'necessary labour' himself, and embark on what was perhaps the most 'magnificent' enterprise of his life. 'I fell back on my own resources, and determined to carry out alone, to the best of my ability, the suggestion which I had made to Mr Parnell.'[2]

Where the money was to come from Heaven alone knew—not a penny of the copy-book profits was diverted from education schemes. Vere launched an immense begging project.[3] Appeals were posted to everyone from the Princess of Wales downwards, but the response was pitifully meagre, and it would appear that at this point he prepared to sacrifice what remained of his own capital. From now there are references to his lack of personal funds. In 1885 he begs Lady Spencer to ask her husband, then Lord Lieutenant, to speed up, if possible, the final hearing of the Ward lawsuit, as his income 'is less than £60 a year',[4] and writing to another correspondent he remarks, 'I have run down my funds so that I have to live after the quietest fashion at home without any travelling, and therefore do not expect to visit Dublin again, unless when absolutely necessary. Indeed I would be very glad of any employment as agent for an emigration society or otherwise.'[4a] The suggestion about employment may or may not have been written in jest, but it was perfectly obvious that Vere was limiting himself to a trifling income, while spending lavishly in other directions.

But again we are faced with a lamentable lack of private correspondence : there are a few circulars, bundle upon bundle of applications for help from practically every parish priest in the west of Ireland,[5] but no private letters. There are, it is true, two bundles of letters—one containing affirmative replies to the begging circular, the other, much larger, composed of regretful notes from those unable to respond. The clerical work was enormous; every letter and application was numbered and dated in his own clear hand. By 1882 applications for help had reached 24,000.

No small wonder that when giving evidence to the Select Committee on Land Laws (Ireland) in 1882, Vere remarked that 'having received such an immense number of letters I cannot leave home'.* The years in the Audit Office, the experience of a diplomatic attaché, all contributed their share towards this amazing order and achievement, which was not rendered easier by a recurring, very painful eye condition, a legacy of the *Washington* voyage. One is staggered by the magnitude of this single-handed undertaking.

As well as falling back on his own resources Vere also fell back on his long association with education. To every teacher in Connaught, and in the counties of Kerry, Clare, and Donegal, and to every clergyman, both Catholic and Protestant, in those areas, he sent a circular outlining his scheme, the financial aid he was prepared to contribute and the qualifications to be fulfilled. He met with 'immediate co-operation'.[6]

Because of limited funds, and also on a point of policy, aid was restricted exclusively to young women between eighteen and thirty. 'I give preference to girls, because they are the least able to get themselves out, and because, as I say, they are generally the most liberal in sending home help to bring out their brothers and sisters and parents, if they wish to go.'[7] Every applicant must receive a testimonial from her clergyman as to her character and her inability to emigrate 'without assistance from Mr Foster'.[8] It was no longer necessary, as in the old days, to give instructions about the voyage, there was no need now to provide information about employment, every Irish family had its representative in America : only the devastating poverty remained unaltered. The parish priest from Achill wrote : 'I could from my soul wish that something was done for this most wretched place. There is

* In the Report of his Writing, Drawing and Painting Competitions for 1881, when there were over 1,000 entrants from some 400 schools in 72 countries, Vere explains that 'The Examination was unavoidably delayed this year in consequence of my time having been almost entirely taken up with an overwhelming amount of correspondence on the subject of assisted emigration from the distressed districts of the West of Ireland, the busiest season for which is during the months of April, May, and June.'

scarcely any use in saying it, but it is unfortunately most true
that since 1847 there was not such want and destitution felt
in this parish.'[9] And another from Galway : 'I say with all the
energy of my existence, let the people leave in any and every
way that may take them out of the slough of poverty and misery
in which they are at present sunk.'[9]

Vere's plan was to issue vouchers for £2 to approved appli-
cants, 'leaving the persons assisted quite free to proceed by any
line of steamers that might best suit their own convenience from
any port in Ireland or England to any port in America, the
vouchers not being transferable, and being payable by me direct
to the steamship companies only at their head office, after receipt
of the company's certificates of the embarkation of the passengers,
and of their presentation to them of the vouchers before such
embarkation'.[10] Agents for the chief shipping lines were found
in all the market-towns—very often they were school teachers.
The great increase in shipping made competition for emigrant
patronage keen, companies at slack periods might charge Mr
Foster £1 for a voucher worth £2.

The surge of applications poured into the Belfast address, one
parish priest writing, 'I am besieged from morning to night, and
if I do not forward these applications to you I will have no
peace'.[11]

In the middle of it all Vere decided in 1881 to go to America
—partly to appeal for funds and partly to investigate employment prospects in Canada and the States. Gratuitous first-class
accommodation awaited him on the Cunard liner of his choice,
all was ready for his departure including the detailed circular
appealing to the American public for funds, 'when I received
yesterday afternoon a summons to appear for cross-examination
in a Chancery suit which, after the manner of Chancery, has
been pending for upwards of three years* . . . I will therefore
post, instead of carrying, my circular, and will follow as soon as
possible.'[12]

A certain amount of information regarding this visit has been

---

* The Marcus Ward case.

preserved in a lecture which Vere delivered to the Mutual Improvement Association of the Rosemary Street Non-Subscribing Presbyterian Church in Belfast.[13] From the moment that he 'folded up his umbrella on leaving Belfast' the sun shone physically and metaphorically. For him America had still its exhilarating attraction. All the old sociability returned. Sir Charles and Lady Tupper were among the passengers. Sir Charles was Minister of Railways in Canada—helpful advice and free rail tickets were lavishly bestowed. In spite of first-class travel Vere 'had no more luggage that I could carry in my hand' and on arrival at Quebec 'was first to get clear of the Customs'. Contact was immediately made with the Minister of Agriculture, J. H. Pope. The Canadian Government offered generous assistance to families prepared to settle on the land, but Vere did not consider the scheme suitable for Irish emigrants who naturally preferred the United States, where their relatives were already established, and he had found by long experience that the Irish peasant, though raised on the land, resisted all efforts to settle him in undeveloped country, choosing instead to congregate in towns and join the hordes of manual workers in great industrial enterprises. Moreover, the emigration of whole families did not appeal to Vere, he was not anxious to depopulate the country, to rob her of her 'bone and sinew'. Assisted female emigration he regarded as a practical and quick means of relieving poverty, but no emigration was 'a panacea for the prevailing distress'—it did not cure the cause. All along he advocated a vast increase in freehold proprietors, to the extent that three-fourths of the population would be owners of the land, so that 'through security of tenure, more careful cultivation, reclamation of waste lands, and spread of manufactures, the soil of Ireland would be able to contain more than its present population in comfort and independence, instead of in gradations ranging, as now, from excessive wealth to hopeless poverty and destitution'.[14] When these essential reforms had been carried out—'when there is enough employment at home they will not go, the thing [emigration] will find its own level'.[15]

In the midst of travelling hither and thither in the interests of his work, Vere permitted himself one 'errand of curiosity'—he seized the opportunity of boarding at Pile of Bones (now Regina) —the construction train actually engaged upon pushing westwards the track for the Canadian Pacific Railway. For three days, sharing the comfortless conditions of the workmen, he watched, with indescribable interest and pleasure, the laying of a great railroad. One is glad for this interlude of sheer delight, for it was in such enterprises, in tasks of such magnitude, that Vere found satisfaction. Anything that would enlarge man's horizon, that would make available the boundless gifts and opportunities of nature, he grasped with both hands. In any age or sphere he could have been a great adventurer—unfolding the secrets of nature, discovering new paths for humanity; that he harnessed all that urge, that immense creative instinct, to the selfless pursuit of the welfare of Irish peasants is the measure of his greatness.

He then turned towards the United States. Developments in the American cities fascinated him : the 'enormous height of immense numbers of new stores, rendered practicable by the extensive use of steam elevators', 'the practice which is introduced of heating houses by means of central furnaces', the vast stockyard in Chicago where 10,000 hogs and 4,000 cattle were slaughtered daily by humane means, the hogs being 'slid along to the dissecting room, where they are cut up and packed in pieces in barrels before the sound of their last squeak has died away in the spectator's ears'. He was away from Belfast for eight weeks. With that habitual care for detail he noted that he had travelled 6,000 miles by sea and more than 6,000 miles on land and that thanks to the generosity of the shipping and railroad companies and to the hospitality of friends the whole wonderful trip had cost less than £25. 'When I got back again to Belfast I unrolled my umbrella !'

Both at home and abroad there was constant opposition to emigration. Irish-American antagonism was voiced by—among others—the Irishman John Boyle O'Reilly, editor of the *Boston Pilot*. As a young private in the 10th Hussars, O'Reilly had been implicated in the Fenian movement and had been transported to Australia, from whence he had escaped, penniless, to America. He was befriended by Horace Greeley in Boston, and years ago Vere had met him as a reporter on the Staff of the *Pilot*. Now, as one of the most important American editors, Vere made a special journey to Boston to solicit his support for an appeal for funds. But O'Reilly, for whom, writes Vere,

> independent of his political opinions, I have the greatest respect and admiration, frankly informed me that he would give me all the opposition in his power, and that I might feel assured the rest of the Irish-American and Irish Press would do the same, because it was felt that there was a rooted desire and design in the minds of the British Government and Imperial Parliament to banish the Irish people from Ireland in order to substitute English colonists in their place. I endeavoured to persuade my friend O'Reilly that such a theory was arrant nonsense, and reasoned with him as to the cruelty of putting difficulties in the way of assistance to poor people to emigrate from the barren and notoriously overcrowded districts of the West of Ireland to the unoccupied and practically unlimited fertile regions of the United States and Canada, but to no purpose, so I returned by the next train to New York.[16]

It is sad to report that appeals to *The New York Tribune, The New York Times, The New York Herald*, and *The Toronto Mail*,[17] also failed to bring any response.

In Ireland the Land League and a section of the Nationalist Party were also opposed to emigration on the grounds that it provided for Britain a too easy means of avoiding responsibility for improving conditions in Ireland, though in practice opposition was directed against family emigration, and not against Vere's schemes for individuals. These political parties offered such remedies as nationalisation of land, enforced selling of estates, withholding of excessive rents, migration within Ireland, and increased employment. As regards the Church, the parish clergy accepted emigration as the best immediate solution for the devastating distress, but the hierarchy were by no means favourably inclined. In 1883 C. T. Redington of the Local Government Board informed Vere that he had been obliged to contradict a

statement made by Dr Logue,* the Roman Catholic Bishop of
Raphoe, 'before a number of priests and laymen', to the effect
that Mr Foster's scheme was subsidised by the government. The
bishop asserted in reply 'that he believed the Govt. were capable
of helping on secretly the emigration of Irish people' but, wrote
Mr. Redington, he 'would consider any statement you made on
the subject conclusive'—a striking testimony to Catholic confidence in Vere's integrity.[17a]

In 1884 a long article appeared in *The Nineteenth Century*
from the pen of Miss Charlotte O'Brien† who had made a visit to
the United States to see for herself the conditions in the large
cities. She vividly described the moral and physical degradation
of the slum areas of New York, into which thousands of Irish
emigrants sooner or later gravitated, and deplored the encouragement of extensive emigration, mentioning 'Mr Vere Foster's
system of assisting single girls to emigrate'. In a spirited comment Vere defended his policy, showing that all his girls went
with the knowledge of their parish clergyman, and that the vast
majority of them were assured of help from relatives on arrival.
He failed to see why girls, 'on whose behalf the clergy plead for
assistance, should be denied the opportunity to emigrate in order
to better their condition', and considered this 'sweeping denunciation without quotation of a single instance in its support' to be
entirely undeserved. 'I must protest,' he concluded, 'that I am
not "without the slightest knowledge of the world" and that I
am not devoid of common sense.'‡[18] Did the memory of much
earlier accusations rise before him? Had he not from the very
beginning crusaded against the pitfalls of emigration schemes un-
attended by the necessary advice and assistance regarding employment, living conditions and so forth? Had he not preached
day in and day out against the folly of congregating in the sea-
ports? Had he not himself conveyed his emigrants far into the

* Later Cardinal Logue.

† A niece of William Smith O'Brien. She made the voyage in the steerage
class of an emigrant ship.

‡ Whilst refuting the allegations, Vere acknowledged that he had a great
respect for Miss O'Brien.

interior? The article is interesting as indicating the manifold misrepresentations that must have assailed him.

Over a long period Vere was much concerned about the whole question of land tenure in Ireland, attributing to the existing system the roots of Irish discord and unhappiness. Among his papers there is a notebook in which a systematic study of the problem is recorded.[19] Separate pages are devoted to such topics as reduction of rent in bad seasons, leases, improvements, compensation for disturbance, sub-letting and goodwill, with notes on the relevant position obtaining in every country in Europe and in many of the American states, evidence in itself of very concentrated study. Moreover, from scattered replies to letters, dating from 1870 onwards and particularly round 1883, it is clear that Vere informed many influential people of his views.[20] In February 1886 he wrote what appears to be a second letter to Mr Gladstone, the draft of which he preserved. After declaring politely that he had 'the highest admiration' for the Prime Minister's 'great genius and many noble qualities', he continues :

> I feel bound to express my dissent from much of the policy which you have pursued towards Ireland, and from the policy which you are popularly credited as intending to pursue . . . I object to the confiscatory clauses of the Land Act as an organised system of statutory public robbery of one class, and that all loyalists, who have acquired their property honestly . . . under the laws of their country, for the benefit of another class, whom, as being disaffected to Imperial rule, it is desired to conciliate. . .
>
> It is admitted on all hands that the land question is at the bottom of the existing discontent and agitation. I believe there can be no complete solution of that question, and no general cessation of discontent and dangerous political agitation, till there shall have been a wholesale multiplication of the number of Irish landlords.[21]

He then states his theory that state purchase, if fair, would be too costly, whereas a modification of the law of inheritance to provide that all property of deceased persons shall be divided equally amongst the next of kin would be simple, inexpensive and 'least injurious'.

Regarding the future policy 'popularly credited' to Mr Gladstone, namely Home Rule, Vere again expresses dissent, 'but,' he writes, 'as the loyalist population of Ulster may be expected to make itself unmistakenly and effectively heard in opposition, I think it superfluous to offer any remarks upon it at present, except that I believe one of the results of its realization would be a bloody Civil War between different portions of the Irish People, and between Great Britain and Ireland'.

Copies of this letter were circulated to the Lord Lieutenant, the Duke of Argyll, Lord Hartington, Lord Granville, James Bryce, George Otto Trevelyan, and others.

Vere's comments on Home Rule are interesting. Vehemently as he had so often denounced the long history of corrupt British rule in Ireland the remedy, as he saw it, lay not in separate nationalism, but in a 'more perfect union'.* The world for him was already becoming an integrated unit, distance was shrinking; the steamship, the railways, the 'electric telegraph' had seen to that. Ireland must take her place as part of the British Empire, the nearest approach to the concept of world government so far achieved. Writing to Lady Aberdeen a few months later he declares again that Home Rule for Ireland would mean civil war, 'but,' he continues, 'the establishment of 4 Provincial Parliaments in Ireland & of 2 in Scotland, and the restoration of the heptarchy in England and Wales might be most desirable, each such Parliament or Council to possess functions similar to those of a State in America or a Province in Canada'.[22]

In a lecture on *Land Tenure in Many Countries* given to the Mutual Improvement Society of the Unitarian Church in Belfast in 1884, Vere once more reiterated his own solution, namely the simplification of procedures for selling and transferring land, and the modification of the laws of inheritance.[23] Increased employment would certainly bring vast benefits, and instead of 'inciting to, or legalizing, robbery and ruin of present owners', which was Vere's interpretation of the 1883 Land Act, the government could do much by supporting land reclamation, developing

* See p 143.

fisheries, opening mines, extending railways and so forth. But, he declared, 'while the grass grows the steed may starve', and assisted emigration of individuals remained, in his view, the most practical, immediate form of relief.[24] Nearly a socialist though Vere was in so many respects, when it came to the rights of ownership and sanctity of legal contracts he was an ardent supporter of orthodox stability. He who had so often spoken of the responsibilities of ownership now acclaimed its rights : the advice of 'theoretical enthusiasts' was 'mischievious [and] calculated to sap the foundations of civilised society by invalidating all contract . . . It would if followed inaugurate a pandemonium.'

In the summer of 1882 Vere gave evidence to the Select Committee on Land Laws in Ireland, the Cairns committee, regarding the poverty that necessitated emigration. Because of the almost total lack of any direct record of how Vere expressed himself, the verbatim reports of this evidence, and of his evidence during the law case, are of great interest. His answers to questions are clear and forthright, with all the force of understatement, and give a far more vivid impression of a commanding personality than does the rather verbose reporting of his educational speeches in the *Irish Teachers' Journal* or his own long-winded notices. At the conclusion of one of the Marcus Ward trials the Master of the Rolls congratulated him on the clarity of his evidence, and his answers to the questions put by the Select Committee show his complete grasp of every aspect of Irish distress. One realises from these comparatively few spoken words how confident Vere was in himself, how he inspired confidence in others, and such replies as the following illustrate the compassion and understanding born of years of the closest contact with poverty and want : 'I do not see how the poor people in the West of Ireland could get sufficient food for themselves and families even if they paid no rent at all.'[25] And, answering a suggestion that the clergy were concerned only for the spiritual welfare of their people. 'They sympathise thoroughly with the poor creatures, and desire to help the poor people in their parishes; and my correspondence being private is much more

honest than it otherwise would be. I can have greater satisfaction
in carrying it on privately than I could have if I were to carry it
on publicly.'[26]

One gets the impression that Vere, because of his unattached
—yet acknowledged—position in the country, enjoyed the confidence of clergy and people. Emphasising to the Select Committee
the necessity of dissociating any emigration scheme from political
or religious motives, he said, 'I have kept perfectly clear of any
political system and I have the co-operation of the clergy of every
denomination'.[27] He was convinced, and remained convinced, in
spite of anything that might be said to the contrary, that his
plan of assisting individual girls was the right one in the given
situation. Incredible though it may appear these activities in connection with land tenure, Select Committees, and so forth, were
undertaken in addition to the great emigration scheme. The Vic-
torians had a prodigious capacity for hard work!

In the autumn of 1882 there was another visit to America.

Meanwhile applications poured in and funds were exhausted.
Appeals were sent out in the spring and autumn of 1883. The first
showed that since 1880, 17,000 girls had been helped at a cost to
Vere of £24,000; by August the number had risen to 18,000.
The circulars included a list of more than one thousand clergy,
Catholic and Protestant, who had applied for help together with
the number of girls from each parish who had been assisted, and
more than one hundred extracts from letters depicting the
urgency of the need. This, for example, from the parish priest at
Clifden:

> The holdings are so small, the land so sterile, that these people
> will be always steeped in poverty . . . I wish to God half the
> people of this barren territory would emigrate somewhere. Penal
> servitude would be a paradise to many of them compared to their
> present condition . . .[28]

But neither that, nor dozens of other equally heartrending cries,
brought in the needed money. Much against his will, Vere was
persuaded to modify his scheme. A contributor offered him £100,
with the promise of a further £400, if he would give his aid, not

as a gift but as a loan to be repaid within one year. 'I have hesitated to do so,' Vere wrote in the explanatory circular, 'because my object being to help not only the girls but their parents and other members of their families, I have found that object in almost all cases faithfully and affectionately carried out.' But having spent all that had been placed at his disposal, and all but a pittance of his private funds, he accepted the offer.[29] For some reason the scheme was not successful, and in 1886, with extraordinary persistence Vere issued another appeal for the fantastic sum of £300,000 to enable him 'to change for the better the prospects of at least 100,000 poor girls'.[30] We do not know how much he received, but three years later, 'having exhausted all my own capital', he asked for another one thousand pounds, which 'prudently expended would ensure the emigration of about 500 honest poor girls'.[31]

It should be noted in passing that Vere Foster was not the only person concerned at this period with large scale emigration. Colonel King-Harman, an extensive and benevolent landowner in Longford, acted on behalf of the *New York Herald* Relief Fund which was mainly concerned with assisting whole families. James A. Tuke, the English Quaker who in 1846–47 had assisted W. E. Forster in relief work sponsored by the Society of Friends in England, was again in Ireland, this time on behalf of a committee, of which the Duke of Bedford was president, for aiding family emigration from the West. Neither of these gentlemen worked single-handed and both were distributing publicly collected funds. Vere did not co-operate with either of these schemes, though in giving evidence to the Cairns Committee Mr Tuke said it would be 'impossible to ever estimate the value of his [Mr Foster's] noble work'.[32] Tuke experienced considerable opposition from the clergy.

By the 1890s the demand for female labour in the United States was lessening, and legislation requiring that all emigrants should come possessed of some small capital virtually ended assisted emigration to the States.

Owing to the complete lack of anything but the scrappiest

financial records it is impossible to assess with accuracy the total amount of money involved in Vere's emigration schemes. In his final appeal he states that between 1849 and 1889 he had assisted 22,615 emigrants, of which more than 20,000 had left Ireland between 1880 and 1887. Allowing £2 for each person one arrives at a figure over £45,000 but this is much too low for a total outlay, for between 1849 and 1857 passages, equipment, and clothing were paid in full at a cost of £7 or £8 per person, for the 2,000 odd he sent out in those years. It would appear that £55,000 would be a conservative estimate for his total expenditure. From such subscription lists as remain £3,000 appears to be the total amount collected, and of this £1,500 was contributed by Frederick; we can only conclude that the balance came from his own pocket. At no time did Vere receive one penny of government aid.

That one man, subject to recurring ill-health, should have organised and financed these great emigration schemes in every minute detail and carried them through single-handed was a remarkable feat, and would of itself have entitled Vere Foster to a place of lasting honour in the annals of his country. That within the same period he built and repaired many hundreds of national schools at a cost which it is not possible even vaguely to estimate, launched his copy-book enterprise and transformed the teaching body from a condition of disorganised depression to full professional status, raises his achievement beyond ordinary comprehension.

What we do know for certain is that by 1890 Vere had reduced himself to penury. Writing in that year to the father of the little Vera* to acknowledge a subscription to the Belfast Royal Hospital he says :

> I have undertaken [the collection] this time because I love the work and need the pay, which is £100, as I have not so much of my own, either as income or capital.[33]

He was in receipt of an annuity of £50 from his great-nephew,

* See p 188.

his lodgings became progressively humbler, when he died ten years later his assets were valued at £178 8s 6d. 'Such are the men,' wrote Arthur Young of an earlier Foster, 'to whom monarchs should decree their honours, and nations erect their statues.'

Vere's tasks were not yet completed.

12

The Two Duchesses

Ever since his nephew, John Frederick Foster, had settled in Glyde Court, Ardee, Vere was glad to stay there from time to time, and a room was permanently set aside for his use. At some date, probably in the middle 1890s, he had, to quote his own words, 'access to a mass of family correspondence of which I was previously unaware'.[1] This was, in fact, a collection of letters that passed between the Bishop of Derry and his wife and their daughter Elizabeth, between Elizabeth and John Thomas Foster, and between Elizabeth and her son Augustus.

We have no idea how much family history Vere already knew. Lawrence's portrait of his grandmother, then Lady Elizabeth Foster, hung on the walls of Glyde Court—he may have vaguely remembered seeing her in England in 1821 when he was little more than two years old. Was he aware, until he unfolded these treasured letters, of the real relationship between her and Georgiana and the Duke? The mid-nineteenth century was very reticent about irregular family happenings; Augustus may not have told him, we learn nothing from Vere himself. After all that had happened in the intervening hundred years, surely it was a curious turn of events that caused Elizabeth Foster's grandson to pore over the record of her unhappy marriage within a stone's throw of the rectory at Dunleer? Furthermore, it was only now that Vere learned of his father's attachment to Annabella Milbanke, and 'it came to my knowledge as a surprise'.[2]

From this wealth of material Vere, assisted by a great-niece, set himself to compile the first record of the now famous friendship between Elizabeth and Georgiana, Duchess of Devonshire, which he published under the title of *The Two Duchesses*. The book is not particularly well put together, much of the correspondence that might have been used is discreetly omitted, some not very relevant letters from the Earl-Bishop and others are included, but it will always be noteworthy as the first authentic narrative concerning 'these two ladies [who] were inseparable companions'.

The book was an immediate success, a considerable achievement for a man of seventy-eight. In a letter to Lord Erne, dated February 1898,[3] Vere states that he has just given orders for the printing of a second edition—'the favourable reception of the book by the universal press having exceeded my most sanguine anticipation'; the date of the first edition is December 1897. As usual he had gone to infinite pains to ensure accuracy. Lord Bristol had been very helpful but, he tells Lord Erne, 'I have been unable to get *any* information from the present Duke of Devonshire about the Duchess Georgiana'.[4]

One imagines that he was much gratified with this success. In a strange way Vere was more family-conscious than either of his brothers. Years earlier, amid the demands of emigration, of education, copy-books, and teachers, he had found time to compile for his two nephews a genealogical table, tracing their Foster lineage to Antenor, King of the Cimmerians, 443 BC! He had found all this in the library of the then Queen's College, Belfast.[5] Perhaps as he read the copious and enthusiastic reviews of *The Two Duchesses*, which were all carefully dated and pasted into a book, he felt that, bachelor though he was, he had done something to perpetuate the family glory.

Though his financial interest in the copy-books had long since ended he maintained a happy relationship with Blackie & Sons, now the printers and publishers, and publishers of *The Two*

Duchesses. The following tale, preserved in the Blackie family probably relates to this period. Mr Walter W. Blackie, a junior partner in the firm, being in Belfast on business, called upon Vere and found him in bed obviously very ill. 'A nearby table was covered with envelopes, each containing a cheque, and each addressed to some cause or protégé. He asked Walter W. to do up the envelopes and post them, but when it was suggested that he should see a doctor, Vere Foster replied, "Oh no. I can't afford a doctor".' In the end Mr Blackie insisted and after a great deal of persuasion Vere allowed himself to be taken to the hospital with which he had been so long and closely connected.[6]

The Two Duchesses was indeed Vere's final assignment, but in spite of failing health, increasing age and self-imposed poverty, he was still working.

In 1898 he compiled his preface to the printed prospectus for the *Vere Foster Twenty-Ninth Annual Competition in Writing, Drawing, Lettering and Painting*, giving the names of more than five hundred prize-winners from all over the world and the addresses of their schools.[7]

In 1896 the Annual Congress of the Irish National Teachers' Organisation met in Belfast. Vere was an honoured guest and invited to address the members. In spite of his break with the teachers he had always kept in touch with educational affairs and in his speech he urged that payments for results should be abolished, some way being found to recompense the female teachers, who would suffer most from loss of earnings. Twenty years earlier he had opposed this method of payment, and he still opposed it though now on the grounds that 'it encouraged mediocrity and discouraged excellence'—to Vere two intolerable evils.

To the very end the Royal Hospital in Belfast claimed his services : only a few months before his death 'on Hospital Saturday . . . the octagenarian was seated in Donegall Place [the main thoroughfare of the city] holding forth a plate to receive subscriptions'.[8]

Ever alive to new ways of helping those in need, one of his

last donations was £5 towards the recently established Day Nursery in Belfast for the children of working mothers.

He died on 21 December 1900, in Belfast, in his eighty-second year.* No public funeral was arranged; city dignitaries, anxious to pay a belated tribute of respect and admiration, followed the simple cortège to the City Cemetery, but it was in the hearts of the poor that he was most deeply mourned.†

'He would deserve to be called a prince of philanthropists,' declared the writer of an obituary notice. 'It will never be known what he gave away in charitable deeds . . . It would have been a pain to him not to give.'[9] Once again he is likened to a prince.

His was the age of philanthropy. Changing social conditions in Britain at the close of the eighteenth century had brought to light the misery and degradation in which vast numbers of the population lived; older forms of charity had become totally inadequate, a new sense of public responsibility became evident; the great philanthropists appear, pioneers of the first order in their day.

But Vere Foster was more, far more than a philanthropist. Put him along side any of his renowned contemporaries in England, with Lord Shaftesbury for example, or with Florence Nightingale, and instantly a new dimension is apparent. No one questions the magnitude of their achievements nor the sincerity of their purpose, but in whatever they did they remained anchored to the social position in which they had been born, secure in wealth, and fortified by the love and affection of intimate friends. Vere Foster renounced all of these.

---

* During the last months he was prevailed upon to allow a great-niece to come and nurse him.

† In 1956 the Irish National Teachers' Organisation placed a plaque to the memory of Vere Foster on No 115 Great Victoria Street, Belfast, where he had lived for some time. In 1967 a committee, representative of citizens in Northern Ireland and the Republic of Ireland, raised by public subscription a memorial fund which was used to endow in perpetuity seven gold medals to be awarded annually to a student in each of the seven Teacher Training Colleges in Ireland. More recently, a Primary School in Belfast and in Tallanstown, Co. Louth, have been named the Vere Foster School.

It is still more illuminating to place him amongst his contemporaries in Ireland.

He began his work in 1849, approximately fifty years after the Act of Union had changed the world for the Irish Protestant Ascendancy to which he belonged, leaving its members stripped of the paraphernalia of wealth and power which for centuries had been theirs. What prestige they still retained by reason of landed possessions, Mr Gladstone's Land Act was quickly to destroy. Yet, 'Anglo-Irish' though this section of the population of Ireland is called to describe the stock from whence it sprang, and to distinguish it from the other section—the 'native' Irish, it was essentially Irish. Furthermore, the roles of the two sections were in process of being reversed. While the ascendancy was being remorselessly forced back from its entrenched position of authority, Catholic emancipation and the extension of the franchise were giving to the 'native' Irish a political power which they had never before known. The Act of Union that was to end for ever dissention in this island served only to accentuate it, giving birth to a nationalism more fundamental and deep-rooted than had inspired the men of the 1780s.*

The history of the post-Union Anglo-Irish has still to be written; their reactions to this mighty change have not as yet been adequately chronicled. Some clung tenaciously to the old traditions, some left the country, others sought to identify themselves more completely and in quite new ways with the land which, for their love of her, they could not abandon. Thus it came about that it was the Anglo-Irish, sons of the former ascendancy, who provided, in the first half of the nineteenth century, the majority of the leaders in the struggle against England for national independence. Robert Emmet, Thomas Davis, Smith O'Brien,† Charles Stewart Parnell all belonged to Protestant Anglo-Irish families. O'Connell, the native Irish Catholic, stands out in solitary grandeur, though he was soon to be followed

* The United Irishmen, 1798, foreshadowed the nationalism of the nineteenth century.

† Smith O'Brien was, in fact, the Protestant descendant of an ancient native family.

by men from his own section. As the century wore on the former ascendancy gave renowned scholars to the study of ancient Irish culture and the revival of the Irish language, and world-famous leaders to the Irish Literary Revival. Dr Douglas Hyde, founder of the Gaelic League, and first President of the Irish Free State, Lady Gregory, Synge, and Yeats are of that great company.

Vere Foster chose a different path, a still more emphatic and decisive alignment with the national need, which, as he saw it, was social rather than political. He deliberately stepped outside all boundaries of class and creed. He renounced privilege in all its forms; he publicly forswore the ascendancy and all its doings,* he cut himself off from his natural friends and associates. Neither before him nor after him has any Anglo-Irishman identified himself so completely with the needs of the Irish peasant. (To the end of his life Parnell was, and acted as, an Irish landowner.)

Vere came endowed with great assets. Everything that nature, inheritance and a privileged upbringing had bestowed upon him was ceaselessly and entirely devoted to this national need, the need of the underprivileged Irish peasant. He not only renounced social position, wealth, and comfort, he consciously directed his great enjoyment of friendship, his passionate delight in travel and enterprise, his urge to explore and experiment, into such channels —and they were pretty restricted—as would contribute to his main purpose. No gleam of personal ambition was, for one moment, permitted to flicker across his horizon.

He had his failings. He was headstrong. He was intolerant of policies of which he did not approve and impatient of people who, he thought, should have known better, and he was not, perhaps, very co-operative with his equals.

He would never submit to limitations. We have seen how, in the early days, the discretion demanded of a diplomat proved insupportable in face of the need to expose oppression.† If anything had to be done there were, humanly speaking, no bounds to the exertions he would make. He gave, for example, *all* his

* See p 141.
† See p 38.

wealth. He worked alone. It could be argued that, had he been willing to submit to the restrictions imposed by co-operation, he might in the end have achieved even more. One thinks of the possibilities of a political career, and it is reasonable to suppose that this may have presented a very real attraction to Vere. He had all the necessary family influence, experience and ability; there is direct evidence of his interest in politics, firstly in Uruguay and then in Ireland in the 1860s. But political affiliation would have tied his hands, and he quickly realised that any connection with political movements in Ireland would only hamper his work. His statement to the Cairns Committee* that he had 'kept perfectly clear' of political systems may indeed indicate that a political career was something that had to be renounced. We do not know.

Neither do we know what he denied himself in the way of love and marriage. There is that one reference to the 'lady friend', who came to say farewell as he left for America in 1864.†

In the same brief diary, amongst notes of the few letters he appears to have written on that tour, are three or four entries as follows: 'Wrote to M.' In other cases full names are recorded. There are no grounds, except supposition, for equating the 'lady friend' with 'M', and there may be no justification for the supposition. The only thing we can be sure of is that Vere Foster dedicated himself entirely to his work, in various fields, for the Irish peasant. Anything that would deflect him from his chosen course was dismissed by that iron self-control and inflexible self-discipline. But above all there was his essential humility—a humility expressed not by a false depreciation of his great powers or by hesitating efforts at 'doing good', but rather by a total banishment of all thought of self that enabled him to undertake with equal zest the meanest task or the princely enterprise.

This way of life, for such it was, may indeed have been Vere's greatest achievement; all else followed from it. To explore it fully would involve incursions into realms beyond the scope of this

* See p 202.
† See p 122.

book. One cannot help, however, being deeply moved by such a manifestation of an essentially religious attitude to life by one who, as a result of deep thought, had dissociated himself from all religious affiliation.

Long ago his grandmother, the Duchess of Devonshire, wrote these lines to her son, Vere's father :

> . . . a really true enthusiastic mind will never want an object for its enthusiasm : you may be an enthusiast in friendship, an enthusiast in love, in the forming of one's character to the practice of every virtue and the fulfilling of every duty : and enthusiasm is in fact what, well directed, leads to the attainment of every virtue, and enables the possessor of it to walk out of the common track of common characters who rest satisfied with doing what is required of them, but never are equal to that most generous, most rare of all qualities *l'oubli de soi-même* : it leads also to a great indulgence for others, and a great severity to one's self.[10]

How right she was. For it was indeed this quality that enabled her grandson 'to fulfil every duty', to walk so resolutely 'out of the common track of common characters', and to exemplify with such dazzling brilliance that 'most rare' of all virtues, *l'oubli de soi-même*.

References

Abbreviations:

F.P.   =   Foster Papers (Private collection)
Devon Commission   =   Royal Commission on Law Practice in respect of Occupation of Land in Ireland, 1845
Powis Commission   =   Royal Commission of Inquiry into Primary Education (Ireland), 1870
N.I.P.R.O.   =   Northern Ireland Public Record Office
R.N. Educ.   =   Reports of Commissioners of National Education in Ireland
Nat. Lib. Ire.   =   National Library of Ireland
I.T.J.   =   *Irish Teachers' Journal*
E.B.   =   *The Earl Bishop.* Childe-Pemberton

Introduction
CHAPTER I, pp 13–26

1   F.P. Augustus Foster to the Duchess of Devonshire, 27.4.1819
1a ibid, Augustus Foster to the Duchess of Devonshire, 7.6.1819
2   Arthur Young. *Autobiography*, p 113
3   *Hist. Mss. Comm. Report 12, App. ix*, p 280. Donoughmore MSS. quoted, E.B., p 136
3a Mrs d'Arblay. *Diary and Letters.* 1876. vol 1
4   F.P. Lord Aberdeen to Augustus Foster, 22.9.1804
5   Vere Foster, *The Two Duchesses*, p 198
6   *William and Mary Quarterly*, April 1952. Third series, vol 9, no 2
7   F.P.
8   Vere Foster, *The Two Duchesses*, p 347
9   F.P. Lord Bristol to Augustus Foster, 18.2.1811
10 ibid, Augustus Foster to the Duchess of Devonshire, 13.9.1814

11   ibid, Augustus Foster to the Duchess of Devonshire, 5.12.1814
12   ibid, Augustus Foster to the Duchess of Devonshire, 21.5.1817
13   ibid, The Duchess of Devonshire to Augustus Foster, 18.11.1818

Early Years
CHAPTER 2, pp 27–44

1   F.P. Augustus Foster's Diary, 7.2.1835
2   ibid, Augustus Foster's Diary, 18.2.1833
3   ibid, Vere Foster to Frederick T. Foster, 2.10.1828
4   ibid, Augustus Foster to Cavendish Foster, 19.2.1839
5   ibid, Augustus Foster's Diary, 26.3.1840
6   ibid, Sir Robt. Peel to Augustus Foster, n.d.
7   ibid, Frederick Foster's Diary, 10.1842
8   ibid, Augustus Foster's Diary, 22.4.1846
9   ibid
10   ibid, Augustus Foster's Diary, 2.9.1846
11   ibid, Augustus Foster's Diary, 14.12.1846
12   ibid, Augustus Foster's Diary, 16.8.1847
13   ibid, Augustus Foster's Diary, 11.10.1847
14   ibid, Augustus Foster's Diary, 5.9.1847
15   ibid, Augustus Foster's Diary, 28.9.1847
16   *Jeffersonian America*, p 343
16a Apsley House Papers. Augustus Foster to the Duke of Wellington, 28.12.1828
17   *The Times*, 20.12.1846
18   F.P. Augustus Foster's Diary, 30.12.1847
19   ibid, Augustus Foster's Diary, 10.3.1847
20   *Gentleman's Magazine*, September, 1848

Vere Emerges
CHAPTER 3, pp 45–59

1   F.P. Frederick Foster's Diary
2   ibid, *Incidents of Travel in America* (unpublished)
3   *R.N. Educ.* 1847. p 138
4   *R.N. Educ.* 1850. p 264
5   F.P.

6 ibid, Broadsheet on Emigration
7 ibid, Letter to American Emigrant's Friend Society of Philadelphia
8 *Recollections of Aubrey de Vere*, p 252

After the Great Famine
CHAPTER 4, pp 60–81

1 *Irish Farmers' Gazette*, 1851
2 F.P.
3 *Report Select Committee on Passenger Acts, 1851*, p xxix
4 *Irish Farmers' Gazette*, 1852
5 ibid
6 ibid
7 ibid
8 ibid
9 ibid
10 *The True Delta*, New Orleans, 22.4.1851
11 *Irish Farmers' Gazette*, 1852
12 ibid
13 *Irish Farmers' Gazette*, 1851
14 *Irish Farmers' Gazette*, 1852
15 F.P.
16 ibid
17 ibid, Frederick Foster to Vere Foster, 29.2.1852

Emigration
CHAPTER 5, pp 82–100

1 F.P.
2 ibid
3 ibid, *Information Wanted* (leaflet)
4 ibid, *Work and Wages* (leaflet)
5 ibid
6 ibid
7 ibid
8 ibid
9 ibid

10   ibid
11   ibid
12   ibid, *Incidents of Travel in America*
13   ibid, Letter from Vere Foster, 23.4.1856
14   ibid, Emigration broadsheet, 4.8.1857
15   ibid, Frederick Foster to Vere Foster, 5.9.1857
16   *Freeman's Journal*, 5.9.1857
17   F.P.
18   ibid
19   ibid
20   ibid, *Incidents of Travel in America*
21   ibid, Frederick Foster to Vere Foster, 3.12.1857
22   ibid, Vere Foster to Lady Albinia Foster, 10.1.1858
23   ibid, Vere Foster to Cavendish Foster, 29.1.1858
24   ibid, Vere Foster to Cavendish Foster, 6.4.1858
25   ibid, Vere Foster to Cavendish Foster, 6.4.1858
26   ibid, *Incidents of Travel in America*
27   ibid

The Peripatetic Educationalist
CHAPTER 6, pp 101–127

1   F.P. Vere Foster to Cavendish Foster, 12.7.1858
2   ibid, Vere Foster to Cavendish Foster, 6.8.1858
3   ibid, Vere Foster to Cavendish Foster, 9.8.1858
4   *R.N. Educ.* 1863. p 250
5   F.P. Vere Foster to Cavendish Foster, 6.8.1858
6   Minutes of National Board of Education, 26.11.1858
7   F.P. Vere Foster to Cavendish Foster, 29.11.1858
8   ibid, Rt Rev John MacHale D.D. to Vere Foster, 12.8.1859
9   *R.N. Educ.* 1863. p 231
10   ibid, 1856. p 146
11   ibid, 1858. p 182
12   ibid, 1856. p 157
13   Minutes of National Board of Education, 4.2.1859
14   F.P.
15   Minutes of National Board of Education, 11.3.1859
16   ibid
17   A. M. Sullivan, *The New Ireland*, 7th ed., p 13
18   F.P. *Incidents of Travel in America*

19 *R.N. Educ.* 1859. p 222
20 ibid, 1859. p 251
21 ibid, 1859. p 169
22 ibid, 1859. p xiv
23 ibid, 1861. p 268
24 F.P. MS circular
25 *I.T.J.*, 1870. p 247
26 *R.N. Educ.* 1863. p 256
27 F.P. 30.9.1859
28 ibid, 13.4.1863
29 ibid, 21.10.1859
30 ibid, 14.1.1861
31 ibid

Copy-books
CHAPTER 7, pp 128–148

1 *R.N. Educ.* 1858. p 177
2 ibid, 1862. p 139
3 ibid, 1863. p 203
4 ibid, 1866. p 169
5 F.P.
6 ibid
7 Minutes of National Board of Education. 25.4.1865
8 *Origin and History of Vere's Foster's Writing and Drawing Copy Books*, leaflet, privately printed, Nat. Lib. Ire.
9 *R.N. Educ.* 1866. p 225
10 Minutes of National Board of Education, 17.11.1868
11 *R.N. Educ.* 1850
12 *Origin and History of Vere Foster's Writing and Drawing Copy Books*
13 *R.N. Educ.* 1866. p 233
14 *Origin and History of Vere Foster's Writing and Drawing Copy Books*
14a D. J. Owen, *History of Belfast*, p 323
15 *Belfast Morning News*, 14.4.1871
16 F.P.
17 ibid
18 ibid
19 *Irish Times*, 19.6.1865
20 F.P. Nov. 1865

21 ibid, 27.6.1865
22 *R.N. Educ.* 1855. p 15
23 F.P. *Conditions of Twenty-ninth Competition*
24 Quinn Papers, N.I.P.R.O. T 1790
25 F.P.
26 *Vere Foster's Writing Copy-Books*, Blackie & Son Ltd, n.d.

Organising Teachers
CHAPTER 8, pp 149–164

 1 *I.T.J.* 1874. p 136
 2 ibid, 1868. p 3
 3 *R.N. Educ.* 1862. p 261
 4 ibid, 1863. p 215
 5 ibid, 1863. p 243
 6 *National Assoc. for Promotion of Science*, 1867
 7 ibid, p 426
 8 ibid, p 437
 9 *Report Powis Commission*, vol 3, p 25
10 *I.T.J.* 1868. p 156
11 Privately printed and circulated, copy in British Museum
12 *I.T.J.* 1869. p 24
13 ibid, 1869. p 77
14 ibid, 1869. p 14
15 ibid, 1869. p 106
15a Costello, *John MacHale, Archbishop of Tuam*
16 *I.T.J.* 1870. p 9
17 ibid, 1870. p 164
18 ibid, 1870. p 250
19 F.P. 17.6.1870

Organising Teachers (continued)
CHAPTER 9, pp 165–180

 1 *I.T.J.* 1871. p 9
 2 *Ulster Examiner*, 25.1.1871
 3 ibid
 4 *I.T.J.* 1871. p 54
 5 ibid, 1871. p 54

6   ibid, 1868. p 137
7   *Northern Whig.* 18.6.1878
8   *I.T.J.* 1873. p 6
9   ibid, 1873. p 483
10 ibid, 1873. p 4
11 ibid, 1873. p 5
12 ibid, 1873. p 26
13 ibid, 1873. p 6
14 ibid, 1873. p 32
15 ibid, 1873. p 63
16 ibid, 1873. p 138
17 ibid, 1873. p 466
18 ibid, 1873. p 492
19 *Northern Whig.* 29.11.1873
20 Quoted *I.T.J.* 1873. p 513
21 *I.T.J.* 1874. p 9
22 *The Nation.* 17.1.1874
23 *I.T.J.* 1874. p 117
24 ibid, 1874. p 161
25 ibid, 1874. p 9
26 ibid, 1873. p 514

Personal
CHAPTER 10, pp 181–188

1   *R.N. Educ.* 1873. p 272
2   *Foster and Ward v. Marcus Ward and Co.* N.I.P.R.O.
3   ibid
4   *Origin and History of Vere Foster's Writing and Drawing Copy Books*
5   *Foster and Ward v. Marcus Ward and Co.* N.I.P.R.O.
6   *Origin and History of Vere Foster's Writing and Drawing Copy Books*
7   *Foster and Ward v. Marcus Ward and Co.* N.I.P.R.O.
8   ibid
9   F.P.
10 ibid, dated Belfast, March 1879
11 ibid, Rev. R. O'Hara to Vere Foster, 25.11.1880
12 In the possession of the Misses Duffin, Newcastle, Co Down
13 Information from Miss D. Grainger, Holywood, Co Down
14 *Northern Whig.* 22.12.1900

Emigration Again
CHAPTER II, pp 189–205

1 Curtis, *A History of Ireland*, p 379
2 *Second Report Select Committee on Land Laws (Ireland) 1882*, p 295
3 F.P.
4 ibid, Vere Foster to Countess Spencer, 25.1.1885
4a Vere Foster to Mr O'Brien, Nat. Lib. Ire, M.S., 13.5.52
5 F.P.
6 *Second Report Select Committee on Land Laws (Ireland) 1882*, p 252
7 ibid, p 249
8 ibid, p 247
9 ibid, p 246
10 ibid, p 295
11 ibid, p 254
12 ibid, p 296
13 *Northern Whig*. 23.1.1883
14 *Second Report Select Committee on Land Laws (Ireland) 1882*, p 296
15 ibid, p 248
16 *Northern Whig*. 23.1.1883
17 F.P.
17a ibid, C. T. Redington to Vere Foster, 5.3.1883
18 Nat. Lib. Ire. MS., 13.5.52
19 F.P.
20 ibid
21 ibid, Vere Foster to W. S. Gladstone, 24.2.1886 [draft]
22 ibid, Vere Foster to Lady Aberdeen, 24.8.1886
23 *Northern Whig*. 8.1.1884
24 F.P. Female Emigration Report, 1880–3
25 *Second Report Select Committee on Land Laws (Ireland) 1882*, p 249
26 ibid, p 253
27 ibid, p 254
28 F.P. Report, Irish Female Emigration Fund, 1883
29 ibid, Circular, Irish Female Emigration Fund, 1884
30 ibid
31 ibid

32 *Second Report Select Committee on Land Laws (Ireland)*
    1882, p 259
33 In the possession of Miss D. Grainger, Holywood, Co Down

        The Two Duchesses
        CHAPTER 12, pp 206–213

1   Vere Foster, *The Two Duchesses*, p 4
2   ibid, p 8
3   Creighton Papers N.I.P.R.O.
4   ibid
5   F.P.
6   *Blackie and Son. 1809–1959*. Privately printed, 1959
7   F.P.
8   *Belfast News Letter*, 29.12.1900
9   ibid, 22.12.1900
10 Vere Foster, *The Two Duchesses*, p 198

Emigrant Ship 'Washington'

RETURN to an Address of the Honourable The House of
Commons, dated 19 February 1851;—*for,*

A "COPY of a LETTER addressed to the LAND and EMIGRATION
COMMISSIONERS by Lord *Hobart,* enclosing a Letter from Mr.
Vere Foster to his Lordship, detailing the Treatment to which
he was subjected, in common with the other Passengers, on
board the Emigrant Ship 'Washington' in the Month of
November 1850, while on her Passage from Liverpool to New
York, with a Copy of the ANSWER returned to Lord *Hobart*
by the Commissioners; and also, Copies of any CORRES-
PONDENCE between the Commissioners and the Emigration
Officer at Liverpool on the subject."

Colonial Office, Downing-Street, ⎱
24 March 1851. ⎰   B. HAWES.

— No. 1. —

Copy of a LETTER from Lord *Hobart* to the Colonial Land and
Emigration Commissioners.

No. 1.
Lord Hobart to
the Colonial Land
and Emigration
Commissioners,
13 January 1851.

Gentlemen,   Board of Trade, 13 January 1851.

WILL you permit me to bring under your notice the accompanying letter, which has recently been received from a relation of
mine (Mr. Vere Foster), who took a passage in the emigrant
ship "Washington," bound for New York from Liverpool?

Mr. Foster embarked in the "Washington" as a steerage passenger, in pursuance of a plan which he had formed for obtain-

ing an insight into the condition and prospects of Irish emigrants, from the time of their leaving this country.

The Commissioners will perceive that the treatment undergone by the emigrants in the "Washington" was considerably worse than that ordinarily experienced by brutes; and from what Mr. Foster states at the end of his letter, the case seems to be by no means an exceptional one.

I apprehend that the master and mates of the "Washington" have brought themselves under more than one of the penalties imposed by the Passenger Act.

I do not know how far the Commissioners or their agent at Liverpool have power to interfere to prevent the future occurrence of similar outrages on common decency and humanity, but I have no doubt that they will do all that lies in that power for that purpose.

Sic in orig.

I should add that Mr. Foster's brother, Sir Frederick Foster, has communicated with the Government Emigration Agent at Liverpool upon the subject, and has been informed that should the requisite evidence be obtainable, that officer will institute a prosecution against the offending parties, on the return, which is shortly expected, of the "Washington" to this country. Mr. Foster will not return to England until the autumn; but the seamen of the "Washington" would be able, and probably willing to give the necessary evidence.

I have, &c.

(signed)   *Hobart.*

Enclosure to Lord *Hobart's* Letter of 13 January 1851.

Ship "Washington,"
My dear——,   1 December 1850.

As the weather is very beautiful to-day, and the wind and sea perfectly still, I will take advantage of so fair an opportunity of writing you some account of my voyage thus far, during the intervals between the performance of my household duties as cook to our mess. We are now, and have been for several days within one day's sail of our destination, if we had a fair wind, but unfortunately there is now no wind.

This is a magnificent vessel of 1,600 tons register burthen, or 3,500 tons measurement, with two lofty and well-ventilated passenger decks, each between seven and eight feet high, and very high bulwarks, over six feet, to protect the deck from the spray of the sea; she is a new vessel and very strong and dry, and probably as well furnished with all necessary conveniences as the best of the emigrant ships between Liverpool and New York. Her crew consists of 31 men, 3 boys and 5 officers; namely, the captain and 4 mates, and she has on board upwards of 900 passengers, whose sleeping berths are a shelf along each side of the whole length of the two decks, with low boards dividing the shelf into berths, all of one size, and each containing from four to six persons; one end of the upper deck is divided off as a separate apartment, containing 12 enclosed cabins, each having two, four, or six berths, and each berth containing two persons. The passengers in this part of the vessel pay a somewhat higher price, viz., 5*l.* instead of 3*l.* 15*s.*, or 4*l.* I occupy one of the berths in a cabin containing four berths, Mr. James Ward, late literary teacher at Glasnevin Model Farm, being my bedfellow; and there are four other men in the same cabin, one of whom is a plasterer, another a miller (American), a third a tanner, and the fourth a young American, who has been travelling in England for his amusement.

The quantity of provisions, which, according to Act of Parliament and according to the stipulations of our contract tickets, in which their price is included, ought to be served out to each emigrant weekly, is, besides three quarts of water daily, and the supply of sufficient firing,

2½ lbs. of bread,	2 oz. of tea,
1 lb. of wheaten flour,	½ lb. of sugar,
5 lbs. of oatmeal,	½ lb. of molasses,
2 lbs. of rice,	Vinegar;

and John Taylor, Crook & Co., agents to this company, which is that of the "Black Star Line of Packets," engage to supply in addition to the above, one pound of pork (free of bone) to each passenger weekly.

The extra provisions which I have brought on board for the use of my bedfellow and myself, in addition to the ship's provisions, are the same as what I have been in the habit of supplying to such passengers as I have sent at my expense to America, viz., for each of us,

1½ stone wheaten flour,	2 lbs. sugar, brown,
6 lbs. bacon,	Salt,
2½ lbs. butter,	Soap,
¼ lb. of tea,	Soda;

A four pound loaf.

These extra provisions cost 10*s.* 6*d.*

I also brought some cooking utensils, and other tinware, bedding, towels and dishclouts.

I consider the above quantity of extra provisions to be plenty, so far as necessity is concerned, with the exception of a pint of vinegar in summer; a cheese, more flour, a few herrings and some potatoes would however be, and were found to be, by many of my fellow passengers, a palatable and desirable addition, particularly during the first fortnight, until the stomach becomes inured to the motion of the ship.

All the passengers who arrive at Liverpool a day or more before the sailing of an emigrant ship, have to be inspected by a surgeon appointed by Government, who will not allow any one to go on board who has any infectious disease of a dangerous character. I passed before him for inspection, which occupied only one or two seconds. He said without drawing breath, "What's your name? Are you well? Hold out your tongue; all right," and then addressed himself to the next person. We were again all mustered and passed before him on board the ship, while sailing down the river.

There was no regularity or decency observed with regard to taking the passengers on board the ship; men and women were pulled in any side or end foremost, like so many bundles. I was getting myself in as quickly and dexterously as I could, when I was laid hold of by the legs and pulled in, falling head foremost down upon the deck, and the next man was pulled down upon the top of me. I was some minutes before I recovered my hat, which was crushed as flat as a pancake. The porters, in their treatment of passengers (naturally) look only to getting as much money as they possibly can from them in the shortest space of time, and heap upon them all kinds of filthy and blasphemous abuse, there being no police regulations, and the officers of the ship taking the lead in the ill-treatment of the passengers.

The "Washington" went out of dock on the 25th, and anchored in the river; I went on board on the next day, and witnessed the first occasion of giving out the daily allowance of water to the passengers, in doing which there was no regularity; the whole 900 and odd passengers were called forward at once to receive their water, which was pumped out into their cans from barrels on deck. The serving out of the water was twice capriciously stopped by the mates of the ship, who during the whole time, without any provocation, cursed and abused, and cuffed and kicked the passengers and their tin cans, and, having served out water to about 30 persons, in two separate times, said they would give no more water out till the next morning, and kept their word. I gently remonstrated with one of the mates, who was cuffing and kicking the poor steerage passengers, observing to him that such treatment was highly improper and unmanly, and that he would save himself a great deal of trouble and annoyance, and win, instead of alienating, the hearts of the passengers, if he would avoid foul language and brutal treatment, and use civil treatment, and institute regularity in the serving out of the water, &c.; but he, in reply, said that he would knock me down if I said another word. I was happy to find, however, that my rebuke had the effect of checking for the moment his bullying conduct.

Provisions were not served out this day, notwithstanding the engagement contained in our contract tickets, and notwithstanding that all the passengers were now on board, the most of them since yesterday, and had no means of communication with the shore, and that many of them, being very poor, had entirely relied upon the faithful observance of the promises contained in their tickets, the price of which includes payment for the weekly allowance of provisions. I was on board of a fine vessel, of the same size as the "Washington," about five weeks ago, named the "Constellation," one of Tapscott's line of packets, in which I sent some passengers. There were 875 passengers on board, and the provisions were served out punctually on the day appointed for sailing, although she was yet in dock, and did not sail for several days afterwards.

While a steamer towed the "Washington" down the river on Sunday, 27th October, all the passengers were mustered on deck, and answered to their names as they were called over by the chief clerk of the agency office at Liverpool. This formality was for the purpose of ascertaining that there was no one on board but such as had tickets. One little boy was found hid, having made his way on board, thinking to escape notice; he was sent ashore.

On the 28th we were so fortunate as to have a most favourable breeze, which carried us out of the Irish Channel, being that part of the voyage in which we expected the greatest delay.

On the 29th I went the round of the lower deck with Mr. Charles Reynolds, surgeon of the ship, observing him take down the numbers in each berth. These berths are constructed to hold four persons, and would conveniently hold five persons; some of the berths had four persons in them, and some as many as six. I observed that the doctor noted down, in many instances, persons between the ages of 14 and 16 as under 14, that is, as not adults, although it is expressly stated in our tickets that 14 years of age constitutes an adult, and any one above that age is paid for extra as such; this was for the purpose of making a saving in the issuing of provisions, as half rations only are served out to passengers under 14 years of age. The doctor remarked to me at the time, that as regarded the issuing of provisions, 16 years of age was considered on board the "Washington" as constituting an adult.

On the 30th October no provisions had yet been served out, and the complaints of the poorer passengers in the steerage were naturally increasing, as they had no means of living, excepting on the charity of those who had brought extra provisions. At their request I drew up a letter, of which the following is a copy, addressed to the captain of the ship, A. Page :—

"Respected Sir,

"We, the undersigned passengers on board the ship, 'Washington,' paid for and secured our passages in her in the confident expectation that the allowance of provisions promised in our contract tickets would be faithfully delivered to us. Four entire days having expired since the day on which (some of us having been on board from that day, and most of us from before that day) the ship was appointed to sail, and three entire days since she actually sailed from the port of Liverpool, without our having received one particle of the stipulated provisions excepting water, and many of us having made no provision to meet such an emergency, we request that you will inform us when we may expect to commence receiving the allowance which is our due.

(signed)

"Vere Foster.	*John Hickey.*	*Denis Mangan.*
"James Molony.	*Samuel Thorn.*	*Charles O'Donoghue.*
"John Collins	*James Ward.*	*H. Hopkins.*
"Jas. McNamara.	*Thomas Hotchin.*	

"P.S.—From want of conveniences of writing, but particularly from the fear of being interfered with by the officers of the ship, no more signatures have been proceeded with, otherwise nearly 900 might have been added. While writing the former part of this letter at the request of my fellow passengers, the first mate, Mr. Williams, knocked me down flat upon the deck with a blow in the face.

"Another day has elapsed without provisions being served out.

"31 October 1850."   (signed)   *"Vere Foster."*

When the mate knocked me down, which he did without the smallest previous intimation or explanation, he also made use of the most blasphemous and abusive language. I said not a word, knowing the severity (necessarily so) of the laws of discipline on board of ships, but retired as he bade me to my own cabin. He then forbade my going into any of the steerage part of the vessel. A passenger heard him make use to the cabin cook, of the observation, that if he caught me in 'tween decks again he would not hit me, but that he would throttle me. I ought to have noticed that last night the mate said to me, "Damn and blast you, come and give us a hand at the rope;" on which I said, "If you'll be civil perhaps I may;" and at the same time I went forward to pull at the rope at which the sailors were hauling, on which the mate seized hold of me by the collar and thrust me aside, swearing at me like a trooper, and saying that he remembered having seen a specimen of me before, alluding to the first day of serving out the water.

On the morning of the 31st October, I presented the letter to Captain Page. He asked me the purport of it, and bade me read it. Having read out one-third of it, he said that was enough, and that he knew what I was; I was a damned pirate, a damned rascal, and that he would put me in irons and on bread and water throughout the rest of the voyage. The first mate then came up, and abused me foully and blasphemously, and pushed me down, bidding me get out of that, as I was a damned b——. He was found by one of the passengers soon afterwards, heating a thick bar of iron at the kitchen fire; the cook said, "What is he doing that for?" and the mate said, "There is a damned b—— on board, to whom I intend giving a singeing before he leaves the ship."

Provisions were issued to the passengers for the first time this day. I took the precaution of bringing a weighing-machine on board, weighing as low as two ounces, in order to compare the allowances issued with the quantities due, which afterwards proved extremely useful for my own purposes, and to other persons. Mr. Ward and I received about 2¾ lbs. of wheaten flour, which was ¾ lb. more than our due; about 2½ lbs. biscuit instead of 5 lbs., and 7½ lbs. of rice and oatmeal mixed, instead of 14 lbs. The steerage passengers did not receive so much.

On Saturday, 2d November, groceries were issued for the first instead of the second time to the passengers; the six persons in my cabin received all their provisions together; we got 6 oz. of tea instead of 12 oz., nearly our proper allowance of sugar, and 1¼ lb. of molasses instead of 3 lbs., and no vinegar. We have as yet received no pork, though we should have received our second weekly allowance of pork to-day.

On Thursday, 7th November, flour, biscuits, oatmeal and rice were issued in the same proportion as before, excepting that the flour was a little under the allowance. I was looking on during nearly the whole of the time, and could see that the quantities were the same to each person. The six persons in my cabin received—

8 lbs. of oatmeal instead of 30 lbs.,	8 lbs. of rice instead of 12 lbs.,
8 lbs. of flour instead of 6 lbs.,	8¾ lbs. of biscuits instead of 15 lbs.

A slight mistake occurred by a second person coming for the provisions for berth No. 115, not knowing that another person had just received the provisions for the whole of the persons in that berth; the first mate told him to get out of that and go to hell; and on the man, an old man he was, saying that he had not yet received his provisions, the first mate rushed at and beat him and knocked him down, using the most violent and blasphemous language.

On Saturday the 9th November an allowance of pork was issued for the first instead of the third time; the six persons in my cabin got 6 lbs. When one of the occupants of berth No. 180 came up for his pork, not knowing that another man from the same berth had just received for the whole of its occupants, the first mate instantly ran at him and hit him with his clenched fist, and with a rope's end, about the face and head, and then added, "if any other b—— annoys me, God damn his soul, I'll smash his head for him." Whenever provisions are served out, a sailor stands by with a rope's end and capriciously lays about him, with or without the slightest provocation. The captain never appears to trouble himself in the slightest degree about the passengers, nor even ever to visit the part of the ship occupied by them. The first and second mates, the surgeon and the man specially appointed to look after the passengers, and the cooks—all these very seldom open their lips without prefacing what they may have to say, with "God damn your soul to hell, you damned b——," or, "by Jesus Christ I'll rope's end you," or some other expression from the same category.

I hear occasionally some of the passengers complain to the first mate or to the captain, of the favoritism shown by the passengers' cooks to those who give them money, or whiskey, and who consequently get five or six meals cooked daily, while those poor passengers who have not the money to give, or who do not give, are kept the whole day waiting to have one meal cooked, or can have only one meal cooked every second day. In my own case, on one of the first mornings of my being on board, the cook took up my kettle of water, which had been waiting one hour and a half to be put on the fire, and said to me, "What are you going to give me to cook that for you?" I replied, that I intended to take my chances, the same as the rest of the passengers, and was contented to take my proper turn in having my victuals cooked, for that if I paid for a preference in having them cooked I should be monopolizing a right which is common to us all, at the expense of those fellow passengers who were not able to pay. The cook then put down the kettle again, saying, "That God damn fellow is not going to pay up, so his kettle may wait." The captain's cook cooks for those passengers who give him 10s. or 12s. each person for the voyage, and a great many do so. I did not, for I wished to place myself as much as I conveniently could in the same position as the general run of my fellow passengers. I find now, that either in consequence of good words in my favour from some of those passengers whom I have had small opportunities of being of service to, or in consequence of an appreciation of my fairness in taking my proper turns, though I am well able to pay for doing otherwise, or of my aiding him by remonstrances to keep the galley (kitchen) from being too crowded and to keep order, the cook now favours me as much as if I did pay him. Asked the third mate where we were, and received the same reply as usual, that he could not tell. No one knows the whereabouts of the vessel except the captain and first mate, and they keep that a profound secret from the ship's company and passengers. No groceries were issued, as they should have been this day.

13th November.—I have spoken frequently with different sailors, asking them if this was the first time of their sailing in this

P

ship; all answer yes, and that it will be the last, and some of them express an opinion that the first and second mates will get a good thrashing at New York.

One of the female passengers played the dirty trick this evening of committing a nuisance on the deck at the top of the steps; being caught in the act, she was (very properly) made to take it up with both her hands and throw it overboard.

14th.—Provisions of oatmeal, biscuits, flour and rice were issued this day as usual. I weighed what was given to four adults and a boy, occupying one of the steerage berths. They received—

10¾ lbs. of oatmeal,	instead of	22½	lbs.	due.
4½ lbs. of biscuits	„	11¼	„	
4 lbs. of flour	„	4½	„	
5½ lbs. of rice	„	9	„	

16th.—Groceries were issued as usual.

17th November.—The doctor this evening heaved overboard a great many chamber-pots belonging to the female passengers, saying that henceforward he would allow no women to do their business below, but that they should come to the filthy privies on deck. I heard him say, "There are a hundred cases of dysentery in the ship, which will all turn to cholera, and I swear to God that I will not go amongst them; if they want medicines they must come to me." This morning the first mate took it into his head to play the hose upon the passengers in occupation of the water-closets, drenching them from head to foot; the fourth mate did the same a few mornings ago.

18th November.—A three-masted vessel in sight, going in the same direction as ourselves; this is the second vessel only that we have seen since leaving Liverpool. About noon a heavy squall came on, which split the fore-topsail and staysail.

19th November.—Mr. Williams, a surgeon passenger, has been canvassing for a subscription among the passengers as a testimonial to the good services of the doctor, for the purpose of serving as an inducement to him to conduct himself well during the rest of the voyage, but he appears now disposed to abandon his project, as his canvass has not been favourably received. This morning the ship doctor remarked to one of the passengers that this project seemed likely to fail, as most similar projects usually do; that the steerage passengers had plenty of pence amongst them, which they would not know what to do with when they got to New York, and that if they would not look after him, he would not look after them. When it was bruited about the ship that a subscription was sought to be raised for the doctor, some passengers remarked, that they would not mind each contributing a shilling to buy a rope if they thought he would be hanged with it. This is a correct index of the general feeling towards him.

A delicate old man, named John M'Corcoran, of berth No. 111, informed me that on Sunday last he had just come on deck, and, after washing, was wringing a pair of stockings, when the first mate gave him such a severe kick with his knee on his backside as he was stooping down, that he threw him down upon the deck, since which he has been obliged to go to the watercloset three or four times a day, passing blood every time.

A passenger having a family with him told me that one of the first days after coming on board, the doctor applied to him for a present, saying, that of course he was paid for his services to the passengers, but that to those persons who liked to give him anything, of course he should pay more particular attention; the passenger then gave him 2s. 6d. He applied in the same manner to Mr. Homer, of cabin No. 8, who gave him 1s. The doctor then said, "And there was that glass of castor oil of the other day, for which you owe me 6d.," which Mr. H. then gave him. The doctor has no right to charge for any medicines, but has, I am told, received a great deal of money on board in the same way. The first mate beat one of the sailors severely this evening with a rope.

20th.—Pork was issued to the passengers as usual.

21st November.—Provisions as usual were issued of flour, rice, oatmeal and biscuits. A violent gale commenced this evening.

22d.—The gale became perfectly terrific; for a few minutes we all expected momentarily to go to the bottom, for the sea, which was foaming and rolling extremely high, burst upon the deck with a great crash, which made us all believe that some part of the vessel was stove in. The wave rushed down into the lower deck, and I certainly expected every moment to go down. Some of the passengers set to praying; the wind blew a perfect hurricane, so that it was quite out of the question to attempt to proceed on our proper course. We therefore scudded before the wind, having up the main-topsail close reefed and the fore-topsail staysail only. The water which had rushed upon the deck remained there to the depth of several feet; it was got rid of by breaking holes in the bulwarks with a hatchet. The whole sea was a sheet of foam. Towards 9 P.M. the gale began to be less, though still violent, and moderated during the night.

25th November.—Another child, making about 12 in all, died of dysentery from want of proper nourishing food, and was thrown into the sea sown [*sic*] up, along with a great stone, in a cloth. No funeral service has as yet been performed, the doctor informs me, over any one who has died on board; the Catholics objecting, as he says, to the performance of any such service by a layman. As there was no regular service, the man appointed to attend to the passengers seized the opportunity, when the sailors pulling at a rope raised the usual song of—

> Haul in the bowling, the Black Star bowling,
> Haul in the bowling, the bowling haul—

to throw in the child overboard at the sound of the last word of the song, making use of it as a funeral dirge.

We passed some ships' spars this and the following day, belonging, perhaps, to vessels which may have suffered in the late gale.

26th.—Tea and sugar issued to those who lost any during the late storm. I and my two mess companions received our allowances together, receiving between us 2 oz. of tea and ½ lb. of sugar.

28th.—The same quantities as usual issued of flour, oatmeal, biscuits and rice.

30th.—The doctor came down to the second cabin in company with the first mate, and to display his authority, drew himself up and swelled himself out excessively tremendous, roaring out, "Now then, clean and wash out your rooms every one of you, God damn and blast your souls to hell." Tea and sugar as usual.

2d December.—A beautiful day and a favourable breeze; took a pilot on board.

Many of the passengers have, at different times during the voyage, expressed to me their intention of making a public complaint respecting their ill-treatment on board this ship, so to meet their wishes I wrote the few following lines, which were signed this evening by the persons whose names are attached.

"Ship Washington, off New York, 2 December 1850.

"WE testify, as a warning to, and for the sake of future emigrants, that the passengers generally, on board of this noble ship, the 'Washington,' commander A. Page, have been treated in a brutal manner by its officers, and that we have not received one-half the quantity of provisions allowed by Act of Parliament and stipulated for by us in our contract tickets.

(signed)

"Vere Foster.
H. Hopkins.
James Ward.
John Swinburne.
Catherine Swinburne.
Benjamin Homer.
Emmeline Homer.
James Moloney.
Catherine Moloney.
William Harvey.
James Macnamara.
Michael M'Callan.
Thomas Cowper.
Oratura Cowper.
Henry Disney.
G. Hannity.
Matilda Dickson.
Marianne Dickson.
John Robertson.
George Elliott.
David Crolly.
George M'Nab.
Anne Brenief.
Eliza Stokes.
Marianne Horsfall.
Ann Mellet.
Thomas Canavan.
Sarah Thomson.
George Elliott, Junr.
Mary Conall.
Anne M'Cabe.
John Williams.
Emma Williams.
Samuel Thompson.
Eliza M'Nab.
Margaret M'Nab.
John Hales.
Michael Flynn.
James Farrell.
Fanny Flynn.
Timothy Cullen.
Catherine Flynn.
Margaret Campbell.

July Flynn.
Peter Cullen.
Anne Doyle.
Bridget Doyle.
L. Hopkins.
Mrs. Richd. Sulivan.
John Phelan.
Eleanor Slattery.
Mary Hoyne.
Robert Cleary.
James Kavanagh.
Peter Walsh.
Denis Bryan.
Thomas Curry.
Michael Walsh.
James Cormons.
Mary Curry.
Caroline Malone.
Richard Kealy.
Pat Cahill.
John Clancy.
John Murry.
Martin Maher.
Sally Kiggins.
Denis M'Evoy.
John Hefferman.
Eliza Lynard.
Judith Farrell.
James Byrne.
Bridget Murphy.
James Hutchin.
James Doran.
James Tyrrell.
Thomas Anderson.
Pat. Bryan.
Catherine Bryan.
Lawrence Bryan.
Mary Byrne.
Thomas Fitzpatrick.
Richard English.
James Delaney.
Martin Riley.
Patrick Shea.

Michael Hurley.
Mary Neary.
Edward Roe.
Honour Delany.
Catherine Delany.
Denis Martin.
Michael Mangan.
Owen Heputtlan.
James Troymor.
Francis Turlit.
James M'Elroy.
Francis Foley.
John S. Kelly.
John Marvill.
John Doran.
John ——.
James Wilson.
James Kelsey.
John Collins.
M. Ma
Peter Mathias.
Denis Mangan.
J. R. Hennelly.
M. Killar.
E. Longworth.
B. Connolly.
John Treavy.
James Coroney.
Thomas Callan.
Michael Lynch.
Peter Mathews.
Daniel Myraw.
John Magee.
James Frances.
James Hugh.
John Welsh
John Morrison.
Patrick M'Cabe.
Eugene Lynch.
Thomas Hartney.
Thomas Mangan.
John Mason."

3d December.—A few of the passengers were taken ashore to the Hospital at Staten Island, and we arrived alongside the quay at New York this afternoon. The 900 passengers dispersed as usual among the various fleecing houses, to be partially or entirely disabled for pursuing their travels into the interior in search of employment.

6th December.—I met this day with some friends of mine, who came out two months ago in the "Atlas," Captain Osborne, with 415 passengers. They described the treatment of the passengers on board that vessel by the officers, as considerably worse than what I have related respecting the "Washington." The provisions, as on board the "Washington," were not served out till about the end of the first week, and no pork was served out at all, excepting to such persons as were willing to buy it. The "Atlas" is also one of the "Black Star line of packets."

I also met to-day with some friends who came out in the "St. Louis," which arrived here the day before yesterday. It was gratifying to hear them describe the treatment of the passengers on board that ship, on the part of the captain, the mates, the cooks, and the men specially appointed to attend to the passengers, as most kind and considerate, and the rations of provisions and water as ample. There were 350 passengers, and there was no death from dysentery on board this vessel, for the captain paid, and caused to be paid, every necessary attention towards the sick. The "St. Louis" sailed from Liverpool one day after the "Washington," and arrived at New York also one day after her.

To attend to the 900 and odd passengers on board the "Washington," only one man was appointed, and he a brute.

I have since met with passengers whom I sent out in the "Washington" on her previous voyage, and I learn from them, that no provisions were served out during the first fortnight of her voyage, and that no meat was served out during the whole of her voyage; I have also met with passengers whom I sent in the "Wm. Rathbone," whose treatment by the officers, and as regards provisions, was similar. The "W. R." is one of the same line of packets.

Here follows a comparison of the provisions due and the provisions received by each passenger during our voyage of 37 days.

				Due.		Received.		Deficiency.	
				lbs.	*oz.*	*lbs.*	*oz.*	*lbs.*	*oz.*
Pork	-	-	-	5⅞	0	2	0	3⅞	0
Flour	-	-	-	5⅞	0	5	0	0⅞	0

Oatmeal	-	-	-	26½	0	11¼	0	15¼	0
Rice	-	-	-	10½	0	6¼	0	4¼	0
Biscuits	-	-	-	13¼	0	6	0	7¼	0
Tea	-	-	-	0	10½	0	4	0	6½
Sugar	-	-	-	2	10	1	13	0	13
Molasses	-	-	-	2	10	0	6⅔	2	3⅛
Vinegar, no specified quantity.						None.			

No. 2.
S. Walcott, Esq.
to Lord Hobart,
15 January 1851.

— No. 2. —

Copy of a LETTER from *S. Walcott,* Esq. to Lord *Hobart.*

Colonial Land and Emigration Office,
Parliament-street, Westminster,

My Lord,   15 January 1851.

I AM directed by the Board to acknowledge the receipt of your letter of the 13th instant, accompanied by a communication from Mr. Vere Foster, detailing the ill-treatment to which the passengers by the ship "Washington" were exposed on their voyage from Liverpool to New York.

The Commissioners desire me to express their regret that Mr. Foster and his fellow passengers did not take proceedings at New York against the officers of the "Washington," both for the assaults, of which the officers were guilty, and for the non-issue of the quantity of provisions required by the United States Law of May 1848. The Commissioners cannot doubt that if this had been done the parties would have been punished for their misconduct. All that the Commissioners can now do is, with your Lordship's permission, to communicate your letter, and that from Mr. Vere Foster, to the emigration officer at Liverpool, but the chance of any successful proceedings in this country is of course much less, both from the difficulty of obtaining evidence in the case, and from the doubt as to the jurisdiction of a British court over acts done at sea under a foreign flag.

I have, &c.
(signed)   *S. Walcott,*
Secretary.

— No. 3. —

COPY of a LETTER from *S. Walcott*, Esq. to Lieutenant *Hodder*, R. N.

Colonial Land and Emigration Office,
Park-street, Westminster,

Sir,   29 January 1851.

I AM directed by the Board to transmit to you herewith a letter from Lord Hobart, accompanied by one from Mr. Vere Foster, who went out to New York as a steerage passenger in the "Washington," detailing the ill-usage to which he and his fellow passengers in the "Washington" were exposed from the officers of that ship. I am to direct you to look out for the arrival of that ship, and if you should then be able to procure any evidence corroborative of the statements contained in Mr. Foster's letter, to take the necessary steps for proceeding against the parties in fault.

I have, &c.
(signed)   *S. Walcott,*
Secretary.

— No. 4. —

COPY of a LETTER from Lieutenant *Hodder*, R.N., to *S. Walcott*, Esq.

Government Emigration Office,
Sir,   Liverpool, 4 February 1851.

I HAVE the honour to acknowledge the receipt of your letter of the 29th ultimo, enclosing a copy of a letter from Lord Hobart, accompanied by a communication from Mr. Foster, relative to the treatment he experienced as a steerage passenger in the ship "Washington," in his voyage to New York.

The ship having returned to Liverpool, I have inquired of the master for his version of the transactions reported to have taken place, with reference to which, as might be expected, his detail differs widely from the complainants, and in the absence of all evidence I am unable to proceed further in the case. It, however, appears strange that legal proceedings were not instituted at New York, where the charges could have been substantiated, or otherwise, without difficulty; and it will appear on reference to the enclosed letter (which be good enough to return) that Mr. Foster acted on the advice of the British Consul and his Solicitor. Letter returned. I return Mr. Foster's original letter.

I am, &c.

(signed) *J. E. Hodder*, Lieut. R. N.

Gov^t. Emigⁿ. Officer.

— No. 5. —

Copy of a LETTER from *S. Walcott*, Esq. to Lord *Hobart*.

No. 5.
S. Walcott, Esq.
to Lord Hobart,
8 February 1851.

Colonial Land and Emigration Office,

My Lord,   Park-street, Westminster, 8 February 1851.

WITH reference to my letter of the 15th ultimo, on the subject of the treatment of emigrants on board the United States ship "Washington," on her recent voyage to New York, I am directed by the Commissioners to inform you that they learn from the emigration officer at Liverpool, that the "Washington" has returned to that port. The emigration officer adds, that the master of the "Washington" denies the statements in Mr. Vere Foster's letter respecting the treatment of the emigrants, and that in the absence of all evidence he found it impossible to take proceedings in the matter.

This result, as your Lordship is aware, the Commissioners had anticipated; but they also learn from the emigration officer's letter, that Mr. Foster had contemplated taking proceedings before the tribunals in New York, but was dissuaded on account of the delay and expense of doing so.

Under these circumstances, the Commissioners apprehend that nothing can now be done until at least the arrival of Mr. Foster in England, and even if he should then be prepared to take proceedings against the officers of the ship, it seems very doubtful whether any English court would have jurisdiction in the matter.

I have, &c.

(signed)   *S. Walcott*, Secretary.

Address of the Ennis National Teachers' Association to
VERE FOSTER ESQ.
[*circa* 1872]

Sir,

We, the representatives of the Ennis National Teachers Association feel gratified at being afforded this opportunity which a mere accident revealed to us—of bidding you a sincere and hearty welcome amongst us. Cold indeed should be our hearts, and dead to every generous feeling, did we fail to pay that tribute of respect and gratitude due to him, who, on all occasions, has so nobly and so ably advocated the right of our body to more generous recognition and more liberal remuneration for services of the highest importance to the community, and involving the gravest moral responsibility.

But, Sir, it is not on personal grounds merely that we would or should offer you our greeting. We do so from considerations more extended and exalted. We do so in the interests of social and intellectual progress, and on the broad principles of humanity.

Who among us cannot conjure up an ideal image of a miserable hovel, on a bleak mountain side, with wretched roof of rush-thatch, furrowed with the rains and snows of half-a-dozen winters? Its walls, which have long since parted with their mortar, are streaked and begrimed with filthy oozings from the roof, and perforated with what are dignified with the title of windows, but which only serve the purpose of excluding the light, and allowing the wind and rain free access to the interior. And what a picture does that interior present. At your very entrance into that dismal, ill-ventilated cell, the noxious gases generated by the breathing of so many children—(for this is an Irish National School)—threaten you with instant suffocation, the walls are bare, moist and dark; the earthen floor is so damp, slippery and uneven as to be unsafe to tread upon; the desks and seats, if ever they had been in company, have long since dissolved partnership, and are only kept from falling by having one extremity pressed against the wall by large stones placed at the other; and the pupils—"playful children" indeed *they* must be— are compelled to sit upon that damp, chilling, health-destroying floor rather than trust themselves to the uncertain keeping of such frail supports.

Then the teacher—but we cannot, dare not complete the picture. Who is he that enters, with placid smile, and mild benignant countenance? He goes up to the teacher, salutes him in kindly tones, modestly introduces himself, and extends the hand of sympathetic friendship. The strange gentleman talks to him familiarly, commiserates his condition, deplores such a melancholy state of things, promises to assist in improving it and takes his leave.

After the lapse of a few months let us visit this sad scene once more. Ah! the scene is sad no longer. It has vanished and another brighter and more pleasing meets our astonished gaze. The walls and roof which were then scarcely distinguishable in the distance from the brown hill-side, now stand out in pleasing relief, for the one is whitened, and the other slated; the handsome glazed windows sparkle in the sunlight; within, the floor is boarded, the desks and forms compact, and of approved pattern; the room is lightsome and cheerful, the white walls are decorated with maps and educational diagrams; and if the pupils sometimes turn from their legitimate business, to gaze in rapt delight at such wonders, let them not be much blamed, for the eye of curiosity is not yet satiated. That cloud of despondency and gloom which hung over the pale thoughtful brow of the teacher is gone too; the thorns have in great part been removed from his path, the road to promotion, which before was all but impassable, through no fault of his, is now free, and his day's labor if not easy is at least tolerable. Verily it is "The Deformed Transformed".

Who is it that has wrought this happy transfiguration? Has it been effected by the owner of yonder mansion, the proprietor of the place, in kindness to his tenants? No, he will not permit the house to stand if he does not receive rent for it, which rent must be paid by the teacher out of his munificent income of £18 per annum. Have the people done it by contribution? No, the wealthiest of them do not patronize National Schools, and of the others, some want the means and others the inclination. Who then? It was that gentleman whom we saw enter the school some months ago. It was he who with local aid merely nominal or with no local aid at all wrought this agreeable change, and did so not in this instance alone, but in thousands of others throughout the country, and every national teacher in Ireland will say without hesitation, it was Vere Foster.

Sir, your noble efforts at immense pecuniary sacrifice, to render the pen indeed a "mightier instrument" by placing in the hands of our pupils such splendid models of plain and ornamental penmanship cannot be too highly estimated, particularly now that the departments of the Civil Service have been thrown open to general competition, and many a future Irish artist may say that his genius received its first impulse from those exquisite specimens of art which you modestly designate "Drawing Copy Books." It has been the fashion to accord the chief space in the history of the world to the warrior, the statesman, the orator and the poet. These are proud titles to be sure, and great and valuable ones when their respective provinces are legitimately exercised; yet it may be questioned whether they have not each and all contributed to the misery, as well as to the happiness of our race. But it is the men who have facilitated national and international intercourse; who have cheapened and increased the comforts and conveniences of life by some useful invention; who have contributed to relieve the wants, and alleviated the miseries of their species; and above all, it is those who influenced by no motive but the purest philanthropy have devoted their time and talents and fortunes to rescue their fellow-creatures from the gulf of ignorance, and to diffuse the blessings of education amongst a people; it is such men that really deserve the gratitude of mankind, for they are its real benefactors. Amongst such men, we do not hesitate to reckon you. Your own acts, Sir, might have furnished the most appropriate design with which to embellish this address, had there been time and opportunity for it; but imperfect and unworthy as it is in every way, it will be no less acceptable, as the genuine expression of our deep respect, and heartfelt gratitude.

In conclusion, Sir, we beg again to hail your presence among us with a thorough, hearty, *Irish—Cead mille failthe.*

Signed in behalf of the Ennis National Teachers' Association.

> Hugh Brady, Ruan N.S.
> Jamie Considine, Quin N.S.
> Michael Cusack, Lough Cutra N.S.
> Patrick Greene, Dysart N.S.
> John O'Brien, Tulla N.S.

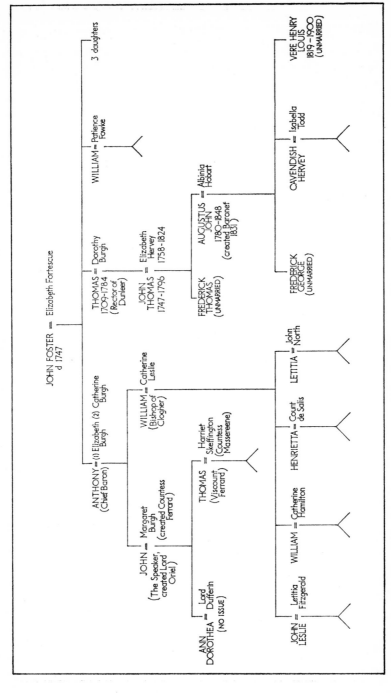

Shortened genealogical tree of the Foster family

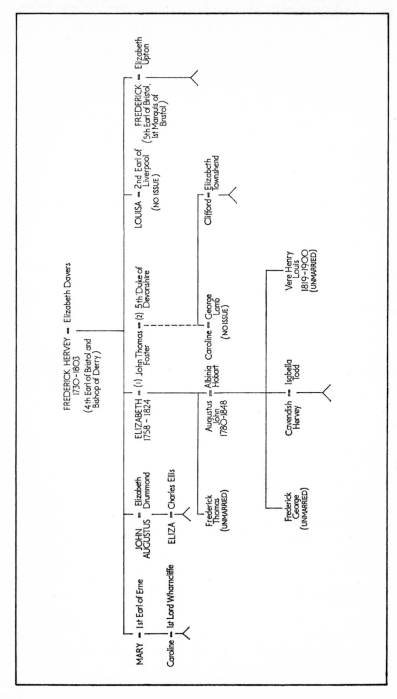

Shortened genealogical tree of the Hervey family

Sources and Bibliography

ORIGINAL MSS

Foster Papers. Private collection
Emigration from Ireland to North America. 1851–1901. G. R. C.
Keep. Unpublished thesis, Trinity College Library, Dublin
Minutes of Commissioners of National Education in Ireland.
National Library of Ireland

OFFICIAL PUBLICATIONS

Report of the Royal Commission on Law and Practice in respect of
the Occupation of Land in Ireland. 1845
Report of Royal Commission of Inquiry into Primary Education
(Ireland). 1870. [c—6 iii]
Report of Select Committee on Passengers' Act. 1851 (632) XIX. I
Report of Select Committee on Land Law (Ireland). 1882 (379)
XI. 547
Annual Reports of Commissioners of National Education in Ire-
land

NEWSPAPERS AND PERIODICALS

The Times
The Irish Times
The Freeman's Journal
Belfast News-Letter
Northern Whig
Belfast Morning News
The Nation
Irish Farmers' Gazette 1851–1852 vols X and XI
Irish Teachers' Journal 1868–1874 vols II–VII
An Múinteoir Náisiúnta—Irish National Teacher 1964

GENERAL HISTORY

The Making of Modern Ireland, 1603–1923. J. C. Beckett. London,
1966.

A Consideration of the State of Ireland in the Nineteenth Century.
G. Locker-Lampson, London, 1907.
A History of Ireland. Edmund Curtis. London, 1936

SELECTED WORKS

Albert Agricultural College, *Centenary Souvenir 1838–1938.* Dublin, 1938
Black, R. D. C. *Economic Thought and the Irish Question.* Cambridge, 1960.
Bryce, Viscount *South America.* London, 1923
Costello, Nuala *John MacHale, Archbishop of Tuam.* Dublin, 1939
Cullen, Wm. *True Cause of the Disturbance in the Irish Teachers' Organisation.* Belfast, 1876
Davis, R. B. (Ed) *Jeffersonian America.* Huntington Library, 1954
de Vere, Aubrey *Recollections.* London, 1897
Edwards, R. C. and Williams, T. D. (Eds) *The Great Famine 1845–52.* Dublin, 1956
Ervine, St J. G. *Parnell.* London, 1925
Foster, Vere *Origin and History of Vere Foster's Writing and Drawing Copy-books, 1882.* Privately printed, 1882
Foster, Vere *The Two Duchesses.* London, 1898
Hughes, A. E. *Lift up a Standard: The Story of the Irish Church Mission.* London, 1948
Hyland, Stanley *Curiosities from Parliament.* London, 1956
Irish National Teachers' Organisation *Short Biographical Study of Vere Foster* (pamphlet). 1956
Journal of the Department of Agriculture, Dublin. 33 (1933): 34 (1934)
Kennedy, David A Plan for Irish Agriculture, *Irish Ecclesiastical Record.* 64 (1944) Dublin
MacDonagh, Michael *Wm. O'Brien.* London, 1928
Mant, Dr Richard *History of the Church of Ireland.* London, 1840
O'Brien, Barry *The Parliamentary History of the Irish Land Question.* London, 1880
O'Brien, Barry *Parnell.* London, 1898
Parton, J. *Life of Horace Greeley.* Boston, 1855
Philips, Allison *History of the Church of Ireland.* Oxford, 1933
Porter, G. W. *To the Golden Door.* Boston and New York, 1962
Porter, Dr J. L. *Life and Times of Henry Cooke, D.D., LL.D.* Belfast, 1875
Society of Friends, Dublin *Transactions of the Central Relief Committee.* Dublin, 1852

Sullivan, A. M. *New Ireland*. Glasgow, 1877

Trench, W. Steuart *Realities of Irish life*. Reprint. London, 1966

Tuke, James *A Visit to Connaught in 1847*. London, 1847

Ward, Wilfred *Aubrey de Vere*. London, 1904

Whateley, Dr Richard *Reflections on a Grant to a Roman Catholic Seminary*. London, 1845

Woodham-Smith, Cecil *The Great Hunger*. London, 1962

Acknowledgements

This book has been made possible by the kindness and generosity of Mrs A. C. May, a great grand-niece of Vere Foster, who placed at my disposal her hitherto unused family papers. While it was being written her unfailing interest and enthusiasm have been a constant encouragement. Now that it is completed I hope she will accept it as the most adequate expression of my indebtedness and thanks.

For other assistance I am no less grateful. Professor J. C. Beckett and Mr Brian Hutton read the manuscript and gave me much sound advice, and Mr Hutton, in his capacity as Assistant Keeper at the Northern Ireland Public Record Office, helped me to unearth much valuable material. Dr O'Rafferty, Secretary of the Department of Education, Dublin; Mr D. J. Kelleher, Mr Lenehan, and Mr E. G. Quigley of the Irish National Teachers' Organisation; Mrs Goodbody, Curator of the Friends' Historical Library, Dublin; Sir Robert Birley, former Headmaster of Eton College, and Prof. J. M. Barkley, DD, all assisted me in various ways.

I am most grateful to His Grace the Duke of Wellington, K.G. for permission to use the letter from Augustus Foster on p 42, and to Mr Francis Needham for locating it for me. To the late Mrs Sweeney, the Misses Duffin and Miss Grainger, I am indebted for the use of letters in their possession; to Miss Eileen Duncan and Mr R. Nelson, Geography Department, Queen's University, Belfast for making the map of Ireland, and to Dr R. W. M. Strain and Mr Peter Rankin for the photographs of 115 Gt Victoria Street, Belfast, and Glyde Court, respectively. Mr Vitty and Mr Gracey of the Linenhall Library, Belfast have been tireless in their efforts to assist me, and I am grateful also to Dr Henchy, Director of the National Library of Ireland. I thank the staffs of both these libraries, and of the library of Queen's University, Belfast, the Belfast Municipal Library, and the Northern Ireland Public Record Office, for their courteous help at all times, and the many friends, known and unknown, who have come to my aid.

Finally I must express my thanks to Professor E. Estyn Evans, Director of the Institute of Irish Studies, The Queen's University, Belfast, for his great encouragement and support, and to the Board of the Institute for making a grant towards the publication of this book.

M. McNeill

Belfast
1970

Index